TQ094186

Migrating to Windows Phone

Jesse Liberty
Jeff Blankenburg

Apress®

Migrating to Windows Phone

Copyright © 2012 by Jesse Liberty and Jeff Blankenburg

All rights reserved. No part of this work may be reproduced or transmitted in any form or by any means, electronic or mechanical, including photocopying, recording, or by any information storage or retrieval system, without the prior written permission of the copyright owner and the publisher.

ISBN-13 (pbk): 978-1-4302-3816-4

ISBN-13 (electronic): 978-1-4302-3817-1

Trademarked names, logos, and images may appear in this book. Rather than use a trademark symbol with every occurrence of a trademarked name, logo, or image we use the names, logos, and images only in an editorial fashion and to the benefit of the trademark owner, with no intention of infringement of the trademark.

The use in this publication of trade names, trademarks, service marks, and similar terms, even if they are not identified as such, is not to be taken as an expression of opinion as to whether or not they are subject to proprietary rights.

President and Publisher: Paul Manning
Lead Editor: Ewan Buckingham
Technical Reviewer: Damien Foggon and Fabio Claudio Ferracchiati
Editorial Board: Steve Anglin, Mark Beckner, Ewan Buckingham, Gary Cornell, Morgan Ertel, Jonathan Gennick, Jonathan Hassell, Robert Hutchinson, Michelle Lowman, James Markham, Matthew Moodie, Jeff Olson, Jeffrey Pepper, Douglas Pundick, Ben Renow-Clarke, Dominic Shakeshaft, Gwenan Spearing, Matt Wade, Tom Welsh
Coordinating Editor: Jessica Belanger
Copy Editor: Kimberly Burton
Compositor: Apress Production (Christine Ricketts)
Indexer: SPI Global
Artist: SPI Global
Cover Designer: Anna Ishchenko

Distributed to the book trade worldwide by Springer Science+Business Media, NY, 233 Spring Street, 6th Floor, New York, NY 10013. Phone 1-800-SPRINGER, fax (201) 348-4505, e-mail orders-ny@springer-sbm.com, or visit www.springeronline.com.

For information on translations, please e-mail rights@apress.com, or visit www.apress.com.

Apress and friends of ED books may be purchased in bulk for academic, corporate, or promotional use. eBook versions and licenses are also available for most titles. For more information, reference our Special Bulk Sales–eBook Licensing web page at www.apress.com/bulk-sales.

The information in this book is distributed on an "as is" basis, without warranty. Although every precaution has been taken in the preparation of this work, neither the author(s) nor Apress shall have any liability to any person or entity with respect to any loss or damage caused or alleged to be caused directly or indirectly by the information contained in this work.

Any source code or other supplementary materials referenced by the author in this text is available to readers at www.apress.com. For detailed information about how to locate your book's source code, go to http://www.apress.com/source-code/.

This book is dedicated to my daughters, Robin and Rachel.

—Jesse Liberty

This book is dedicated to my wife, Sara, and my children Riley and Miles.
Without your support and understanding, nothing would be possible.

—Jeff Blankenburg

Contents at a Glance

Contents

About the Authors

Jesse Liberty is a senior developer-community evangelist on the Microsoft Windows Phone team. He hosts the popular "Yet Another Podcast" on his popular blog at `http://JesseLiberty.com`. Liberty is the author of numerous top-selling books, including the forthcoming *Programming Windows 8* (Apress, 2012) and *Programming C# 4.0* (O'Reilly Media, 2010). Prior to Microsoft, he was a Distinguished Software Engineer at AT&T, a software architect for PBS, and vice president of information technology at Citibank. He can be followed on Twitter `@JesseLiberty`.

Jeff Blankenburg. Ultra passionate. That's how Jeff describes his relationship with technology. Over the past ten years, Jeff has enthusiastically applied his technical expertise to build industry-changing web sites and marketing efforts for mega brands, including Victoria's Secret, Abercrombie & Fitch, Ford Motor Company, Sony, and several pharmaceutical companies. He's especially proficient in user interface design, web standards, and mobile application development. In addition to his senior developer evangelist role for Microsoft, Jeff contributed to *Windows Developer Power Tools* (O'Reilly Media, 2006) by James Avery and Jim Holmes, on the subject of code validation services; and he has more than ten applications available in the Windows Phone marketplace. He also serves as an organizer for the CodeMash, Stir Trek, and M3 conferences. Jeff holds a bachelor of science degree in psychology from Ohio's Bowling Green State University.

About the Technical Reviewer

Damien Foggon is a developer, writer, and technical reviewer in cutting-edge technologies and has contributed to more than 50 books on .NET, C#, Visual Basic, and ASP.NET. He is the co-founder of the Newcastle–based user-group NEBytes (**www.nebytes.net**) and is a multiple MCPD in .NET 2.0, 3.5, and 4.0. His blog, Notes from a Small Mind, is at **http://blog.fasm.co.uk**.

Fabio Claudio Ferracchiati is a prolific writer and technical reviewer on cutting-edge technologies. He has contributed to many books on .NET, C#, Visual Basic, SQL Server, Silverlight, and ASP.NET. He is a .NET Microsoft Certified Solution Developer (MCSD) and lives in Rome, Italy. He is employed by Brain Force.

Acknowledgments

Thank you to Jeff Blankenburg whose genius was the sine qua non of this entire project. Special thanks to John Osborn, Jessica Belanger, Damien Foggon, Fabio Claudio Ferracchiati, Ewan Buckingham, Kimberly Burton, and all the folks at Apress for bringing this book to life and making it a far better book than the one we originally wrote. And thank you, dear reader—without you, this book would be a paperweight.

—Jesse Liberty

There are many people who helped me get this book to its final state, and without any of them, I'm not sure this would have been possible. Jesse Liberty gave me my first real authoring opportunity and his wisdom shaped my words on paper. Jessica Belanger provided laser focus on getting this book completed, despite delays and interruptions. John Osborne provided his editing wizardry; this book would have been much worse without his guidance. Martin Schray and Bob Laskey gave me the freedom and flexibility to pursue my passion. Dave Bost, Chris Koenig, and Jared Bienz were an incredible team of technologists to work with and learn from. Jeffery Bright and Angelo Lamatrice literally helped me learn to walk again during this book writing process.

Finally, I thank everyone who has sat through my presentations and articles over the years. You helped make this content what it is.

—Jeff Blankenburg

Foreword

You're riding the train to work in the morning. You're onboard an airplane that's taxiing to the gate following the flight attendant's announcement that cell phones and other electronic devices can be turned back on. You're sitting in a coffee shop enjoying a morning brew. And what are people all around you doing? They're checking their e-mail, surfing the web, reading the news, and checking the latest weather report—all on their iPhones, Android phones, Blackberrys, Windows phones, and other devices that just a few short years ago wouldn't have fit in a suitcase, much less a purse or pants pocket.

The smartphone phenomenon is no less a revolution in the way we live, work, and play than the personal-computer revolution was in the early 1980s. And it represents no less of an opportunity to developers, to whom it falls to write the applications that drive these devices. In coming years, companies will be built and millionaires will be made by savvy developers who successfully anticipate the needs of the market and possess the technical chops to meet those needs. Developers everywhere realize that mobile is where the action is. Moreover, the excitement around mobile devices in the development community is as palpable today as it was around personal computers in the heyday of the IBM PC.

The latest contestant to enter the mobile arena and scrap for market share is the new Windows Phone, powered by Windows Phone 7.1, also known as "Mango." No one refutes that Microsoft was late to the party. But so was Google with its Android operating system, and Android sales now outstrip iPhone sales by a comfortable margin. The market is huge, and there's plenty of room under the tent. Microsoft has put a stake in the ground with Mango and has big plans for the Windows Phone for 2014 and beyond.

What is it that makes Mango a compelling platform for developers? For starters, if you're already a C# programmer, you'll feel right at home with Mango, using a familiar language, familiar tools, and even a familiar API. If you're a Silverlight developer, you're way ahead of the game because you already know XAML, and learning to write Windows Phone apps is largely a matter of learning about phone-specific APIs such as the location API and sensor API. But even if you're not already versed in XAML and the .NET framework, you'll find Windows Phone Mango as easy a platform to learn as any you've ever picked up. It's managed code all the way, supported by an elegant set of APIs that were designed from the ground up to enable types of applications, which just a few years ago we could only dream about.

Mango improves on Windows Phone 7.0 in numerous ways. For example, in 7.0, applications that weren't in the foreground were almost always terminated, causing app developers to have to save state prior to deactivation and restore it again following reactivation. Mango turns that model upside-down, ensuring that in most cases, suspended apps are just that— suspended—and therefore can be resumed very quickly. This is mostly transparent to the developer, but there are implications to this architecture that affect the design of your apps. You still need to preserve state in case you're terminated, but upon activation, you can detect whether you were terminated and avoid the potentially costly process of restoring that state when it doesn't need restoring.

Mango also introduces a new set of APIs for accessing compasses, gyroscopes, and other sensors. It provides low-level access to the phone's built-in camera and adds support for front-facing cameras as well. It introduces a brand-new API for background processing, and it features a local database based on SQL CE that's perfect for storing relational data in flash memory on the phone, as well as an encryption API that enables data to be stored securely. It also adds HTML5 support to the platform, making Mango an equally viable target for cross-platform mobile development as iPhones, Android phones, and Blackberry devices. The list of new features could go on and on, but suffice it to say that I know developers on the Windows Phone team at Microsoft who told me even before 7.0 came out "just wait until you see Mango. It's awesome." They were right. And there's no better time than the present to see for yourself by downloading the SDK and checking out the new and improved Windows Phone.

I can't think of anyone better to guide you on the path to Windows Phone enlightenment than Jesse Liberty and Jeff Blankenburg. Both work for Microsoft and have "ins" to the phone team that the rest of us can only dream about. Both have been involved with the Windows Phone operating system since the beginning. And both have a passion for this platform that comes through in their blog posts, their speaking engagements, and, of course, in their books.

They've put together a step-by-step guide to building Windows Phone applications not only for developers already at home with the Microsoft technology stack, but for iPhone and Android developers as well. You'll learn about the application lifecycle and what it means for your code. You'll learn how to use push notifications to deliver timely informational updates and convert static tiles into live tiles. You'll learn about launchers and choosers and the role they play in building great mobile applications. In short, you'll get a working introduction to the core features and services that Mango has to offer, as well as to the tools that you use to leverage them—all in an edgy and humorous style that's in keeping with the hipness of the mobile market. *Angry Birds*, after all, wasn't written by a bunch of guys wearing coats and ties.

PCs are out. Mobile is in. You can either ride on top of the wave or get crushed by it. Let the revolution begin.

— Jeff Prosise
Cofounder, Wintellect

Introduction

Windows Phone was introduced to the public in North America on November 8, 2010. It entered a highly competitive market, with very popular alternatives, and yet it was immediately seen as something new, different, innovative, and potentially game changing.

Even at its release, the developers were saying "you ain't seen nothing yet," and just ten months later, Microsoft released the Windows Phone 7.5 code name, Mango.

It has been estimated that Mango has more than 1,000 new APIs for the Windows Phone SDK, implementing some very exciting features, which you'll read about in this book. Mango not only revolutionizes Windows Phone, but arguably revolutionizes the industry itself.

This book represents a snapshot in the life of Windows Phone, but has been written with an eye toward staying current, even as Windows Phone evolves.

Windows Phone is innovative and different, not for the sake of being different, but for the sake of making a phone that integrates into the user's lifestyle without becoming a lifestyle in itself.

One of the most noticeable aspects of Windows Phone is the Metro design style, modeled after state-of-the-art signage to be clear, immediately apprehended, and beautiful.

We won't waste your time trying to convince you that it makes sense to program for Windows Phone; we will make the assumption that you are reading this book because you've already made that decision.

Migrating

The goal of this book isn't to demonstrate how to port existing applications to Windows Phone, but to help you migrate your existing skills to those of a professional Windows Phone programmer.

Migrating from Other Phones

Many of you picking up this book have experience in iPhone, Android, and other development environments. We'll try to make the path to Windows Phone programming clear, and we're convinced you'll find it simpler and more enjoyable.

Migrating from Silverlight or WPF

Those of you migrating your skills from Silverlight or WPS will find the transition to be straightforward, although there are some tricky places that we will point out as we go along.

■ ■ ■

CHAPTER 1

Get to Work: Your First Windows Phone Program

We believe the best way to get started with Windows Phone programming is to dive into the deep end.

In this chapter, we're going to build a non-trivial application from start to finish. While there will be many topics introduced, the skills demonstrated here will be explained and expanded upon in later chapters. We believe that by seeing a real application built you'll quickly learn many of the fundamentals of Windows Phone Programming.

Along the way you'll learn how to use some of the controls that Microsoft provides for building phone applications, including layout controls that you'll use as containers for other controls. You'll also learn how to set control properties and how to databind a control to a value. Finally, you'll learn how to code and wire up the event handlers that bring a control to life.

The project we're going to build is a calculator, as shown in Figure 1-1.

Figure 1-1. The calculator

We will build this application using both Visual Studio and Expression Blend 4. We'll write the code in Visual Studio and we'll do nearly all the layout and design using Expression Blend.

Creating a New Application with Visual Studio

Let's begin by creating the application in Visual Studio.

1. Open Visual Studio, and select File ▸ New Project on the main menu. When the New Project dialogue appears, create a new application by selecting the Windows Phone Application template from the list of Silverlight for Windows Phone Installed Templates, as shown in Figure 1-2. Give the new project a name, a location, and a solution folder name.

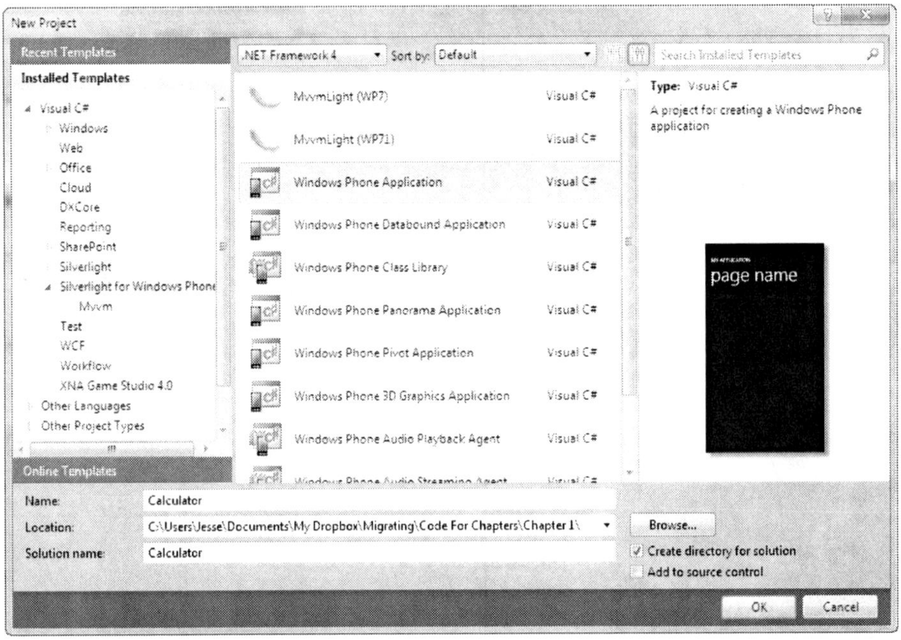

Figure 1-2. Creating a Windows Phone application

2. When you've completed the New Project dialog, click OK and you will next be presented with a dialog box in which you will pick the version of Windows Phone you will target. Be sure to set this to Windows Phone OS 7.1.

■ **Note** The latest edition of Visual Studio and Expression Blend will build for version 7.0 or 7.1. Version 7.1 (commonly known as Mango) is the correct version for use with phones with operating system version 7.5, and generally speaking, is the version you want to use. All of the applications in this book will use SDK version 7.1.

3. After you've selected a target phone OS, click OK. Once Visual Studio settles down, you should see the Visual Studio editor as the main window, with the Solution Explorer and Properties panel on the right side, and possibly the Toolbox and other windows on the left.

Notice that the main window can be split, as shown, with the design view on the left and the Xaml view on the right. Your arrangement may vary depending on which version of Visual Studio you are using and how you've configured it. You may want to open windows (using the View and Window menus) and close windows so that your view matches that shown in Figure 1-3.

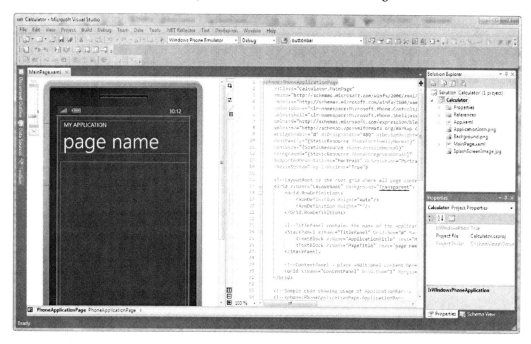

Figure 1-3. Visual Studio

Now you're ready to build the user interface for your application.

Building the User Interface with Expression Blend

Many experienced Windows Phone developers create the UI of their applications using Expression Blend. This works out quite well as Expression Blend works on *exactly* the same solution files as does Visual Studio. Thus there is no translation needed between the two programs, and you can move freely back and forth without breaking or losing anything in the transition. We'll use Blend to create the face of our calculator application.

1. To switch to Blend, right-click on the project in the Solution Explorer and click on Open in Expression Blend, as shown in Figure 1-4.

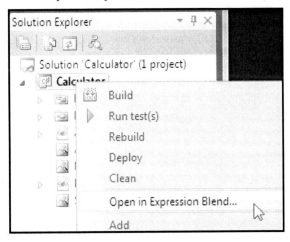

Figure 1-4. Open in Expression Blend

2. When Blend opens you may, once again, want to open (or close) windows until the layout in your Expression Blend window matches the image shown in Figure 1-5.

Figure 1-5. The Expression Blend work area

Every Windows Phone application consists of Xaml markup and code (C#). Though the two are theoretically interchangeable, Xaml is used mostly for UI and C# for application logic.

Note In this book we'll do all our coding in C#.

There are many ways to edit the Xaml. You can edit Xaml directly in the editing window of either Visual Studio or Expression Blend, or you can do so in the Properties window of either application. When you edit properties with either Blend or Visual Studio, the Xaml is modified; and when you modify the Xaml code in the editor, the Properties panels of both applications are updated.

To see this explicitly, we'll begin by making the same edits both in the Xaml editor and in the Properties panels in Blend. After we've demonstrated that this really works, however, we'll make (nearly) all of our future edits in the Blend Properties panel, as this is usually much easier than editing the Xaml directly (though you are always free to do either).

Setting the Application Title

Let's begin by using Blend to give the application a title.

1. In designer view, click on MY APPLICATION, the application title and notice that the Properties panel on the right-hand side, which is context sensitive, switches to show you the properties of this TextBlock.

At the top of the Properties panel you'll see that its name is "ApplicationTitle" and that it is of type TextBlock. TextBlocks and all other controls will be described in detail in the next chapter; for now you need to know that TextBlocks are used to show read-only text.

Run your eyes over the various properties shown in the Properties panel until you come to the Common Properties panel, shown in Figure 1-6.

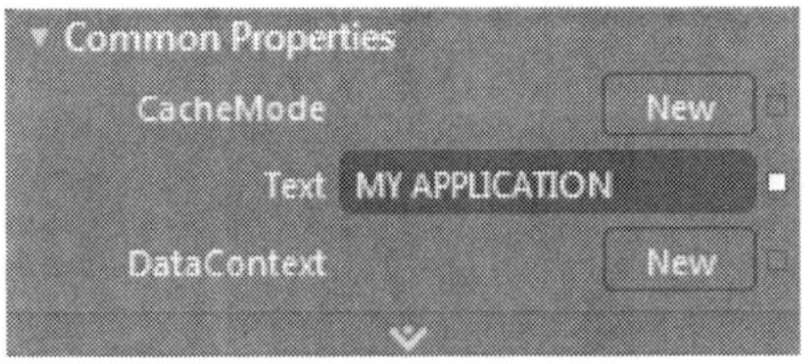

Figure 1-6. The Common Properties panel

The Text property in the Common Properties panel is currently set to MY APPLICATION. We're going to modify that; but before we do, let's split the editor so that it shows the page visually and also shows the associated Xaml. To do so, first locate the three small buttons located between the artboard (the panel showing the page) and the Properties dialog to its right, as shown in Figure 1-7.

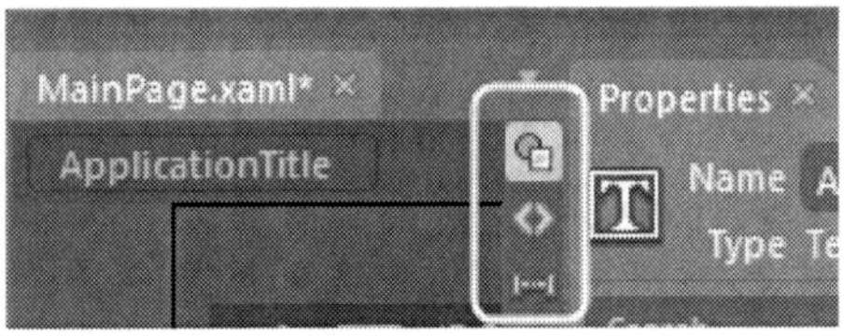

Figure 1-7. View buttons

Those three View buttons show the design, Xaml, or split display options that Blend provides, from top to bottom.

2. Click on each of these to see what they do and then click on the Split button to leave the artboard split between design view and Xaml view.

3. In the design view, click on the TextBlock that displays the application name and notice that the Xaml view scrolls to the markup for that TextBlock.

You don't need to understand all this Xaml at the moment, but do note that the Text property matches the text shown in the design view and also matches the text shown in the Properties panel.

4. Change this text directly in the Xaml to "YOUR APPLICATION" and note that when you do, the design view and the Properties panel are updated, as shown in Figure 1-8.

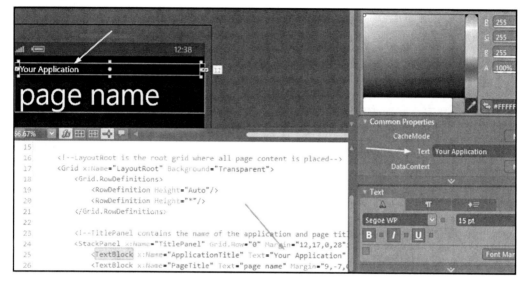

Figure 1-8. Updating the Application Title

5. Switch back to design view and update the Application Title in the Properties panel by entering the word "CALCULATOR." This should be in all-caps to follow the *Metro* look and feel. Metro is the design standard for Windows Phone.

6. Click on the **TextBlock** holding the **PageName** and hit the Delete key. Hey! Presto! The page name is gone.

We are now ready to add the calculator's buttons.

Adding the Calculator Buttons

Turn your attention to the Objects and Timeline panel (typically in the lower left of Expression Blend). You should see that the Page consists of an **ApplicationBar** and something called **LayoutRoot**.

1. Click on **LayoutRoot** and look at the Properties panel; you'll see that **LayoutRoot** is a grid.

2. Click the triangle next to **LayoutRoot** in the Objects and Timeline panel to expand it. Indented underneath it you'll find two other panels: the **TitlePanel** and the **ContentPanel**. The former contained the **TextBlocks** for the Application and the Page. The latter is currently empty, but it is here, in the **ContentPanel** that we'll place the buttons for the calculator.

You'll learn about grids and other layout containers (panels) in coming chapters. For now, the following is a summary of the three most important types:

- Grids have rows and columns
- StackPanels stack objects one above or one next to the other
- Canvas allows exact positioning of objects based on x/y coordinates

Now we're ready to create a surface for the calculator keypad.

Create a Surface for the Keypad

In the objects and timeline panel, notice that the layout root consists of a title panel and a content panel. The title panel holds the application title and the page title, and the content panel typically holds the rest of the contents of the page.

1. Click on the ContentPanel in the Objects and Timeline and notice in the Properties panel that the ContentPanel is of type Grid. We'd like this to be a StackPanel.

2. Right-click on the ContentPanel and select Change Layout Type StackPanel. Hey! Presto, the change is done.

Add the Display Panel

We need next to create the display panel for the calculator. To do this we'll use a TextBlock (a text field for read-only text). But TextBlocks can't have their background color set, so we'll solve this by wrapping the TextBlock in a Border control. As you'll see the background color for the border control will act as a background to the Text.

Controls are found in the Toolbox (the thin panel that runs top to bottom on the extreme left of Blend).

1. Click on the ContentPanel to make it the active container, and double-click on the TextBlock control in the Toolbox, as shown in Figure 1-9.

Figure 1-9. The TextBlock control in the Toolbox

2. A TextBlock is added to the ContentPanel. Set its Width and Height to Auto and its Horizontal and VerticalAlignment to stretch so that it fills the width of the Panel. Set all its margins to zero. Set the font size to 36 pt.

3. We'd like the TextBlock to live inside a Border control. The Border control in this case will provide a background color for the TextBlock. To do this, right-click on the TextBlock in Objects and Timeline and choose GroupInto Border. This places a Border control around the TextBlock.

4. Click on the Border control in Objects and Timeline and then click on the Background brush in the Properties panel. Next, click on the solid color brush button and set the colors to 255, 255, 255 (white), as shown in Figure 1-10.

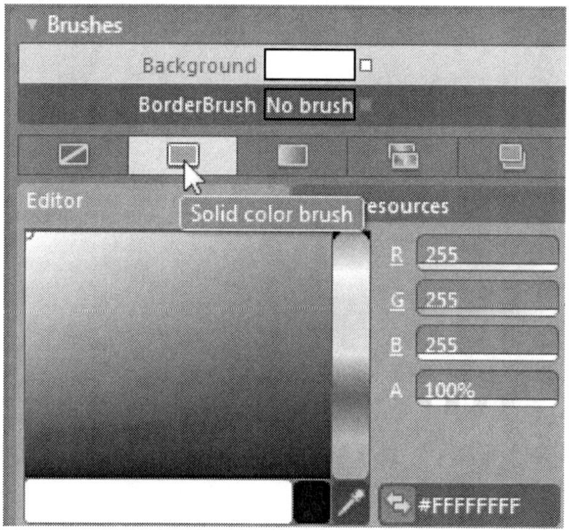

Figure 1-10. Setting the background to solid brush, white

5. Next, click on the TextBlock in the Objects and Timeline and set the foreground brush to solid and 0, 0, 0 (black). Set the alignment of the TextBlock to right. This will serve as the display for the values entered and the totals.

Now we're ready to go to work on the calculator buttons.

Design a Button

Before we add more buttons, we need to create a style for them. We will then be able to apply that style to all the buttons we create. The style we'll create will change the color of the button when it is pressed. The default style makes the button look white when pressed; we'll change it so that when the button is pressed it takes on the *accent color* (the color picked by the user for the tiles).

1. Locate the Button control, as shown in Figure 1-11. While you are there notice the small white triangle to the lower right of the button. This indicates that there is more "under" this button. To see the related controls, click and hold the button—the related controls will appear allowing you to pick various kinds of buttons, such as RadioButtons or CheckBoxes, as shown in Figure 1-12.

Figure 1-11. The Button in the Toolbox

Figure 1-12. Expanding the Button

2. Release the button so that it is no longer expanded. We now want to create a button on the artboard, under the ContentPanel. To do so, first click on the ContentPanel to make it the active container, then double-click on the button. A button appears in the design view and under ContentPanel in the Objects and Timeline.

3. With that Button still highlighted, let's set its width in the Properties panel to 100 and its height to 100. Set the contents to lowercase c.

We are going to create quite a few buttons, but rather than put them into a Grid or any of the other three standard controls, we'll use a wrap panel so that they lay themselves out nicely.

Buttons Layout

The WrapPanel does not ship with Windows Phone, but it is available in the Windows Phone Toolkit
(http://silverlight.codeplex.com/releases/view/71550)

1. Download the latest version of the Toolkit and install it.

The WrapPanel control is not on the Toolbox, but the last symbol on the toolbar is a chevron (>>),
which we'll use to find one.

2. Click on the chevron to expand the complete set of controls. Notice that at the
    top of this window is a search box. Type "wrap" into that search box and the
    wrap panel will be made visible.

3. Click on the WrapPanel and its icon will appear in the Toolbox.

You are now ready to add the WrapPanel to the ContentPanel.

4. Click and drag the WrapPanel into the designer. Check the Objects and
    Timeline to make sure the WrapPanel is inside the content panel. Click the
    Button object in the Object and Timeline and drag it *onto* the WrapPanel, which
    will cause the button to be placed within the WrapPanel.

You now have a WrapPanel with one Button in it; your Objects and Timeline should look like Figure
1-13.

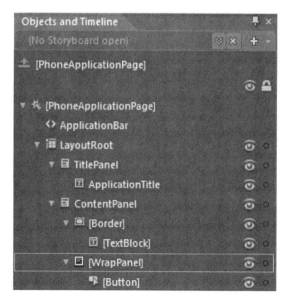

Figure 1-13. Button in WrapPanel

5. In the Objects and Timeline panel, click on the WrapPanel, and in the
    properties panel set all the margins to zero and the Horizontal and Vertical
    Alignments to Stretch, as shown in Figure 1-14.

11

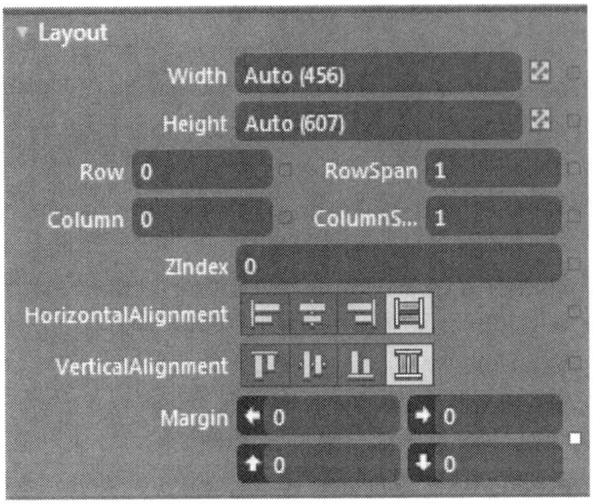

Figure 1-14. WrapPanel layout

6. Click on the `Button` and set its font size to 36 point and set the font to Segoe WP Semibold.

7. Copy and paste the `Button` 16 times, filling the `WrapPanel` with a total of 16 buttons. Notice that they wrap as they are laid into the `WrapPanel` (hence the name!).

8. Change the button content for the second button to "1" and change its name to Button01. Change the button content for the third button to "2" and change its name to Button02. Do the same for buttons 3 through 9.

9. Go back and change the name for the Clear button (the first button) to Clear.

10. Click on the Zero button and make its width 200. Do the same with the last button, but set its content to the equal sign "=" and its name to ButtonEquals. At this point, all your buttons should have names and your artboard should look like Figure 1-15.

Figure 1-15. Calculator buttons

11. In the Objects and Timeline, click on the first button in the WrapPanel and then shift-click on the last, highlighting all the buttons. Set the right margin to 10 to give the buttons a bit more padding and to fill the width of the page. Remember to go back to the two double-wide buttons and set their width to 210 to compensate for the margins.

Before you leave the page, you may want to fuss with the margins of the Border control to improve the alignment with the buttons.

Programming the Calculator

When the user clicks a button, an event is raised. We'll talk quite a lot about events later in the book, but in short, you can register a method to "handle" that event; that is, you can set up your program so that when the user clicks your button, a specific method is invoked.

There are a number of ways to register a method to an event. One of the easiest ways to do this is to click on the Button in the Designer and then to click on the event that interests you in the Properties panel. To see the events, you need to click the Events button in the upper-right hand corner, as shown in Figure 1-16.

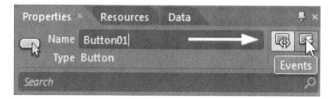

Figure 1-16. Events button

The events window lists all the events that might be associated with your Button.

1. Click on the Clear button and then double-click in the Click event handler box. Blend creates a new Event for you named by appending the event (Click) to the Butttion's name with an underscore (Clear_Click). Blend also creates the stub for the event handler code, and moves you to the code file (`MainPage.xaml.cs`).

2. Switch back to `MainPage.xaml` and click on the 1 button. This time rather than double-clicking in the event handler for the Click button, type in the name "NumberButton_Click". Do this for all ten-number buttons; they will all share the same event handler. Use the default name for all the other buttons.

3. Click the menu choice File Save All. Right-click on the solution file and choose Edit in Visual Studio, as shown in Figure 1-17.

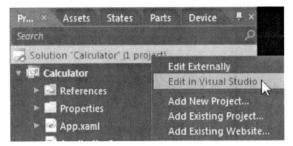

Figure 1-17. Edit in Visual Studio

Examining the Button Xaml

Before we go on to examine writing the code associated with this application, let's open `MainPage.xaml`. Visual Studio defaults to a split view, with the design view on the left and the Xaml view on the right. Notice that what you see in the Visual Studio design view is identical to what you saw in Expression Blend.

Let's focus on the Xaml for a moment. Every property that you set interactively in Blend is now shown in the Xaml. For example, notice that the first entry in the `StackPanel` is a `Border` that contains a `TextBlock`, which is just what we hoped.

```
<StackPanel x:Name="ContentPanel" Margin="16,0,8,0" Grid.Row="1" >
        <Border Margin="15,0,30,0" Background="White">
                <TextBlock TextWrapping="Wrap" Text="0" FontSize="48" Foreground="Black"
HorizontalAlignment="Right" Margin="0"/>
        </Border>
```

Take a look at the `WrapPanel` and double-check that all the Buttons have been assigned the right names and the correct Click event handlers, as shown in Listing 1-1.

Listing 1-1. The Wrap Panel in Xaml

```
<toolkit:WrapPanel Margin="0">
        <Button x:Name="Clear" Content="c" Width="100" Height="100"
            FontSize="48" Margin="0,0,10,0" Click="Clear_Click"/>
        <Button x:Name="Button01" Content="1" Width="100" Height="100"
            FontSize="48" Margin="0,0,10,0" Click="NumberButton_Click"/>
        <Button x:Name="Button02" Content="2" Width="100" Height="100"
            FontSize="48" Margin="0,0,10,0" Click="NumberButton_Click"/>
        <Button x:Name="Button03" Content="3" Width="100" Height="100"
            FontSize="48" Margin="0,0,10,0" Click="NumberButton_Click"/>
        <Button x:Name="Button04" Content="4" Width="100" Height="100"
            FontSize="48" Margin="0,0,10,0" Click="NumberButton_Click"/>
        <Button x:Name="Button05" Content="5" Width="100" Height="100"
            FontSize="48" Margin="0,0,10,0" Click="NumberButton_Click"/>
        <Button x:Name="Button06" Content="6" Width="100" Height="100"
            FontSize="48" Margin="0,0,10,0" Click="NumberButton_Click"/>
        <Button x:Name="Button07" Content="7" Width="100" Height="100"
            FontSize="48" Margin="0,0,10,0" Click="NumberButton_Click"/>
        <Button x:Name="Button08" Content="8" Width="100" Height="100"
            FontSize="48" Margin="0,0,10,0" Click="NumberButton_Click"/>
        <Button x:Name="Button09" Content="9" Width="100" Height="100"
            FontSize="48" Margin="0,0,10,0" Click="NumberButton_Click"/>
        <Button x:Name="Button0" Content="0" Width="210" Height="100"
            FontSize="48" Margin="0,0,10,0" Click="NumberButton_Click"/>
        <Button x:Name="Add" Content="+" Width="100" Height="100"
            FontSize="48" Margin="0,0,10,0" Click="Add_Click"/>
        <Button x:Name="Subtract" Content="-" Width="100" Height="100"
            FontSize="48" Margin="0,0,10,0" Click="Subtract_Click"/>
        <Button x:Name="Multiply" Content="X" Width="100" Height="100"
            FontSize="48" Margin="0,0,10,0" Click="Multiply_Click"/>
        <Button x:Name="Divide" Content="/" Width="100" Height="100"
            FontSize="48" Margin="0,0,10,0" Click="Divide_Click"/>
        <Button x:Name="Equals" Content="=" Width="210" Height="100"
            FontSize="48" Margin="0,0,10,0" Click="Equals_Click"/>
</toolkit:WrapPanel>
```

Planning Button Actions

With the layout and UI design complete, it is time to write the logic of the calculator. Turn to
MainPage.xaml.cs and notice that it includes event handlers that were created and "stubbed-out" by
Blend, for example.

```
private void Clear_Click(
    object sender,
    System.Windows.RoutedEventArgs e)
{
        // TODO: Add event handler implementation here.
}
```

Your job, no surprise, is to fill in the event handler implementations. Before we dive into the specific event handlers, we need a few class members. We'll begin by defining an enumeration named `OperatorTypes`.

```
public enum OperatorTypes
{
    None,
    Addition,
    Subtraction,
    Multiplication,
    Division
}
```

We'll create a private member variable of type `OperatorTypes` and initialize its value to `None`.

```
OperatorTypes operatorType = OperatorTypes.None;
```

We also need a flag to tell us if we're dealing with a new value and a field to keep track of the number previous to the current value.

Connecting Button Results to the Display

Now we're going to do a bit of hand waving because we want to bind the value shown in the `TextBlock` to the value of a property named `DisplayNumber`. For now, just this once, we're going to ask you to type in the code in Listing 1-2 as is, without fully explaining it.

Listing 1-2. Creating a Property and a Dependency Property

```
public double DisplayNumber
{
    get { return (double)GetValue(DisplayNumberProperty); }
    set { SetValue(DisplayNumberProperty, value); }
}

public static readonly DependencyProperty DisplayNumberProperty =
    DependencyProperty.Register("DisplayNumber", typeof(double), typeof(MainPage),
null);
```

There is some complexity here involved in the creation of what are known as Dependency Properties, and we really don't want to get into this just yet, even though we do want to make the binding work. We will come back to this in depth in Chapter 3. The net effect, however, is that `DisplayNumber` is now a property to which you can Bind.

The second step in this binding process is to return to the Xaml and to add the Binding to the `TextBlock`. Open `MainPage.xaml` and locate the `TextBlock` at the top of the form.

```
<TextBlock TextWrapping="Wrap" Text="0" FontSize="48"
    Foreground="Black" HorizontalAlignment="Right" Margin="0"/>
```

Replace Text="0" with the following:

```
Text="{Binding DisplayNumber}"
```

At this point the entire TextBlock should look as follows:

```
<TextBlock
    TextWrapping="Wrap"

    Text="{Binding DisplayNumber}"

    Height="58"
    FontSize="48"
    TextAlignment="Right"
    Foreground="{StaticResource PhoneTextBoxForegroundBrush}"
    FontFamily="Segoe WP Semibold" />
```

Notice that we say in the Text property that the Binding is to the DisplayNumber. What is the DisplayNumber? It is a property, but of what object? This is answered by setting the DataContext (much more about this, again, in Chapter 3).

Every time you navigate to the page (in this case, by starting the application), a known method, OnNavigatedTo(), is called. We'll override this method to set the DataContext for the page to the Page object itself (since we've created the DisplayNumber property on the page itself). To do so, add the following code below the event handlers:

```
protected override void OnNavigatedTo(
    System.Windows.Navigation.NavigationEventArgs e )
{
    DataContext = this;
    DisplayNumber = 0;
}
```

You can now press F5 to test the databinding. You should see that the TextBlock comes up displaying the number 0.

Handling the Number Buttons

We now need a helper method we can call each time a new number is entered to compute the new display value, as shown in Listing 1-3.

Listing 1-3. Helper Method to Compute the Display Value

```
private void AddToDisplayNumber( double digit )
{
    if (isNewNumber)
    {
        isNewNumber = false;
        previousNumber = DisplayNumber;
        DisplayNumber = digit;
    }
    else if (DisplayNumber == 0)
    {
        DisplayNumber = digit;
```

```
        }
        else
        {
            DisplayNumber = DisplayNumber * 10 + digit;
        }
    }
```

We will call this method every time a number is pressed. To make that happen, we need to get the number that was pressed and pass it to this method, which we do in the event handler we created for all the numbers.

```
private void NumberButton_Click(
    object sender,
    System.Windows.RoutedEventArgs e)
{
    AddToDisplayNumber(
        double.Parse( (( Button ) sender)
        .Content.ToString() ) );
}
```

This code takes the sender (passed in as a parameter of type object) and casts it to a `Button` (we know it is a `Button` because only a `Button` can call this event handler). It then extracts the Content property of the `Button` and calls `ToString()` on that Content. Finally the string returned from the `Button` (e.g., "3") is parsed into a `Double` and it is that `Double` that is passed to our helper method.

Press F5 to run the program, you should now be able to enter multi-digit values.

Handling Other Buttons

The Clear button's event handler is one of the simplest; we just set the `DisplayNumber` back to zero.

```
private void Clear_Click(
    object sender,
    System.Windows.RoutedEventArgs e)
{
    DisplayNumber = 0;
}
```

The `EventHandler` for the Add button sets the `isNewNumber` flag to `true` so that the `AddToDisplayNumber` method will do the right thing and it sets the `operatorType` to addition so that the Equals button handler will do the right operation. Subtraction, multiplication, and division all work in the same way, as shown in Listing 1-4.

Listing 1-4 Addition, Subtraction, Multiplication, Division, and the Equals Button

```
private void Add_Click( object sender, System.Windows.RoutedEventArgs e )
{
    operatorType = OperatorTypes.Addition;
    isNewNumber = true;
}

private void Subtract_Click( object sender, System.Windows.RoutedEventArgs e )
{
```

```
        operatorType = OperatorTypes.Subtraction;
        isNewNumber = true;
}

private void Multiply_Click( object sender, System.Windows.RoutedEventArgs e )
{
        operatorType = OperatorTypes.Multiplication;
        isNewNumber = true;
}

private void Divide_Click( object sender, System.Windows.RoutedEventArgs e )
{
        operatorType = OperatorTypes.Division;
        isNewNumber = true;
}

private void Equals_Click( object sender, System.Windows.RoutedEventArgs e )
{
        switch (operatorType)
        {
            case OperatorTypes.Addition:
                DisplayNumber = previousNumber + DisplayNumber;
                break;
            case OperatorTypes.Subtraction:
                DisplayNumber = previousNumber - DisplayNumber;
                break;
            case OperatorTypes.Multiplication:
                DisplayNumber = previousNumber * DisplayNumber;
                break;
            case OperatorTypes.Division:
                DisplayNumber = previousNumber / DisplayNumber;
                break;
            default:
                break;
        }
        isNewNumber = true;
}
```

▓ **Note** Notice that this calculator can handle the operation 73 * 59 but not 2 + 3 + 4. If you were to enter 2 and press the plus sign (+) and then enter 3, followed by another plus sign, and followed by 4 and the equals sign (=), the answer it would show would be 7, the sum of the last two numbers. It is left as an exercise for the reader to correct this problem.

Summary

In this chapter you learned how to use Visual Studio and Expression Blend to build a simple app for Windows Phone 7. You saw how to use various layout controls to contain other controls and build a simple user interface. You learned how to set a control's properties and how to databind it to a value. You also learned how to wire-up event handlers and how to implement event handlers to add behavior to your UI.

All of this was treated at a somewhat superficial level because we wanted to take you on a whirlwind tour of the tools and techniques you'll use to write Windows Phone applications. We'll deal these in more detail in coming chapters, beginning with Chapter 2, where we'll take a closer look at Windows Phone controls.

CHAPTER 2

■ ■ ■

Get Control: Exploring Windows Phone Controls

The thought of design and particularly layout makes many developers cringe. We have spent our careers boldly looking past our user interfaces in search of pure code. For us, functionality always takes precedence over form. That is, until we show our application to an actual user. It's at that point we realize our weakness. Yes, our application works. Yes, it meets all of the business requirements. But no, it doesn't make any sense to our users, and in many cases, they can't even figure out how to do simple tasks.

When building mobile applications, your user interface may have more impact on your app's success than the underlying code. Potential users will look through the marketplace, and screenshots are an easy way to determine if an application is great or mediocre. A stellar interface will always give you an advantage over your competitors.

In this chapter, you're going to learn about how Windows Phone provides the tools, called *controls*, to take the guesswork out of user interface construction Each control has a look and feel that is native to the entire Windows Phone operating system, which makes it easy for us, as developers, to create beautiful (and familiar) applications for our users. This will include controls for layout, like the Grid and Canvas, tools for navigation, like the Panorama and the NavigationService, as well as controls for making your application more beautiful, like the Image control. We'll also focus on the power of the TextBox, and show you how you can customize the on-screen keyboard it uses for input.

This chapter will introduce the Application Bar, a powerful OS-level feature that you can use to promote the most important features of your pages.

If you apply a few rules for layout to the use of these controls, you'll have a functional application that your users can understand too. To show how it's done, we'll build an interface for a home inventory application that uses all of the controls introduced in this chapter to create a compelling user experience.

Introducing Layout Controls

Before we get started building the application, there are a few things you should know about placing controls on Windows Phone 7 pages. Microsoft provides three primary Panel controls, and each possesses its own strengths and weaknesses. These controls are the Grid, the Canvas, and the StackPanel. Each of these controls serves a specific purpose. The grid panel provides rows and columns, the stack panel allows you to align items one on top of or next to each other, and the grid allows for absolute positioning. As you build your first applications, you'll start to see how these panels can be used separately and together.

The Grid Control

The Grid control is often compared to table-based layout in HTML, but this can be misleading. While it is true that the use of HTML tables is often discouraged, the Grid does not suffer the limitations or bloat of the table, and is an essential layout control for the Phone, one whose use is *encouraged.*

The Grid is the default container for every new Windows Phone project, and for good reason. It provides a specific layout structure for each page, and is flexible enough to stretch and grow as your content changes. Listing 2-1 shows a simple example of a Grid control in Xaml.

Listing 2-1. A Grid Control

```
<Grid>
  <Grid.ColumnDefinitions>
    <ColumnDefinition Width="100" />
    <ColumnDefinition Width="100" />
    <ColumnDefinition Width="100" />
  </Grid.ColumnDefinitions>
  <Grid.RowDefinitions>
    <RowDefinition Height="100" />
    <RowDefinition Height="100" />
  </Grid.RowDefinitions>
  <Rectangle Fill="Red" Grid.Row="0" Grid.Column="0" />
  <Rectangle Fill="Orange" Grid.Row="0" Grid.Column="1" />
  <Rectangle Fill="Yellow" Grid.Row="0" Grid.Column="2" />
  <Rectangle Fill="Green" Grid.Row="1" Grid.Column="0" />
  <Rectangle Fill="Blue" Grid.Row="1" Grid.Column="1" />
  <Rectangle Fill="Purple" Grid.Row="1" Grid.Column="2" />
</Grid>
```

As you can see in Listing 2-1, within the Grid we define columns (with ColumnDefinition tags) and rows (with RowDefinition tags). We assign the individual elements to the specific row and/or column that is appropriate.

You'll notice that the Xaml example doesn't really look like the HTML table layout that you've seen in the past. Instead, we've separated the content from the layout. We don't have to wrap each element in a set of table tags. We define a Grid, and then we simply assign each element to a cell of that Grid.

Please note that the Grid locations start in the top left corner with (0, 0), not (1, 1).

In the examples in this book, we provide a Xaml solution for the layout. Xaml is very descriptive and very human readable, but it's also very static. Many times you're not going to know how many rows your table needs, or even how many elements you'll have to place in it. In those cases, you can recreate *any* Xaml element via code in your code-behind file. Listing 2-2 shows the exact same grid would look like created dynamically in C#. You should notice that it's significantly more difficult to visualize what the end result looks like.

Listing 2-2. A Grid Created By C#

```
Grid newGrid = new Grid();
newGrid.ColumnDefinitions.Add(new ColumnDefinition{ Width = new GridLength(100) });
newGrid.ColumnDefinitions.Add(new ColumnDefinition { Width = new GridLength(100) });
newGrid.ColumnDefinitions.Add(new ColumnDefinition { Width = new GridLength(100) });
newGrid.RowDefinitions.Add(new RowDefinition { Height = new GridLength(100) });
newGrid.RowDefinitions.Add(new RowDefinition { Height = new GridLength(100) });

Rectangle r1 = new Rectangle{ Fill = new SolidColorBrush(Colors.Red) };
Grid.SetColumn(r1, 0);
Grid.SetRow(r1, 0);
Rectangle r2 = new Rectangle { Fill = new SolidColorBrush(Colors.Orange) };
Grid.SetColumn(r2, 1);
Grid.SetRow(r2, 0);
Rectangle r3 = new Rectangle { Fill = new SolidColorBrush(Colors.Yellow) };
Grid.SetColumn(r3, 2);
Grid.SetRow(r3, 0);
Rectangle r4 = new Rectangle { Fill = new SolidColorBrush(Colors.Green) };
Grid.SetColumn(r4, 0);
Grid.SetRow(r4, 1);
Rectangle r5 = new Rectangle { Fill = new SolidColorBrush(Colors.Blue) };
Grid.SetColumn(r5, 1);
Grid.SetRow(r5, 1);
Rectangle r6 = new Rectangle { Fill = new SolidColorBrush(Colors.Purple) };
Grid.SetColumn(r6, 2);
Grid.SetRow(r6, 1);

newGrid.Children.Add(r1);
newGrid.Children.Add(r2);
newGrid.Children.Add(r3);
newGrid.Children.Add(r4);
newGrid.Children.Add(r5);
newGrid.Children.Add(r6);

LayoutRoot.Children.Add(newGrid);
```

In Listing 2-2, you can see that there's a bit more work required. For each element (ColumnDefinition, RowDefinition, Rectangle), we have to create an instance of that element, and then we have to add it to its parent container. So each Rectangle is added to the newGrid element, and then the newGrid element is added to our LayoutRoot element. (LayoutRoot is the default Grid that is created when you create your page. In both examples, you should end up with a layout of six colored boxes, in two rows, as shown in Figure 2-1.

Figure 2-1. Layout of six colored boxes in grayscale

Ultimately, the Grid can be used in a variety of ways, especially when you need elements to be aligned with each other. When you need something a little more free-form, however, you might want to consider the Canvas as your primary panel control. Where the Grid takes many liberties with its contents (resizing elements to fit the Grid cell, centering elements automatically), the Canvas is almost completely hands-off.

The Canvas Control

Just as the Grid control is comparable to an HTML table, the Canvas control behaves like the absolute positioning provided by HTML/CSS. When you use a Canvas, each element is given a specific location on the page, and nothing but code can move them. This is also one of the limitations of the Canvas, but for many applications, particularly animation-intensive applications, you'll find it to be ideal.

When elements are absolutely positioned, they just don't adjust. Elements will overlap, without having any positioning-related effect on its neighbors. This is one of the fastest ways to get your elements positioned on a page, and the taboos that came with absolute positioning in CSS are erased, because we're developing for a mobile operating system, not seventeen flavors of browser and platform combinations.

So what exactly does a Canvas look like? Listing 2-3 shows the Xaml to re-create the same layout that we used in the Grid example.

Listing 2-3. Using the Canvas Control

```
<Canvas>
    <Rectangle Fill="Red" Width="100" Height="100" Canvas.Top="100" Canvas.Left="100" />
    <Rectangle Fill="Orange" Width="100" Height="100" Canvas.Top="100" Canvas.Left="200" />
    <Rectangle Fill="Yellow" Width="100" Height="100" Canvas.Top="100" Canvas.Left="300" />
    <Rectangle Fill="Green" Width="100" Height="100" Canvas.Top="200" Canvas.Left="100" />
    <Rectangle Fill="Blue" Width="100" Height="100" Canvas.Top="200" Canvas.Left="200" />
    <Rectangle Fill="Purple" Width="100" Height="100" Canvas.Top="200" Canvas.Left="300" />
</Canvas>
```

For each element in your Canvas, you will need to specify the Canvas.Top and Canvas.Left properties. Omitting these values will result in your elements being positioned in the top left corner of the Canvas, at position 0, 0. As with any Xaml element, you can embed these controls inside each other, giving you the ability to segment and separate your content into different panels.

Another important difference to notice in the Canvas example is that we have to be explicit about sizes of our elements. In the Grid example, we didn't have to size our Rectangles because they will automatically fill the size of the Grid cell they occupy. In a Canvas, everything needs to be explicit, or the element will either not show up (because it has a height and width of zero), or will render at its default size (if it has one.)

In Chapter 5, we're going to cover animation, and show how adding movement to an application can enhance your user's experience. In most cases, the Canvas is the ideal surface for creating animations, because there aren't any other "rules" as to how or where its contents should be displayed. Creating animations with elements that live in a Grid control, for example, can be more difficult, because you'll find yourself wanting to move elements from cell to cell, which can create some unwanted behaviors.

The StackPanel Control

The last of the big three panel controls is the StackPanel. This control might seem a little more familiar to the CSS fans who love flow-based layouts. As the name might suggest, the StackPanel stacks the elements it contains. By default, StackPanels stack their contents vertically, but you can also set a property to "stack" the objects horizontally instead.

In Listing 2-4, we are going to recreate the same output we created with the Grid and Canvas, using StackPanels. Since we have six Rectangles that we want to arrange in a 3 × 2 block, we should start with an outer StackPanel that, by default, will stack our elements vertically. However, we want to have two rows of three Rectangles each, so we are going to nest two more StackPanels inside. Each of these child StackPanels will need their Orientation property set to Horizontal to create the rows. Again, Listing 2-4 renders the exact same layout as the Grid and Canvas examples from earlier.

Listing 2-4 Using the StackPanel Control

```
<StackPanel>
    <StackPanel Orientation="Horizontal">
        <Rectangle Fill="Red" Width="100" Height="100" />
        <Rectangle Fill="Orange" Width="100" Height="100" />
        <Rectangle Fill="Yellow" Width="100" Height="100" />
    </StackPanel>
    <StackPanel Orientation="Horizontal">
        <Rectangle Fill="Green" Width="100" Height="100" />
        <Rectangle Fill="Blue" Width="100" Height="100" />
        <Rectangle Fill="Purple" Width="100" Height="100" />
    </StackPanel>
</StackPanel>
```

Recap

As we've shown in the previous three examples, each panel control treats your content differently, and recognizing those differences will allow you to select the right control for the right situation. Each of these controls has its strengths and weaknesses, so the important lesson here is that if your content looks and behaves the way you expect it to, you've made a good choice.

In the next section of this chapter, we're going to build a real application, using real controls and layout practices. We'll point out some easy stumbling blocks to avoid, while giving you the insight to make your application more useable for your users along the way.

Building a Real User Interface

For the remainder of this chapter, we are going to build a user interface that lets us explore many of the controls that are available to us by default for Windows Phone. We'll focus on several controls in the Visual Studio Toolbox, and show how best to use them.

We're going to build something simple, but useful: a home inventory application. If you're not familiar with the idea of a home inventory, imagine something terrible happened to your home last week. How would you prove to your insurance company that you had fifteen computers, nine Xbox 360s, and a bag full of diamonds? By taking a home inventory, you'll have descriptions, serial numbers, locations, and photos of all of the valuable items you own (using the camera is covered in Chapter 9).

In our application, we're going to create several different pages. The home page will provide links for navigation and expose some of our data using a Panorama control. We'll also include pages for adding new items, new categories, and new locations.

Getting Started

We'll begin by opening a new application and deleting some default code created by Visual Studio that we won't need.

1. Open Visual Studio 2010, and choose File New Project Windows Phone Application, a shown in Figure 2-2. Complete the dialog and click OK.

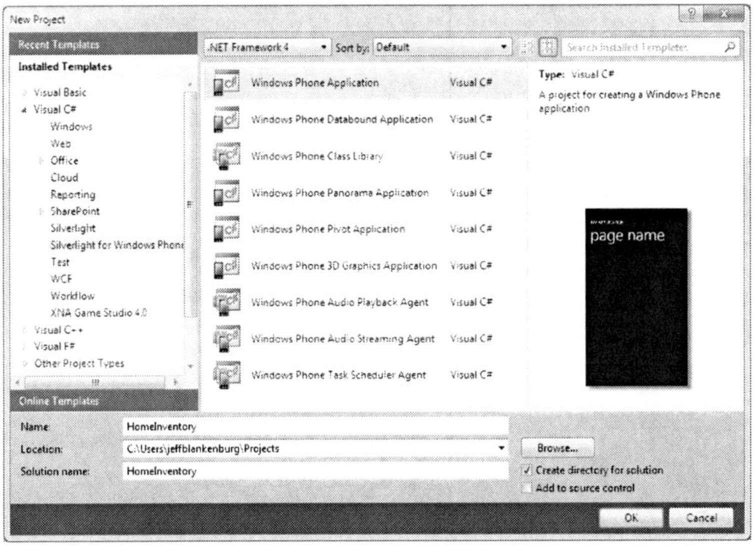

Figure 2-2. Shows how to open a new project with Open Visual Studio 2010

One of the first things you may want to do when starting a new Windows Phone project is to delete the default code in your `MainPage.xaml` file. The default code is great for your first "Hello World!" application, but is a little simplistic for what we are trying to accomplish in this chapter. We're not deleting everything, but we are deleting the code responsible for the default user interface.

2. Go to `MainPage.xaml`. You can delete all of the code shown in Listing 2-5.

Listing 2-5. The Xaml You Can Remove from the Default Page Template

```xml
<!--LayoutRoot is the root grid where all page content is placed-->
<Grid x:Name="LayoutRoot" Background="Transparent">
    <Grid.RowDefinitions>
        <RowDefinition Height="Auto"/>
        <RowDefinition Height="*"/>
    </Grid.RowDefinitions>

    <!--TitlePanel contains the name of the application and page title-->
    <StackPanel x:Name="TitlePanel" Grid.Row="0" Margin="12,17,0,28">
        <TextBlock x:Name="ApplicationTitle" Text="MY APPLICATION" Style="{StaticResource
PhoneTextNormalStyle}"/>
        <TextBlock x:Name="PageTitle" Text="page name" Margin="9,-7,0,0"
Style="{StaticResource PhoneTextTitle1Style}"/>
    </StackPanel>

    <!--ContentPanel - place additional content here-->
    <Grid x:Name="ContentPanel" Grid.Row="1" Margin="12,0,12,0"></Grid>
</Grid>

<!--Sample code showing usage of ApplicationBar-->
<!--<phone:PhoneApplicationPage.ApplicationBar>
    <shell:ApplicationBar IsVisible="True" IsMenuEnabled="True">
        <shell:ApplicationBarIconButton IconUri="/Images/appbar_button1.png" Text="Button 1"/>
        <shell:ApplicationBarIconButton IconUri="/Images/appbar_button2.png" Text="Button 2"/>
        <shell:ApplicationBar.MenuItems>
            <shell:ApplicationBarMenuItem Text="MenuItem 1"/>
            <shell:ApplicationBarMenuItem Text="MenuItem 2"/>
        </shell:ApplicationBar.MenuItems>
    </shell:ApplicationBar>
</phone:PhoneApplicationPage.ApplicationBar>-->
```

Most of the time, we prefer the first page of an application to be a rich, robust experience that gives our user access to as much data and navigation as we can. Many applications pack tons of buttons on the first screen, but there's a better way to provide lots of options to your users: the `Panorama` control. If you look in your default Visual Studio Toolbox, you'll probably notice that the `Panorama` isn't listed. Let's fix that first.

Adding Missing Controls to Your Toolbox

Figure 2-3 is a quick look at the default contents of your Visual Studio Toolbox. There are many other controls available to you, but they're hidden because they're not part of the default namespaces that are included in your project.

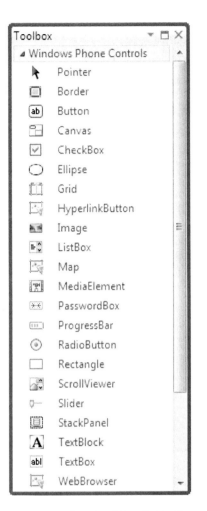

Figure 2-3 The Visual Studio Toolbox for Windows Phone applications

In order to get the hidden controls into your Toolbox, you'll need to add them.

1. To do this, right-click on your Toolbox and select "Choose Items…" (as shown in Figure 2-4).

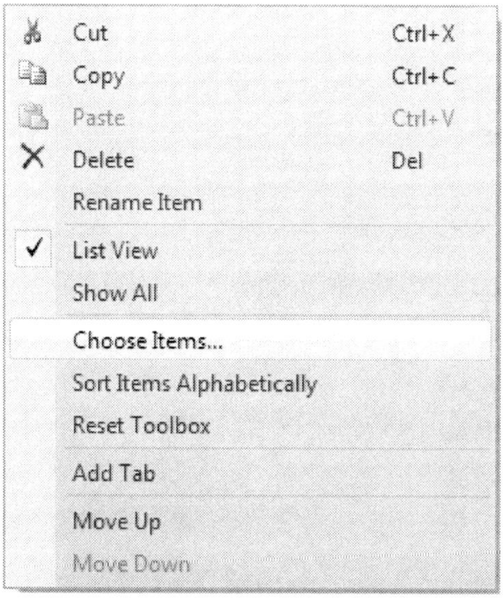

✂	Cut	Ctrl+X
📋	Copy	Ctrl+C
📋	Paste	Ctrl+V
✕	Delete	Del
	Rename Item	
✓	List View	
	Show All	
	Choose Items...	
	Sort Items Alphabetically	
	Reset Toolbox	
	Add Tab	
	Move Up	
	Move Down	

Figure 2-4 Adding additional controls to your Toolbox

2. The "Choose Toolbox Items" dialog box that appears (shown in Figure 2-5) allows you to choose the specific controls you want in your Toolbox. There are dozens of additional controls to use, and almost all of them will require an additional reference in your application. Feel free to add any of the controls that sound interesting, but for our application, we're only going to need the Panorama control. Also notice that the Toolbox doesn't alphabetize the controls for you, so if you want to move Panorama up between the MediaElement and the PasswordBox, just drag it up there once you've added it. (You can also right-click again, and choose "Sort Items Alphabetically.")

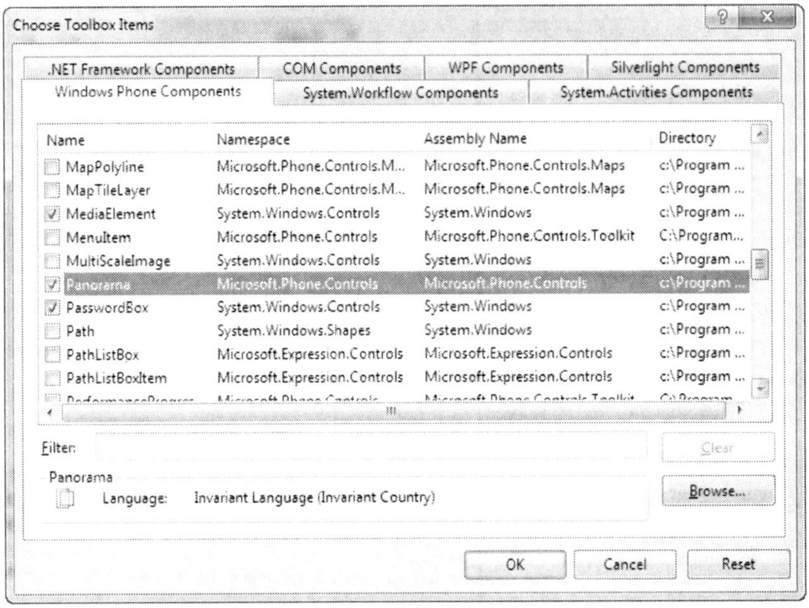

Figure 2-5 The Choose Toolbox Items dialog box

Using the Panorama Control

You're almost ready to add this Panorama to the application home page.

3. If you drag the Panorama control from your Toolbox to the place in your Xaml where you deleted all of that code earlier, you'll notice that it adds a tag that looks like Listing 2-6.

Listing 2-6 The Base Panorama Xaml Tag

```
<controls:Panorama />
```

The controls: portion of that tag refers to the new namespace that has been added to your page. If you look at the very top of your page, there should now be a line that looks like the following:

```
xmlns:controls="clr-namespace:Microsoft.Phone.Controls;assembly=Microsoft.Phone.Controls"
```

When you dragged the Panorama into your code, Visual Studio added this tag for you automatically, as well as reference to the Microsoft.Phone.Controls assembly. This assembly is where the Panorama control lives, and without the assembly included in your project, you can't use the Panorama control. You could have typed both of those lines, but sometimes drag-and-drop can save you some time. (If you dragged the Panorama from the Toolbox to your design surface, you got a little more Xaml than Listing 2-6 showed. To continue following this example, just trim back your Xaml to look like Listing 2-7.)

4. Because we actually want to put content inside our Panorama, we're going to need to expand the self-closing tag that was placed there for us. You should also add a title to your Panorama control, because this is the huge text that appears at the top of the control. This is shown in Listing 2-7.

Listing 2-7. Expanding the Panorama Control Tag

```
<controls:Panorama Title="home inventory">

</controls:Panorama>
```

After you add this content to your page, your design surface should look like Figure 2-6.

Figure 2-6. An empty Panorama with a title property

Everything else that put on this page will be contained within this all-important tag. This is because every Xaml page can only have one root container. In this case, we've chosen a Panorama, but on most pages (and the rest of this application) will use one of the layout controls that we discussed earlier in this chapter.

5. Let's continue by adding some sections to our Panorama. We do this with PanoramaItem controls. Listing 2-8 shows the four sections we'll have in our application.

Listing 2-8. Adding PanoramaItems to a Panorama Control

```
<controls:Panorama Title="home inventory">
    <controls:PanoramaItem Header="your stuff">

    </controls:PanoramaItem>
    <controls:PanoramaItem Header="categories">

    </controls:PanoramaItem>
    <controls:PanoramaItem Header="rooms">

    </controls:PanoramaItem>
    <controls:PanoramaItem Header="photos">

    </controls:PanoramaItem>
</controls:Panorama>
```

At this point, stop and press F5 to run your application. The emulator should spin up, and you should see an application with a black background, and some large white text. You should be able to click-and-drag the screen in either direction, and see that native Panorama behavior, where the screen slides from section to section, and the Panorama title moves at a slower pace.

6. The last step we'll take in our Panorama control is to add a background image. We add this right alongside the PanoramaItem controls that we added before, by defining the Background property of the Panorama, and then adding Xaml inside it to specify the actual background image. Listing 2-9 shows what the Xaml will look like.

Listing 2-9 . Adding a Background Image to a Panorama Control

```
<controls:Panorama.Background>
    <ImageBrush ImageSource="images/warehouse.jpg" Opacity=".4" />
</controls:Panorama.Background>
```

We have specified two properties on an ImageBrush control, ImageSource and Opacity. The ImageSource points to an image that added to the project, and the Opacity is used because the raw image is just a little too bright to contrast with the white text on the screen.

7. To add an image to your project, right-click on your project's name, and choose "Add New Folder…" and name it "images." Now, right-click on that new folder, and choose "Add Existing Item…" Select an image file from your computer that you'd like to use as your backgroundct.

You always want to use an image that is 800 pixels tall, or your image will be stretched to fill the space. The width, however, is entirely up to how many PanoramaItems you intend to use. Our recommendation is to use an image with a minimum width of 1024 pixels, but if you're using more than five PanoramaItems, add approximately 200 more pixels per additional PanoramaItem. You'll see this in the next section.

Adjusting Background and Accent Colors

By default, your application and your emulator are both set to use the Dark background on the phone, and a Red accent color. The Dark background includes dark backgrounds with light text. The Light background uses white backgrounds with dark text. If you're not familiar with the ways a user can customize their phone, you're going to want to become intimately close with these concepts. This is the number-one reason why applications fail marketplace validation, and with a little attention to detail, they can easily be avoided.

8. Open up your emulator, and press the Home button (the Windows icon) that is on the bottom center of the device.

9. Press the circled arrow, and choose Settings from the list of applications that appears.

10. Inside Settings, look for the "theme" option. Choose that, and you'll discover that you can change both background and accent color on the emulator, as shown in Figure 2-7.

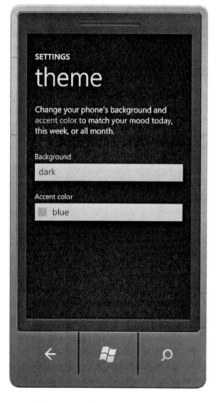
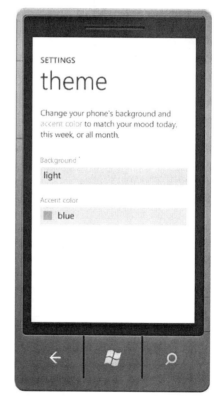

Figure 2-7. Changing the theme of the Windows Phone emulator

These are system-wide settings that apply to every default color in every application on the phone. So far in our application, we have only used default colors, so we should be incredibly conscious of what our application looks like under each theme. Figure 2-8 gives you a quick look.

Figure 2-8. Our home inventory application using the different themes

.As we progress further into our application, this is going to become more and more important to pay attention to. This is because black text on black backgrounds isn't visible, just as white text on white backgrounds vanishes. If we stick with all default values, we should generally be safe, but the moment we start explicitly naming colors of our controls is when we venture into more dangerous territory.

Thankfully, Expression Blend makes this easy for us to test. Open the Devices tab in Expression Blend and you'll find the ability to switch themes and accent colors very easily, as shown in Figure 2-9..

Figure 2-9 The Device tab in Expression Blend

Another recommendation we give to developers with actual Windows Phone devices is to set your device to the Light Theme, because your emulator will always default to Dark. This way, as you're testing your applications, you'll be certain to see the interface in both themes.

Adding Images to a Page

One of the most common controls you will use in your applications will be the Image control. You will use it to show photos and other images to your user. In the "photos" section of our Panorama, we want to show the user all of the photos they have added to their collection. To do this, we'll lay the images out in a Grid control.

11. First, we will need some images in our application. The Image element can use PNG, JPG, and BMP files. GIF format is not supported. (In a fully-functional application, these images would be created and saved as the user added new items to the app. In our example, we're going to use static images, but the user interface will be identical.)

Inside the "photos" PanoramaItem of our MainPage.xaml file, we need to add a Grid, its Column and Row definitions, as well as the images we just selected.

12. Listing 2-10 shows the Xaml you need, including the PanoramaItem for reference. Add it now.

Listing 2-10. Adding a Grid and Images to a PanoramaItem

```
<controls:PanoramaItem Header="photos">
    <Grid>
        <Grid.ColumnDefinitions>
            <ColumnDefinition Width="110" />
            <ColumnDefinition Width="110" />
            <ColumnDefinition Width="110" />
            <ColumnDefinition Width="110" />
        </Grid.ColumnDefinitions>
        <Grid.RowDefinitions>
            <RowDefinition Height="110" />
            <RowDefinition Height="110" />
            <RowDefinition Height="110" />
            <RowDefinition Height="110" />
        </Grid.RowDefinitions>
```

```
        <Image Source="images/laptop.jpg" Width="100" Height="100" />
        <Image Source="images/nook.jpg" Width="100" Height="100" Grid.Column="1" Grid.Row="0"
/>
        <Image Source="images/clicker.jpg" Width="100" Height="100" Grid.Column="2"
Grid.Row="0"/>
        <Image Source="images/headphones.jpg" Width="100" Height="100" Grid.Column="3"
Grid.Row="0"/>
        <Image Source="images/bag.jpg" Width="100" Height="100" Grid.Column="0" Grid.Row="1"/>
        <Image Source="images/mifi.png" Width="100" Height="100" Grid.Column="1"
Grid.Row="1"/>
    </Grid>
</controls:PanoramaItem>
```

As we show in Listing 2-10, we have a primary element, the Grid, as the only element inside our PanoramaItem. We defined four columns and rows that are each 110 pixels wide and tall, respectively. We then added six Image elements, and assigned them to individual cells of the Grid control, just as we discussed earlier in this chapter. If you run your project, you should now have a nice layout of images for your user, as shown in Figure 2-10.

Figure 2-10. Our PanoramaItem populated with six images in a Grid

This simple interface makes it very easy for your user to look through their images, but we're somewhat restricted by the size of the screen. We would be able to show a maximum of 20 images. This gives us an opportunity to introduce one more incredibly valuable control: the ScrollViewer. By wrapping our Grid in a ScrollViewer control, we immediately get the ability to scroll down to a much longer list of images. Listing 2-11 shows a larger example of our previous Grid and Image controls, using a ScrollViewer.

Listing 2-11. Using a ScrollViewer for a Large Set of Images

```xml
<controls:PanoramaItem Header="photos">
        <ScrollViewer>
            <Grid>
                <Grid.ColumnDefinitions>
                    <ColumnDefinition Width="110" />
                    <ColumnDefinition Width="110" />
                    <ColumnDefinition Width="110" />
                    <ColumnDefinition Width="110" />
                </Grid.ColumnDefinitions>
                <Grid.RowDefinitions>
                    <RowDefinition Height="110" />
                    <RowDefinition Height="110" />
                    <RowDefinition Height="110" />
                    <RowDefinition Height="110" />
                    <RowDefinition Height="110" />
                    <RowDefinition Height="110" />
                    <RowDefinition Height="110" />
                    <RowDefinition Height="110" />
                </Grid.RowDefinitions>
                <Image Source="images/laptop.jpg" Width="100" Grid.Column="0" Grid.Row="0" />
                <Image Source="images/nook.jpg" Width="100" Grid.Column="1" Grid.Row="0" />
                <Image Source="images/clicker.jpg" Width="100" Grid.Column="2" Grid.Row="0"/>
                <Image Source="images/headphones.jpg" Width="100" Grid.Column="3"
Grid.Row="0"/>
                <Image Source="images/mifi.png" Width="100" Grid.Column="0" Grid.Row="1"/>
                <Image Source="images/laptop.jpg" Width="100" Grid.Column="1" Grid.Row="1" />
                <Image Source="images/nook.jpg" Width="100" Grid.Column="2" Grid.Row="1" />
                <Image Source="images/clicker.jpg" Width="100" Grid.Column="3" Grid.Row="1"/>
                <Image Source="images/headphones.jpg" Width="100" Grid.Column="0"
Grid.Row="2"/>
                <Image Source="images/bag.jpg" Width="100" Grid.Column="1" Grid.Row="2"/>
                <Image Source="images/mifi.png" Width="100" Grid.Column="2" Grid.Row="2"/>
                <Image Source="images/laptop.jpg" Width="100" Grid.Column="3" Grid.Row="2" />
                <Image Source="images/nook.jpg" Width="100" Grid.Column="0" Grid.Row="3" />
                <Image Source="images/clicker.jpg" Width="100" Grid.Column="1" Grid.Row="3"/>
                <Image Source="images/headphones.jpg" Width="100" Grid.Column="2"
Grid.Row="3"/>
                <Image Source="images/bag.jpg" Width="100" Grid.Column="3" Grid.Row="3"/>
                <Image Source="images/mifi.png" Width="100"    Grid.Column="0" Grid.Row="4"/>
                <Image Source="images/laptop.jpg" Width="100" Grid.Column="1" Grid.Row="4" />
                <Image Source="images/nook.jpg" Width="100"    Grid.Column="2" Grid.Row="4" />
                <Image Source="images/clicker.jpg" Width="100" Grid.Column="3" Grid.Row="4"/>
```

```
            <Image Source="images/headphones.jpg" Width="100" Grid.Column="0"
Grid.Row="5"/>
                <Image Source="images/bag.jpg" Width="100" Grid.Column="1" Grid.Row="5"/>
                <Image Source="images/mifi.png" Width="100"    Grid.Column="2" Grid.Row="5"/>
                <Image Source="images/laptop.jpg" Width="100" Grid.Column="3" Grid.Row="5" />
            </Grid>
        </ScrollViewer>
    </controls:PanoramaItem>
```

As we have shown, there's nothing significant about the ScrollViewer's implementation, but it gives us the power to scroll content, both horizontally and vertically, when we need it. You will find that this tool comes in very handy with large sets of data. In the next chapter, we'll discuss the best ways to work with your user's data on a Windows Phone.

Navigating Between Pages

In its simplest form, navigating between pages in Windows Phone is as simple as navigating between pages in a web site. We create a UI element (e.g., a Button), and on its click-event, we call a navigation method that directs the user to the next page.

Let's start by adding the following new pages to your application:

- Categories.xaml

- Rooms.xaml

- Items.xaml

13. To do this, right-click on your project in Visual Studio, and choose "Add   New Item…" or you can press Ctrl+Shift+A on your keyboard, as shown in Figure 2-11.

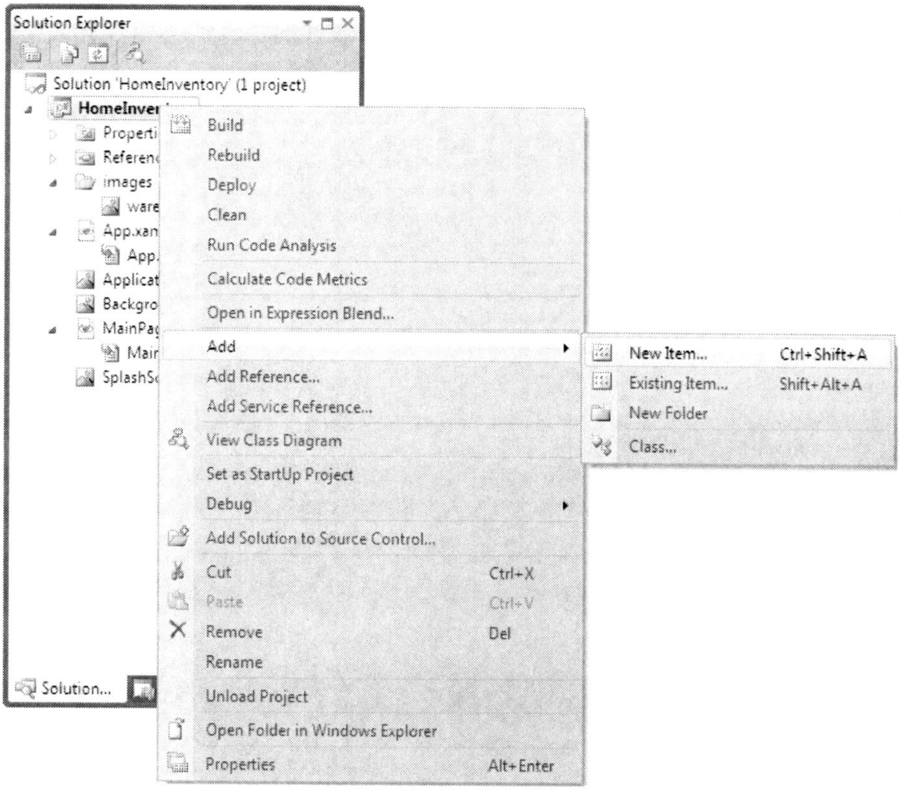

Figure 2-11. Adding a new item to your project

14. Once you've done this, you'll be presented with an Add New Item dialog box
for adding just about anything to your project, but fortunately a new Windows
Phone Portrait Page is the default option. Give it the appropriate name, in this
case Categories.xaml, and then add the other two pages the same way (shown
in Figure 2-12).

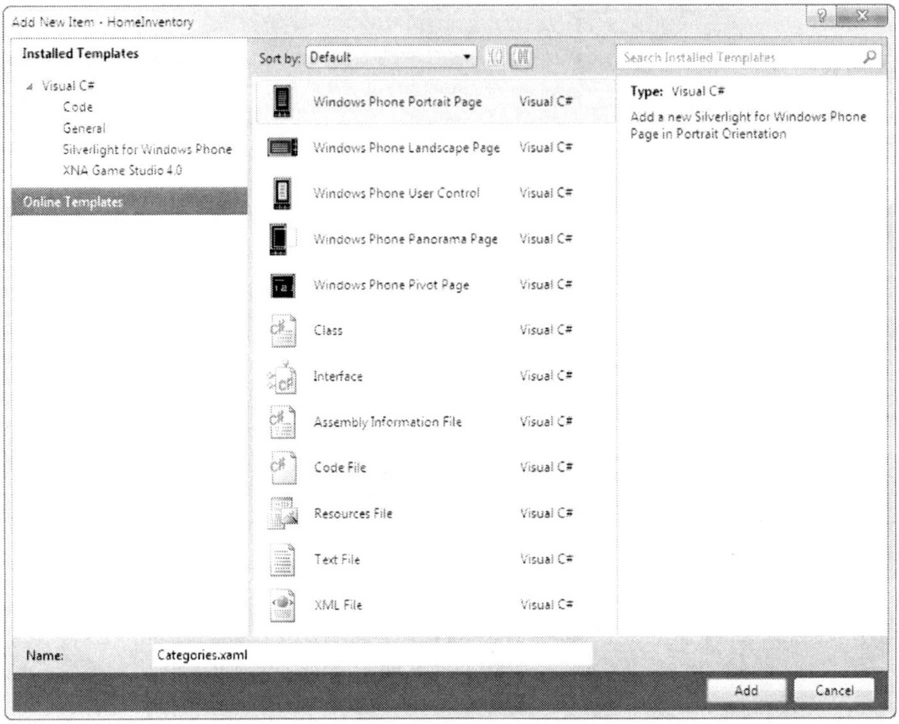

Figure 2-12. Adding a new page to our project

15. Now let's go back to `MainPage.xaml` and add a `Button` to our page so that we can navigate to one of these new Xaml files we created. Inside the `PanoramaItem` that has the Header "categories," let's add a `Grid` and a `Button` control, as shown in Listing 2-12 and Figure 2-13.

Listing 2-12. Adding a Grid and Button to Our PanoramaItem

```
<controls:PanoramaItem Header="categories">
    <Grid>
        <Button x:Name="CategoriesButton" Width="200" Height="100" Content="Add New" />

    </Grid>

</controls:PanoramaItem>
```

Figure 2-13. The appearance of our new Grid and Button

By adding a Click event handler to this button, we can then execute any code we want. The following are three ways to add a Click event handler:

a. Double-click on the button

b. Type in the event handler in the Xaml

c. Add the event handler in the code-behind (discussed later in this chapter)

16. If you double-click on the Button, Visual Studio will create the event handler for you, naming it with the name of the button, followed by an underscore, followed by the name of the event (as shown in Listing 2-13).

Listing 2-13 An Empty Click Event Handler Method

```
private void CategoriesButton_Click(object sender, RoutedEventArgs e)
{

}
```

17. This is where we will add our navigation code. To navigate to our
    Categories.xaml page, it requires one line of code (shown in Listing 2-14).

Listing 2-14. Using the NavigationService to Move Between Pages

```
private void CategoriesButton_Click(object sender, RoutedEventArgs e)
{
    NavigationService.Navigate(new Uri("/Categories.xaml", UriKind.Relative));
}
```

You should also find that the Click event handler code was added to your Xaml Button as well, as shown in Listing 2-15.

Listing 2-15. The Click Event Handler Added to Our Button Tag

```
<Button x:Name="CategoriesButton" Width="200" Height="100" Content="Add New"
Click="CategoriesButton_Click" />
```

18. Go ahead and run the project again (press F5). If you slide your Panorama to the
    left, revealing the Categories section, you should be able to click on your
    button, and navigate to the new, empty Categories page. Pressing the Back
    button on the emulator should return you to your Panorama, on the same panel
    that we left it. This is how the NavigationService works. We programmatically
    move the user forward, and the Back button allows them to move backwards.

░ **Note** We can also programmatically move backwards through the "back stack" using the
NavigationService.Back() method, but with a dedicated hardware button, that will usually be unnecessary, and
most often will violate the design guidelines for the phone.

Dealing with the Back Stack

One of the bigger navigation challenges in Silverlight applications for Windows Phone is the concept of
the *back stack*, and how it can quickly build a maze for your user. Think of the back stack as an ever-
growing list of pages you have visited. Not only within your application, but the entire Windows Phone
operating system. When your application provides links to other pages, the back stack quickly grows
larger and larger. This is especially true when you provide any type of mechanism to get back "home."
The following is an example navigation path in our current application.

Home Categories Add Category Categories

In that example, we navigated to our Categories page, went to another page that allows us to add a
category, and then when we finished that task, we returned the user to the Categories page so that they
could see the new item in the list. Each of these moves used code similar to that in Listing 2-14, which
means that when the user uses the Back button to navigate to the first page of our application, it's

actually going to take three confusing clicks to get there. In short, the back stack on the phone doesn't match the back stack in your user's head. Now imagine that your user decides to start entering dozens of categories at once. They could require more than 20 Back button presses to get back home. Before that happens, they're going to exit your application, never to return.

Thankfully, there's a better solution. In the Windows Phone 7.5 release, the NavigationService was expanded to allow more flexibility in navigating through our applications.

To solve the problem presented, we can use the RemoveBackEntry method of the Navigation Service on our Add Category page (shown in Listing 2-16). This removes the Add Category page from our page stack, and when the user saves a value, we can use the NavigationService.Back() method to go back to the main Categories page.

Listing 2-16. Using the RemoveBackEntry Method

```
if (NavigationService.CanGoBack)
    NavigationService.RemoveBackEntry();
```

You'll notice that we wrapped the method call in a check to see if we can, in fact, go backwards in the navigation stack. If there is not an available entry in the navigation stack, you will get an InvalidOperationException and your application will crash. To remove multiple entries in the back stack, you can call the method multiple times.

You'll always be safer to make the CanGoBack check before calling the RemoveBackEntry method.

You should still be very cautious about modifying the default navigation behavior of your application, because it is very easy to miss a step and get your user lost, or caught in a navigation loop, and these are situations that will cause your application to be denied from the Marketplace every time. We will cover the Marketplace, and our tips and tricks for navigating it in Chapter 10.

Using TextBoxes

On each of our individual category pages, we need a way to capture our user's input. There are many ways to capture input from a user (shake, touch, microphone, camera), but text input will overwhelmingly be the way that we get information into our apps. Thankfully, we have some robust power available inside the standard TextBox control, and we're going to cover two of them: InputScope and the Software Input Panel (SIP) or keyboard.

When users tap on a TextBox, they expect to be able to type text or numbers. This means that the keyboard pops up every time this happens. What's nice about this is that we can choose which keyboard gets shown to the user by setting its InputScope property, and there's dozens. An InputScope is simply a definition of which type of keyboard you want to present to your user. To add a standard TextBox to our page is pretty straightforward, as shown in the following:

```
<TextBox Width="400" Height="75" />
```

Adding an InputScope is just as simple, as follows:

```
<TextBox Width="400" Height="75" InputScope="EmailNameOrAddress" />
```

For those of you following along in Visual Studio as you read, you probably just noticed that Visual Studio doesn't seem to provide IntelliSense for the different InputScope values. Unfortunately, this format doesn't accommodate that. (You'll find that you generally only use three or four different InputScopes, but to explore the list, you can use this slightly more verbose format).

```
<TextBox Width="400" Height="75">
    <TextBox.InputScope>
        <InputScope>
            <InputScopeName NameValue="EmailNameOrAddress" />
        </InputScope>
    </TextBox.InputScope>
</TextBox>
```

Figures 2-14, 2-15, 2-16, and 2-17 show a few of the most common InputScope keyboards.

Figure 2-14. Default Windows Phone keyboard

Figure 2-15. EmailNameOrAddress InputScope keyboard

Figure 2-16. Number InputScope keyboard

Figure 2-17. TelephoneNumber InputScope keyboard

It's important to remember that InputScope does not equal validation. Using the TelephoneNumber scope, for example, will not validate that the user is actually entering a properly formatted phone number. InputScope only defines the type of keyboard that will be presented to the user. Nonetheless, InputScope is a great way to make data entry easier on your user, and should be applied at every appropriate opportunity.

Using the ApplicationBar

The ApplicationBar is an important part of the Windows Phone operating system. It provides additional screen real estate, and is distinctively a Windows Phone feature. You may have noticed the small circled icons at the bottom of many of the applications in the Windows Phone Marketplace, and these icons are just one part of the ApplicationBar. The icons are meant to provide easy access to the most common functions a user would perform on the specific page. The other part of the ApplicationBar, the ApplicationBarMenuItems, provide a way to bury other functionality that would otherwise take up your valuable screen real estate.

It's important to remember that the ApplicationBar runs at the operating system's shell level, not at your application level. This distinction is important because as you become more familiar with the ApplicationBar, you'll notice that it doesn't have the same types of robust flexibility that standard Silverlight controls offer us. It's a bit more primitive than some of the other controls you've worked with to this point, but it also has some features that are *huge* timesavers.

19. Let's start by adding a simple ApplicationBar to a page. Open one of the new pages we created for our home inventory application. Here we're using the Categories.xaml page, primarily because we've already provided a way to navigate there in our app. At the bottom of that page, there's a large section of Xaml commented out. It looks like Listing 2-17.

Listing 2-17. The Default Commented-out Application Bar

```xml
<!--Sample code showing usage of ApplicationBar-->
<!--<phone:PhoneApplicationPage.ApplicationBar>
    <shell:ApplicationBar IsVisible="True" IsMenuEnabled="True">
        <shell:ApplicationBarIconButton IconUri="/Images/appbar_button1.png" Text="Button
1"/>
        <shell:ApplicationBarIconButton IconUri="/Images/appbar_button2.png" Text="Button
2"/>
        <shell:ApplicationBar.MenuItems>
            <shell:ApplicationBarMenuItem Text="MenuItem 1"/>
            <shell:ApplicationBarMenuItem Text="MenuItem 2"/>
        </shell:ApplicationBar.MenuItems>
    </shell:ApplicationBar>
</phone:PhoneApplicationPage.ApplicationBar>-->
```

20. Uncommenting this code will automatically enable the ApplicationBar, including adjusting the d:DesignHeight property of your page. Give it a try. The default DesignHeight value is 768, which removed 32 pixels to accommodate the SystemTray that shows the clock, battery level, etc. When you add the ApplicationBar, the DesignHeight drops to 696 pixels. This is because the ApplicationBar takes up 72 pixels. There are ways to reclaim those pixels, and we'll show you how to do that a little later in this section.

If we look closely at the elements of the ApplicationBar in Listing 2-17, there are two specific pieces that should stand out: an ApplicationBarIconButton and an ApplicationBarMenuItem.

The ApplicationBarIconButton

Each of the ApplicationBarIconButton elements are the icons you see at the bottom of the application If you look at the code for the ApplicationBar, you've likely noticed that it's pointing to two images that are not currently part of your project. If you run your app, you'll notice that it shows an X icon for each of the ApplicationBarIconButtons (shown in Figure 2-18).

Figure 2-18. ApplicationBarIconButtons with "broken" images

We could very easily go create some images for these buttons, add them to our project, and then reference them on those lines of code, but there is a much easier way; and it is found in Expression Blend.

21. Open your app in Expression Blend, and navigate the "Objects and Timeline" tree until you find those ApplicationBarIconButton objects, as shown in Figure 2-19.

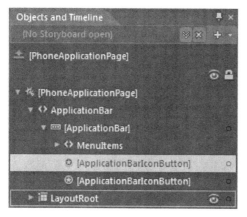

Figure 2-19. The Objects and Timeline panel in Expression Blend

22. When you click on one of the ApplicationBarIconButtons, check the Properties tab. You'll see a simple way to set the icon and text for each one. Figure 2-20 shows what it looks like.

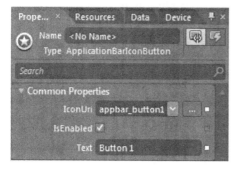

Figure 2-20. The ApplicationBarIconButton properties tab

If you drop down the IconUri select box, you'll see a wealth of standard icons that you can use in your applications. Unless you have a custom icon that you absolutely can't live without, these icons should serve *most* of your needs (you can always create your own icon and add it manually). And by selecting one, it automatically adds the white version of that icon to your project. All of your icons should *only* be white. You don't need multiple versions because the OS can manipulate the colors of the ApplicationBar automatically. We'll cover this in detail later in this chapter. If you're not following along in Blend, here's the list of standard icons.

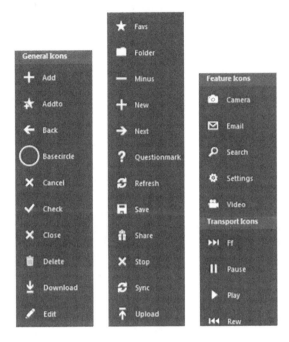

Figure 2-21. List of default icons available in Expression Blend

Expression blend automatically adds a folder named "icons" to your project. If you are creating your icon manually, we recommend that you also create an icons folder in your project.

You can right-click to add this folder, and then right-click on the folder to Add Existing Item. You can also use Shift+Alt+A on your keyboard. You can select the icon you wish to use from your computer, and it will add it your project. Change the path of the image in one of the IconButtons to the path of your image, and it will now be sitting inside a white circle in the ApplicationBar.

Each of these IconButtons has an available Click event handler, and it is how you allow your user to take an action when they tap the button. To add the Click event, you can either edit the Xaml, as shown in Listing 2-18, or you can use the Events portion of the Properties tab in Expression Blend.

23. To access this, click the icon with the lightning bolt in the top right region of the Properties tab, as shown in Figure 2-22.

Figure 2-22 . The Events tab in Expression Blend

Type the name of the event handler you would like to create in the box labeled Click to add an event handler to your ApplicationBarIconButton, as shown in Listing 2-18.

Listing 2-18. Completed ApplicationBarIconButton elements in Xaml

```
<shell:ApplicationBarIconButton x:Name="AddButton" IconUri="/icons/appbar.add.rest.png"
Text="add" Click="AddButton_Click"/>
<shell:ApplicationBarIconButton x:Name="DeleteButton" IconUri="/icons/appbar.delete.rest.png"
Text="delete" Click="DeleteButton_Click"/>
```

Note that we included a Text value for each of the two ApplicationBarIconButtons. This text value is used below each icon, as shown in Figure 2-24. Figure 2-23 shows what this ApplicationBar will look like on the screen by default.

Figure 2-23. The Application Bar with icons

Note the ellipses in the top right corner of Figure 2-23. Tapping that, or any unused space in the Application Bar, will raise it slightly, showing the text values of the button, as shown in Figure 2-24. This is also how you access the ApplicationBarMenuItems that we cover next in this chapter.

Figure 2-24. Showing the text values of the ApplicationBarIconButtons

Instead of showing another simple event handler example, we'll use our event handler method to change the icon of the ApplicationBarIconButton. Listing 2-19 shows what the event handler looks like.

Listing 2-19. Using an Event Handler with an ApplicationBarIconButton

```
private void AddButton_Click(object sender, EventArgs e)
{
    ApplicationBarIconButton button = sender as ApplicationBarIconButton;
    button.IconUri = new Uri("icons/appbar.delete.rest.png", UriKind.Relative);
}
```

You'll notice that even though we gave our ApplicationBarIconButton a name in our Xaml file, we didn't use that name in the code-behind method. Because our IconButton is part of the ApplicationBar, and not a Framework object, we can't make direct references to them by name. We can, however, catch a reference to the sender in our event handler, and assign a new IconUri. This icon swap makes sense in many situations, but try not to overuse this. For example, perhaps you have a state your user can toggle, like auto-save is on or off. Tapping the icon would allow them to switch the states. The buttons on the ApplicationBar should be consistent and predictable to your users, and swapping them can cause confusion if they're not used appropriately.

Another important lesson for these controls is that you can have a maximum of four `ApplicationBarIconButtons`. Any more than four, and the compiler will actually tell you that you have too many items in the list. Make sure that you are focused on exposing the four (or fewer) bits of functionality that a user will most want to perform on that page.

The ApplicationBarMenuItem

If the `ApplicationBarIconButton` is meant for the most common functions you'll perform on a page, then the `ApplicationMenuBarItem` is meant to give the user access to every other possible action on that page. We commonly recommend using them for tasks like the following:

- Contact Us

- About This Software

- Check for Updates

- Reset This Application

- Log Out

- Report a Bug

These are generally features that you want to offer to your users, but filling the screen with them can take a costly amount of space. By placing them in the `ApplicationBar`, you make those features readily available, but not so prominent that they're taking away from the main purpose of the page.

Like the `IconButtons`, these elements have a `Click` event handler that we can leverage to take the action the `MenuItem` suggests. Unlike the `IconButtons`, we don't get any images or icons to use. The `ApplicationBarMenuItem` is specifically text only (shown in Listing 2-20).

Listing 2-20. Creating ApplicationBarMenuItems in Xaml

```
<shell:ApplicationBar.MenuItems>
    <shell:ApplicationBarMenuItem Text="about home inventory" Click="About_Click"/>
    <shell:ApplicationBarMenuItem Text="contact customer support" Click="Support_Click"/>
</shell:ApplicationBar.MenuItems>
```

You can add an unlimited number of `ApplicationBarMenuItems` to the list, but we highly recommend no more than six. Anything greater than six will require the user to scroll to see the items in the list, and there's no visual indication that the list *can* scroll. If you're putting more than six items in the `ApplicationBarMenuItems` list, you're likely trying to use this menu for something it wasn't designed for.

Customizing the Appearance of the ApplicationBar

You may have noticed earlier that we recommended only using white versions of your icons. For some developers, perhaps white doesn't go with the rest of your application. Maybe you've got a need for the application bar to have brown icons, or an orange background.

The `ApplicationBar` has a `ForegroundColor` and `BackgroundColor` property that we can use to make it look however we choose. Listing 2-21 shows our `ApplicationBar` from earlier, but now rendered with brown icons and an orange background.

Listing 2-21. ApplicationBar with Foreground and Background Colors

```
<phone:PhoneApplicationPage.ApplicationBar>
    <shell:ApplicationBar IsVisible="True" IsMenuEnabled="True" ForegroundColor="#FF3F2503"
BackgroundColor="Orange">
        <shell:ApplicationBarIconButton x:Name="AddButton"
IconUri="/icons/appbar.add.rest.png" Text="add" Click="AddButton_Click"/>
        <shell:ApplicationBarIconButton x:Name="DeleteButton"
IconUri="/icons/appbar.delete.rest.png" Text="delete" Click="DeleteButton_Click"/>
        <shell:ApplicationBar.MenuItems>
            <shell:ApplicationBarMenuItem Text="about home inventory" Click="About_Click"/>
            <shell:ApplicationBarMenuItem Text="contact customer support"
Click="Support_Click"/>
        </shell:ApplicationBar.MenuItems>
    </shell:ApplicationBar>
</phone:PhoneApplicationPage.ApplicationBar>
```

Remember that we are still only using white icons. The ApplicationBar will automatically make the icons and the surrounding circle the color you specify.

Next, there is an Opacity property to the ApplicationBar as well. Using this property is really only recommended for situations where you *are not* using ApplicationBarMenuItems, as it becomes difficult to read the text of the buttons when overlaid on the contents of the page. When you only have ApplicationBarIconButtons, however, these buttons can appear to simply hover over our background image, giving both a nice appearance, as well as the removal of that thick, chunky, dark bar at the bottom of the page. Figure 2-25 shows an example of what this could look like.

Figure 2-25. An ApplicationBar with an opacity of zero

To do this, all we need to do is specify an Opacity value for our ApplicationBar. Listing 2-22 shows what the ApplicationBar in Figure 2-25 would look like in Xaml.

Listing 2-22. ApplicationBar with an Opacity of Zero

```
<phone:PhoneApplicationPage.ApplicationBar>
    <shell:ApplicationBar IsVisible="True" IsMenuEnabled="True" Opacity="0">
        <shell:ApplicationBarIconButton x:Name="AddButton"
IconUri="/icons/appbar.add.rest.png" Text="add" Click="AddButton_Click"/>
    </shell:ApplicationBar>
</phone:PhoneApplicationPage.ApplicationBar>
```

We feel that this use of Opacity in your ApplicationBar gives you the opportunity to mix the Windows Phone look-and-feel with your own application branding, which results in a nice blend of both appearances. Give this approach serious consideration in the times that you choose to use an ApplicationBar in your app.

Finally, you can disable ApplicationBarIconButtons when appropriate. If you have a Save button in your ApplicationBar, disabling this button when there isn't any new content to save might make sense in your app. You can set this in the Xaml, using the IsEnabled = "false" property, but its more likely you'll want to disable the button via code. To disable an ApplicationBarIconButton with code, we need to reference it via its position in the Buttons array of the ApplicationBar (shown in Listing 2-23).

Listing 2-23. Setting an ApplicationBarIconButton to Disabled

```
ApplicationBarIconButton abib = (ApplicationBarIconButton)ApplicationBar.Buttons[0];
abib.IsEnabled = false;
```

Disabling one of the ApplicationBar's buttons is also very effective for actions that require some sort of latency, like reaching out to your web services. Again, like swapping icons, this should be used sparingly. Disabling a button can be perceived by your user as losing control of the app. Make sure that they understand why you have disabled their buttons.

Summary

In this chapter, we showed how to use a variety of controls to build the beginnings of a home inventory app. By using controls like the Panorama and the ApplicationBar, your users will be instantly aware of how to navigate through your application, as they are found throughout the Windows Phone UI. Grid, Canvas, and StackPanel controls made it easy to get our elements in the right place on the screen. We focused primarily on creating the user interface of the application in this chapter, and in the chapters following this one, we'll focus on how we can make use of real data, not only from our code, but from the camera, our user's interactions, and a variety of sensors on the device.

CHAPTER 3

■   ■   ■

Get the Data

Virtually every meaningful Windows Phone application deals with data from *some* source, and often it is very convenient (if not downright necessary) to bind that data to one or more controls, store it away for later use, or even stash it in a relational database.

In this chapter, you will learn about the following three most important ways we manipulate data in Windows Phone:

- Binding data to controls

- Storing data in isolated storage

- Storing data in a local database

There are myriad sources of data. Some are local to your application, such as recording your daily workout, and might be stored in a database or in isolated storage (both of which are covered later in this chapter). Other data is retrieved from outside sources such as Web Services (e.g., nutritional information retrieved from a centralized service).

Our goal in this chapter is to explore databinding and local data storage. Towards that end, we will create an in-memory data source, a Customer object to which we will bind controls. The essentials of databinding are the same whether you are binding to in-memory local objects or to objects obtained over the internet.

We will also explore using isolated storage to persist data between usages of the application and then we'll go on to look at creating and using local databases to store data in a relational format.

Binding Data to Controls

You *can* put data into your controls programmatically, but that is very code-intensive and prone to errors. Programmatically manipulated data is difficult to maintain and can cause massive changes to your code when the data types change.

Far better is to bind data to your controls so that updates are made automatically, and you need to write much less code.

Databinding a control to data creates a relationship so that when the data changes the control is updated. This is known as one-way binding. Two-way binding occurs when the control which the data is bound to itself changes (e.g., when the data is changed by a different user).

There are two key aspects to data binding: 1) the binding must be created in the control (typically in the Xaml), and 2) the DataContext must be set. A control can be bound to any public property of an object.

While we name the property we want the control to bind, and we do not identify the object that contains it. We use a DataContext to specify the object with the property we want to bind to. The DataContext is usually set at runtime while the binding is typically set at compile-time. This provides enormous flexibility and power because any object that has the appropriate properties can be used as the data context, and the data context can be determined at runtime.

Let's set up an example by creating a new Windows Phone Application called Data Binding.

Creating the Data

We'll begin by creating a new Windows Phone project.

1. Open Visual Studio and use the standard Windows Phone Application template to open a new project.

In order to have some data to work with, let's create a `Books.cs` class in which we'll define a Book object and create static properties to retrieve a single book or a list of books.

2. To do this, right-click on the project, choose Add Class, and name the new class Books.cs.

3. Add four public properties to the top of the class, as follows:

```
public string Title { get; set; }
 public string Authors { get; set; }
 public string Publisher { get; set; }
 public string ISBN { get; set; }
```

4. Add a static property to return a single book with pre-filled data, as follows:

```
public static Book ABook
 {
     get
     {
         return new Book()
         {
             Title = "Programming Windows Phone",
             Authors = "Jesse Liberty and Jeff Blankenburg",
             ISBN = "143023816X",
             Publisher = "Apress"
         };
     }
 }
```

5. Finally, add a property to return a list of Book object so that we can populate a list box, as follows:

```
public static List<Book> Books
{
    get
    {
        return new List<Book>()
        {
            new Book()
            {
                Title = "Programming Windows Phone",
                Authors = "Jesse Liberty and Jeff Blankenburg",
                ISBN="143023816X",
                Publisher = "Apress"
            },
            new Book()
            {
                Title = "Programming Reactive Extensions and LINQ",
                Authors = "Jesse Liberty and Paul Betts",
                ISBN = "1430237473",
                Publisher = "Apress"
            },
            new Book()
            {
                Title = "Programming Windows 8",
                Authors = "Jesse Liberty",
                ISBN = "TBD",
                Publisher = "Apress"
            },
        };
    }
}
```

Now we're ready to create a couple TextBox controls which we'll bind two properties of a book to.

Creating Controls

Since we want to layout the controls, let's switch over to Expression Blend, being sure to save all the files we've created so far.

1. Open Expression Blend.

2. Set the title to *DATABINDING* and the page name to *binding*.

3. Click in the left margin and create two small rows to hold the two controls we'll be binding to. Drag a TextBlock onto the first row, name it "Title" and center it. Copy and paste the TextBlock and drag the copy into row 2, making sure that its margins are all zero and it is set to be centered both vertically and horizontally. Set its name to ISBN. Save the file and switch back to Visual Studio.

You'll be prompted to update Visual Studio with the changes that were made in Expression Blend; click "Yes to All."

Switch to MainPage.xaml and click on the first TextBlock. Notice that the associated TextBlock in the Xaml is highlighted. This is where we want to add the databinding code. Find the Text property and modify it so that it looks like the following:

```
<TextBlock
    x:Name="Title"
    HorizontalAlignment="Center"
    Margin="0"
    TextWrapping="Wrap"
    d:LayoutOverrides="Height"
    VerticalAlignment="Center"
    Text="{Binding Title}" />
```

The keyword **Binding** indicates that the Text in the TextBox will come from the property of some object (to be named at a later time), and the word **Title** names that property. Notice that nowhere do we indicate *which object* will have that property to bind to. This will be handled by the DataContext, as you'll see in just a moment.

Modify the second TextBlock so that it binds to the ISBN property of the yet-to-be-named object.

Adding DataContext

Now that you've specified which properties are to be bound to our TextBox, you must provide the object that has these properties. This you can do at compile time (by writing it in the Xaml) or, more commonly, at runtime in the code-behind. Open MainPage.xaml.cs and in the constructor add the following line:

```
DataContext = Book.ABook;
```

This sets the DataContext for the current page to what is returned from the static property ABook. If you run the application, you'll find that the TextBlocks have been populated with the Title and ISBN respectively.

To review, briefly, the Binding syntax says, "There is a property of this name that has your data. I'll let you know which object that has this property to use later," and the DataContext says, "Remember I gave you properties to bind to? This is the object with those properties."

The bound data will be displayed in a list box. Let's add that to the page now.

ListBoxes and DataTemplates

The list box provides a convenient way to display data from more than one object at a time. In this case, we'll use it to show the name and ISBN of the books in our collection.

4. Add a ListBox to the third (much larger) row on your page

5. Set its horizontal and vertical alignments to stretch

6. Set its margins to zero

7. Set its width and height to auto (it will take up all the room in the third row)

8. Set its name to BooksList

You can indicate to the ListBox that it is to draw its contents from the static property Books from the Book class by assigning the list to the ListBox's ItemsSource property. To do so, all you need do is add the following line in the constructor:

```
BooksList.ItemsSource = Book.Books;
```

The problem is that while the list box knows it is to get its data from the list of Book objects, it has no way to know which of the three properties to display, and so it just displays the type of each object. To fix this, you'll need to create a DataTemplate—a template that teaches the list box how to layout the sub-controls that will display the contents of the list.

```
<ListBox
    Grid.Row="2"
    HorizontalAlignment="Stretch"
    Margin="0"
    Name="BooksList"
    VerticalAlignment="Stretch"
    Width="Auto"
    Height="Auto"">

    <ListBox.ItemTemplate>
        <DataTemplate>
            <StackPanel
                Margin="0,0,0,17"
                Width="Auto"
                Height="78">
                <TextBlock
                    Text="{Binding Title}"
                    TextWrapping="Wrap"
                    />
                <TextBlock
                    Text="{Binding ISBN}"
                    TextWrapping="Wrap"
                    Margin="12,-6,12,0"
                    />
            </StackPanel>
        </DataTemplate>
    </ListBox.ItemTemplate>
</ListBox>
```

Notice that the ListBox opening and closing tags enclose the DataTemplate. Within the DataTemplate can be exactly one control; in this case the StackPanel. Fortunately, StackPanel can have multiple controls and acts in this case as the container for two TextBlocks. The TextBlocks bind to the data in exactly the same way we saw earlier. The difference is that the DataContext iterates through each book in the list, providing the Title and ISBN for each in turn.

Binding Data with the DataBound Template

Both Visual Studio and Expression Blend offer a special template to get you started with DataBound applications, as shown in Figure 3-1.

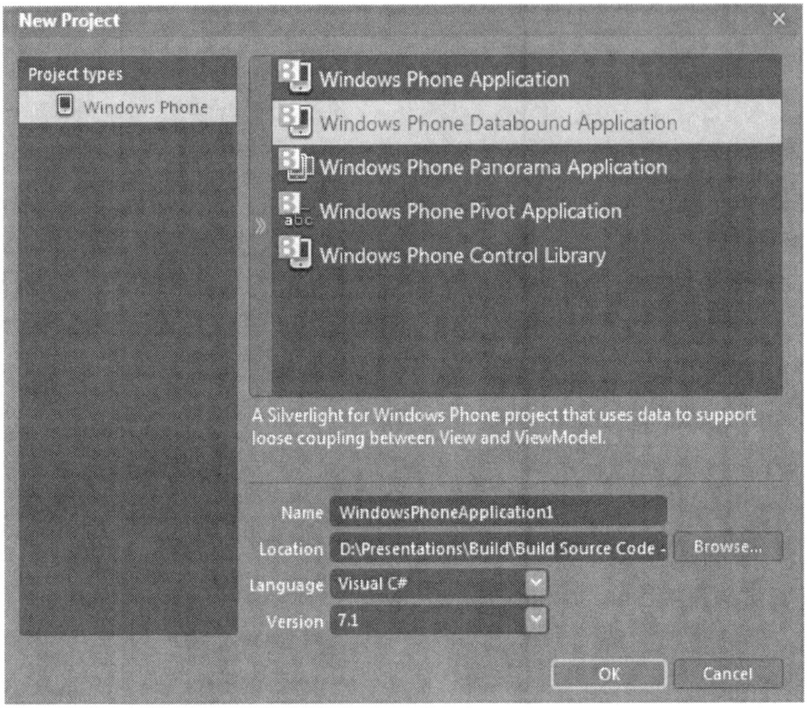

Figure 3-1. Template for DataBound application

This template does so much of the primary work of databinding that it is well worth exploring what you get right out of the box.

The first thing to notice is that there is data available at design time (while you are creating the form) rather than only being available at runtime. We'll take a look at how this is done in just a moment.

The out-of-the-box application consists of two pages: the list (MainPage.xaml) and the details page (DetailsPage.xaml).

Let's start with MainPage.xaml and find a few things to point out.

The design-time DataContext is set in the heading.

```
d:DataContext="{d:DesignData SampleData/MainViewModelSampleData.xaml}"
```

- The DataTemplate TextBlocks use styles to make the individual entries stand out.

```
<TextBlock

    Text="{Binding LineOne}"

    TextWrapping="Wrap"
    Style="{StaticResource PhoneTextExtraLargeStyle}" />
```

- The ItemsSource is bound in the ListBox Xaml declaration rather than in code, and while they're at it, the SelectionChanged event handler is registered.

```
<ListBox
    x:Name="MainListBox"
    Margin="0,0,-12,0"

    ItemsSource="{Binding Items}"
    SelectionChanged="MainListBox_SelectionChanged">
```

The key thing to note on the MainPage.xaml.cs code-behind page is that when the selection changes, the application navigates to a new page (the details page) passing in the selected index.

```
NavigationService.Navigate( new Uri( "/DetailsPage.xaml?selectedItem=" +
MainListBox.SelectedIndex, UriKind.Relative ) );
```

The selected index is passed in as an argument to the Uri for the details page.

```
new Uri( "/DetailsPage.xaml?selectedItem=" + MainListBox.SelectedIndex,
UriKind.Relative ) );
```

This causes navigation to the DetailsPage. Take a look at **OnNavigatedTo** in DetailsPage.xaml.cs to see how the value that was passed in is fished out of the QueryString property.

```
protected override void OnNavigatedTo( NavigationEventArgs e )
{
    string selectedIndex = "";
    if (NavigationContext.QueryString.TryGetValue( "selectedItem",
            out selectedIndex ))
    {
        int index = int.Parse( selectedIndex );
        DataContext = App.ViewModel.Items[index];
    }
}
```

Once we have the selectedIndex, we use that as an index into the Items collection, allowing us to retrieve the complete associated record, and then to bind various fields to its properties.

Before we leave the topic of databinding, we should mention that it is also possible to bind one control to the value of another (see sidebar on Binding to an Element).

■ **Note** Not only is it okay, it is recommended to start with and modify the code in this template for your own purposes.

BINDING TO AN ELEMENT

In addition to binding to data, you can bind one control to another. There are a number of common ways of doing this, but let's examine how we might bind a slider to the opacity of a control on the page. To do this, open Expression Blend and create a new application named ElementBinding, using the standard Phone template.

1. Delete the PageName and set the application name to *ElementBinding*.

2. Click the rectangle in the toolbar, and drag the rectangle onto the Design surface. Right-click on the rectangle in the Objects and Timeline, and select group into border. Set the border to 3 pixels, and set the border color to white (255,255,255).

3. Open the chevron and search for the slider. Make sure the ContentPanel is the selected panel and double-click the slider onto the grid. Use the Selection tool to move the slider next to the rectangle and size it so that it is as tall as the rectangle.

4. Name the rectangle *MyRect* and name the slider *MySlider*. Set the border on the slider to white and set the orientation to vertical.

5. We want the slider to run from 0 to 1, so set the maximum to 1, the large change to 0.1 and the small change to 0.01.

6. Now it is time to tie the opacity of the rectangle to the slider. Click on the advanced properties tab next to opacity on the rectangle and select *Element Property Binding.* The cursor will change, as shown in Figure 3-2.

Figure 3-2. Dropping the Element Binding on the slider

7. Hover over the slider and click, tying the Opacity property of the rectangle to the slider. A dialog box will pop up and ask which property of the slider you want to bind to (notice that it defaults to the property we want, *Value.* Click to accept and—Presto! The elements are bound. Hit F5 to test. Move the slider up and down and note the opacity of the rectangle as it changes with the slider.

Storing Data in Isolated Storage

An essential ingredient in **storing the state and other data of your application**, especially when your application may be tombstoned (see Chapter 4) or, even more extreme, closed, is the ability to create **persistent** storage—that is to write to the disk so that you can retrieve your data when the application resumes or is restarted.

This is the purpose of *isolated storage*. The term is nearly self-explanatory; it is persistent **storage** that is **isolated** from the storage used by all other applications.

There are a number of ways to store data to isolated storage, but it boils down to **key/value pairs.**

You can store these pairs in the ApplicationSettings collection of the IsolatedStorageSettings object. This is, essentially, a **dictionary** that is unique to your application and that is stored on the device securely isolated from all other similar storage.

To see this at work, create a new application with two TextBlocks as prompts, two TextBoxes (Key and Value), a Button (Save) and a ListBox (KeysAndValues), as shown in Figure 3-3.

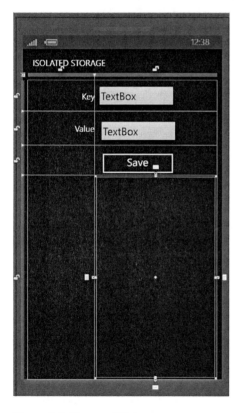

Figure 3-3. Keys and Values

To begin, you'll need a member variable to represent isolated storage, as follows:

```
private IsolatedStorageSettings _isoSettings;
```

IsolatedStorageSettings will not be recognized. Click Control-dot (that is, control-period) to bring up the IntelliSense assistant and accept the following new using statement:

```
using System.IO.IsolatedStorage;
```

Initialize the _isoSettings private member variable in the constructor, as follows:

```
_isoSettings = IsolatedStorageSettings.ApplicationSettings;
```

There are two events that you want to capture:

- The click of the Save button

- The SelectionChanged event on the list box

The **Save button** saves new key/value pairs or updates existing key/value pairs.

Clicking an entry in the list raises **SelectionChanged**, which makes the selected key current and populates the Key and Value TextBoxes

Let's start with the Save_Click event handler. The tasks here are as follows:

9. Make sure we have both a key and a value to add

10. See if the key exists, if so update it

11. If the key does not exist, add it

The following is the code for the event handler:
```
private void Save_Click( object sender, RoutedEventArgs e )
{
    if (
        String.IsNullOrEmpty( Key.Text ) ||
          String.IsNullOrEmpty( Value.Text ))
    {
        return;
    }

    if (_isoSettings.Contains( Key.Text ))
    {
        _isoSettings[Key.Text] = Value.Text;
    }
    else
    {
        _isoSettings.Add( Key.Text, Value.Text );
    }

    RebindListBox();
}
```

Adding to or updating the isolated storage itself is as simple as managing a dictionary; the actual business of writing to disk is handled for you by the IsolatedStorageSettings object.

Notice that the method ends with a call to **RebindListBox**—the job of that method is just to rebuild the list box based on the keys and values in isolated storage.

```
private void RebindListBox()
{
    Value.Text = Key.Text = String.Empty;
    KeysAndValues.Items.Clear();
    foreach (string key in _isoSettings.Keys)
    {
        ListBoxItem lbi = new ListBoxItem();
        string newKey = key + ": " + _isoSettings[key];
        KeysAndValues.Items.Add( newKey );
    }
}
```

I've chosen to list both the key and its value. This makes the workings of the project a bit easier to understand but it does complicate, slightly, the handler for clicking on an entry in the list box.

```
private void KeysAndValues_SelectionChanged(
    object sender,
    SelectionChangedEventArgs e )
{
    if (e.AddedItems.Count < 1)
        return;
    string selected = e.AddedItems[0].ToString();
    string key = selected.Substring(
        0, selected.IndexOf( ":" ) );
    Key.Text = key;
    Value.Text = _isoSettings[key].ToString();
}
```

The small amount of extra work is to isolate the key from the colon and the value; with this in hand, we can proceed to populate the Key TextBox as well as the Value TextBox.

▓ **Note** After you add a key/value pair, you can change applications or stop debugging altogether and then restart to find the values have been saved (persisted) and are restored just as you left them.

Storing Data in a Local Database

Windows Phone supports a full SQL CE database that you interact with using LINQ to SQL, a SQL-like query syntax with objects. This is a fairly straightforward syntax for manipulating data in the database (for more on LINQ to SQL we recommend *Programming with Reactive Extensions and LINQ* (Apress, 2011) by Jesse Liberty and Paul Betts.)

To get started, let's build a dead-simple example that hardwires two objects and places them into the database, and then extracts them and shows their values in a list box.

The program will store information about Books, including the Author(s) and the Publisher, and then display that information on demand.

Building the UI

The initial UI consists of a button that will create two books, a button that will retrieve the two books and a list box that will display the two books, as follows:

```xml
<Grid
    x:Name="ContentPanel"
    Grid.Row="1"
    Margin="12,0,12,0">
    <Grid.RowDefinitions>
        <RowDefinition
            Height="1*" />
        <RowDefinition
            Height="1*" />
        <RowDefinition
            Height="4*" />
    </Grid.RowDefinitions>
    <Button
        Name="CreateBook"
        Content="Create Books"
        VerticalAlignment="Center"
        HorizontalAlignment="Center"
        Margin="0" />
    <Button
        Name="ShowData"
        Content="Show Books"
        Grid.Row="1"
        VerticalAlignment="Center"
        HorizontalAlignment="Center"
        Margin="0" />
    <ListBox
        Name="BooksLB"
        Grid.Row="2"
        VerticalAlignment="Stretch"
        HorizontalAlignment="Stretch"
        Margin="20">
        <ListBox.ItemTemplate>
            <DataTemplate>
                <!-- Details elided -->
            </DataTemplate>
        </ListBox.ItemTemplate>
    </ListBox>
</Grid>
```

░ **Note** For now, we've left out the details of the DataTemplate; we'll return to that shortly.

Accessing Local Storage

We begin the work of managing the data by creating a **DataContext**.

Add a reference to System.Data.Linq and add these three using statements to the top of every related file.

```
using System.Data.Linq;
using System.Data.Linq.Mapping;
using Microsoft.Phone.Data.Linq.Mapping;
```

With these in place we can create the BooksDataContext, which will consist of three Tables and a constructor that passes its connection string to the base class:

```
public class BooksDataContext : DataContext
{
    public Table<Book> Books;
    public Table<Author> Authors;
    public Table<Publisher> Publishers;
    public BooksDataContext( string connection )
        : base( connection ) { }
}
```

As written, the program will not compile because we have not yet defined the Book, Author, and Publisher classes. Let's do so now, and we'll do so with an understanding of relational data and normalization; that is, we'll have the Book class keep an ID for each author and for each publisher, rather than duplicating that information in each instance of Book.

This approach is informed by relational database theory, but is good class design in any case.

▨ **Note** We make the simplifying assumption that every book has but a single author.

The following code appears in Books.cs:

```
[Table]
public class Book
{
    [Column( IsPrimaryKey = true )]
    public string BookID { get; set; }

    [Column]
    public string Title { get; set; }

    [Column]
    public string Author { get; set; }

    [Column]
    public string Publisher { get; set; }

    [Column]
    public DateTime PublicationDate { get; set; }
}
```

Table and Column are LINQ to SQL mapping attributes that tell LINQ to SQL how to map properties in your class to Columns in the tables. The following are the contents of Author.cs and Publisher.cs:

```
[Table]
public class Author
{
    [Column( IsPrimaryKey = true )]
    public string AuthorID { get; set; }

    [Column]
    public string FirstName { get; set; }

    [Column]
    public string LastName { get; set; }

}
[Table]
public class Publisher
{
    [Column( IsPrimaryKey = true )]
    public string PublisherID { get; set; }

    [Column]
    public string Name { get; set; }

    [Column]
    public string City { get; set; }

    [Column]
    public string Url { get; set; }
}
```

We create an instance of the database in MainPage.xaml.cs, in the constructor, where we also wire-up event handlers for the two buttons.

■ **Note** Event handlers can be wired up in the Xaml or in the constructor. It is a matter of personal taste.

```
public MainPage()
{
    InitializeComponent();
    DataContext db =
      new BooksDataContext( "isostore:/bookDB.sdf" );
    if (!db.DatabaseExists())
        db.CreateDatabase();

    CreateBook.Click +=
      new RoutedEventHandler( CreateBook_Click );
    ShowData.Click +=
      new RoutedEventHandler( ShowData_Click );

}
```

Notice the syntax for storing our database file (bookDB.sdf) inside of isolated storage. With the DataContext that we get back, we create the new database.

When CreateBook is clicked the event handler is called, and at this time we want to create two books. Since our books have a publisher and different authors, we must create those objects first (or we'll refer to a publisher or author ID that doesn't exist). Let's start with the creation of the publisher.

```
BooksDataContext db =
    new BooksDataContext( "isostore:/bookDB.sdf" );

Publisher pub = new Publisher()
{
    PublisherID = "1",
    Name = "Apress",
    City = "Acton",
    Url = "http://Apress.com"
};

db.Publishers.InsertOnSubmit( pub );
```

This code gets a new reference to the database, and then instantiates a Publisher object, initializing all the Publisher fields. The last line instructs the database context to insert this record when the Submit command is called. Before calling the Submit command, however, we'll create a few author records.

```
Author auth = new Author()
{
    AuthorID = "1",
    FirstName = "Jesse",
    LastName = "Liberty"
};

db.Authors.InsertOnSubmit( auth );

auth = new Author()
{
    AuthorID = "2",
    FirstName = "Paul",
    LastName = "Betts"
};

db.Authors.InsertOnSubmit( auth );

auth = new Author()
{
    AuthorID = "3",
    FirstName = "Jeff",
    LastName = "Blankenburg"
};

db.Authors.InsertOnSubmit( auth );
```

With these four records ready to be submitted, we call SubmitChanges on the databaseContext.

```
db.SubmitChanges();
```

We're now ready to create the two book objects. Once again we instantiate the C# object and initialize its fields, and once again we mark each instance to be inserted on submission.

```
db = new BooksDataContext( "isostore:/bookDB.sdf" );

Book theBook = new Book()
{
    BookID = "1",
    Author = "2",
    Publisher = "1",
    PublicationDate = DateTime.Now,
    Title = "Programming Reactive Extensions"
};
db.Books.InsertOnSubmit( theBook );

theBook = new Book()
{
    BookID = "2",
    Author = "3",
    Publisher = "1",
    PublicationDate = DateTime.Now,
    Title = "Migrating to Windows Phone"
};
db.Books.InsertOnSubmit( theBook );

db.SubmitChanges();
```

The two books are now in the database, and we can prove that to ourselves by implementing the event handler for the ShowData button.

```
private void ShowData_Click( object sender, RoutedEventArgs e )
{
    BooksDataContext db =
      new BooksDataContext( "isostore:/bookDB.sdf" );
    var q = from book in db.Books
            orderby book.Title
            select book;
    BooksLB.ItemsSource = q;
}
```

Once again we create a new DataContext, but pointing to the same local database. We now execute a LINQ Query against the database, obtaining every record in the Books table, ordered by Title. We set the resulting IEnumerable (q) as the ItemsSource property for the BooksListBox. This then becomes the DataContext for the databinding in the DataTemplate of the list box.

```
<ListBox.ItemTemplate>
    <DataTemplate>
        <StackPanel>
            <TextBlock
                Text="{Binding Title}" />
            <StackPanel
                Orientation="Horizontal">
```

```
                        <TextBlock
                            Text="Author ID: " />
                        <TextBlock
                        Text="{Binding Author}" />
                </StackPanel>
                <StackPanel
                    Orientation="Horizontal">
                    <TextBlock
                        Text="Published: " />
                    <TextBlock
                        Text="{Binding PublicationDate}" />
                </StackPanel>
                <TextBlock
                    Text="-----------------" />
        </StackPanel>
    </DataTemplate>
</ListBox.ItemTemplate>
```

Adding Relationships

It turns out that any given book can have only one publisher, but a publisher, of course, can have many books. We can model this by modifying the Book class.

```
[Table]
    public class Book
    {
        [Column( IsPrimaryKey = true )]
        public string BookID { get; set; }

        [Column]
        public string Title { get; set; }


        [Column]
        public string PublisherID { get; set; }

        private EntityRef<Publisher> _publisher;

        [Association(
            OtherKey = "PublisherID",
            ThisKey = "PublisherID",
            Storage = "_publisher" ) ]
        public Publisher BookPublisher
        {
            get
            {
                return _publisher.Entity;
            }
            set
            {
                _publisher.Entity = value;
```

```
            PublisherID = value.PublisherID;
        }
    }


    [Column]
    public DateTime PublicationDate { get; set; }

}
```

We have a public **PublisherID** that allows us to link this Book's publisher to the ID of a publisher in the database. In addition, we have a private **Entity Reference** back to the instance of the Publisher class. Finally, we add the public property **BookPublisher**, adorning it with the **Association** attribute. In this case we've added the following three properties to the attribute:

- *OtherKey:* The key as it is represented in the publisher class

- *ThisKey:* The foreign key in the Book class

- *Storage:* The backing variable for the property

Since we are only going to follow the association from the Book to the Publisher, that's all we have to do to the class.

We are ready to instantiate a couple publishers.

```
BooksDataContext db = new BooksDataContext( "isostore:/bookDB.sdf" );
Publisher pub = new Publisher()
{
    PublisherID = "1",
    Name = "Apress",
    City = "Acton",
    Url = "http://Apress.com"
};
db.Publishers.InsertOnSubmit( pub );

Publisher pub2 = new Publisher()
{
    PublisherID = "2",
    Name = "O'Reilly",
    City = "Cambridge",
    Url = "http://Oreilly.com"
};
db.Publishers.InsertOnSubmit( pub2 );
```

With these we can instantiate a Book object. Notice that we handle the relationship from an object perspective, making an instance of the publisher a member of the Book object (tying this back to the EntityRef).

```
Book theBook = new Book()
{
    BookID = "1",
    BookPublisher = pub,
    PublicationDate = DateTime.Now,
    Title = "Programming Reactive Extensions"
```

```
};
db.Books.InsertOnSubmit( theBook );
```

We can make as many Book instances as needed, assigning either pub or pub2 (or other publishers we created) to each Book.

```
theBook = new Book()
{
    BookID = "2",

    BookPublisher = pub,

    PublicationDate = DateTime.Now,
    Title="Migrating to Windows Phone"
};
db.Books.InsertOnSubmit( theBook );

theBook = new Book()
{
    BookID = "3",

    BookPublisher = pub2,

    PublicationDate = DateTime.Now,
    Title = "Programming C#"
};
db.Books.InsertOnSubmit( theBook );
```

Querying the Local Database

When we are ready to display the Books, **we will execute a query obtaining the Books, ordered by Title**. We can then assign the results to the ItemsSource property of the ListBox.

```
var q = from b in db.Books
        orderby b.Title
        select b;

BooksLB.ItemsSource = q;
```

Rather than retrieving all the books, it is more efficient to create a temporary class with just the fields we need.

```
var q = from b in db.Books
        orderby b.Title
        select new
        {
            b.Title,
            b.PublicationDate,
            b.BookPublisher
        };

BooksLB.ItemsSource = q;
```

Anonymous Types are internal and by default Windows Phone does not allow reflection into internal types. To allow this anonymous type to provide data via binding you need to add the following line to AssemblyInfo.cs:

```
[assembly: InternalsVisibleTo("System.Windows")]
```

We need to modify the Xaml to bind to the publisher as a reference within the Book object (we do this with the Path property). The following is the relevant excerpt:

```
<ListBox
  Name="BooksLB"
  Grid.Row="2"
  VerticalAlignment="Stretch"
  HorizontalAlignment="Stretch"
  Margin="20">
  <ListBox.ItemTemplate>
    <DataTemplate>
      <StackPanel>
        <TextBlock
          Text="{Binding Title}" />
        <StackPanel
          Orientation="Horizontal">
          <TextBlock
           Text="Published: " />
          <TextBlock
           Text="{Binding PublicationDate}" />
        </StackPanel>
        <TextBlock
          Text="{Binding Path=BookPublisher.Name}" />
        <TextBlock
          Text="-----------------" />
      </StackPanel>
    </DataTemplate>
  </ListBox.ItemTemplate>
</ListBox>
```

Performance is always an issue with databases, and the Windows Phone DB is no exception. Let's take a look at some simple steps you can take to enhance the performance of your application.

Database Performance Optimization

Perhaps the easiest performance optimization available in Windows Phone programming is to add a version control column to your class. The following is all you have to do:

```
[Table]
public class Book
{
    [Column( IsPrimaryKey = true )]
    public string BookID { get; set; }

    [Column]
    public string Title { get; set; }
```

```
[Column]
public string Publisher { get; set; }

[Column]
public DateTime PublicationDate { get; set; }

[Association( OtherKey = "AuthorID" )]
public EntitySet<Author> BookAuthors { get; set; }

[Column(IsVersion=true)]
private Binary _version;
}
```

By adding the Binary _version column, you can improve performance on your DataBase application by up to 700 percent. Here's why: LINQ to SQL is based on optimistic concurrency, which means that possible inconsistencies caused by concurrent users updating the database is checked for only when you submit the transaction (there is no prophylactic record locking). By default, LINQ to SQL submits your changes to the database query processor, which does the consistency check.

The performance enhancement comes by ignoring the query processor and working directly with the tables. But this means that there has to be another way to determine if the record has changed since the previous query. Enter the version column; if this has not changed, then the entire transaction is safe. If it has changed, of course, then LINQ to SQL will throw a ChangeConflictException, but it would have done that anyway.

In short, by adding a version column, only one column needs to be tested, and performance gets a big boost.

Summary

In this chapter you saw how to bind data to controls and how to bind one control to another. You also saw how to store data in isolated storage, which excels at storing key/value pairs. Finally, you saw how to use LINQ to SQL to create and modify a local database.

In the next chapter, we'll take a look at the application lifecycle and you'll see isolated storage put to work.

■ ■ ■

CHAPTER 4

Get a Life

If your application were the only one available on a phone, your life as a developer would be much easier. Not so much for the user, however. Users want to equip their phones with a variety of apps. They want to be able to start yours, switch to another, come back to yours, switch away again, and then shut down the phone, treating the application lifecycle with happy abandon.

To make sure your applications behave appropriately in this environment, you must be able to deal with any change that might occur in its state. In this chapter, you will learn what the stages are in the lifecycle of a Windows Phone application and how you can enhance the experience of your users as your applications moves through them. You will also see what you have to do so that your application supports Fast Application Switching (FAS) and background processes, and generally is seen as responsive.

Understanding the Application Lifecycle

Your application moves through discreet stages from the time it is launched until the time it is closed. It begins with being activated, moves into the Run state, and from there may become dormant, "tombstoned" or may be closed.

Figure 4-1 shows the key stages of the application lifecycle.

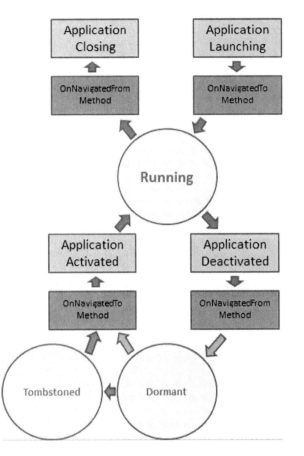

Figure 4-1. The application lifecycle

The following are the principle stages of a Windows Phone 7 application:

Application Launching: The application is starting up. This is your opportunity to do any application-wide setup.

Running: Your application is the foreground application, running in its normal state.

Dormant: Your application has been moved into the background; state is maintained but the application is no longer active and resources have been deal located.

Tombstoned: The phone needed your applications memory and so the application's state is no longer preserved (unless you have saved that state to, e.g., isolated storage).

Closing: The application has been shut down by the user (or by the system). This is your opportunity to do any application-wide clean up.

When the user starts your application, and before it is running, two events are fired: Application Launching and Page On Navigated To. You are free to hook into either event and take whatever action you wish to, to set up your application or your page, respectively. When the application is running, all is normal and good and right with the world.

The user can leave your application in a number of ways, but the key ways are either to close your application (by hitting the back key from your first page) or by launching another application (e.g., from the start menu).

To be explicit; if the user hits the back key from the first page of your application, your application will close. If, however, the user hits the start key and then launches another application, your application will move to the Dormant state.

In the first case, in which the user closes your application, you receive the PageOnNavigatedFrom event to signal that you are leaving the page, and the Application Closing event to signal that the application is going away.

In the second case, in which the user launches a new application, you will still receive the PageOnNavigatedFrom event, but instead of Application Closing, you'll receive Application Deactivated. At this point you want to save anything you might need if the application is either tombstoned or made dormant. We'll cover tombstoning in just a moment.

When you are first deactivated, you will very likely be put in the Dormant state. In this condition, all your memory values are intact, nothing has been lost; and if the user switches back to your application, you will be resumed nearly instantly (assuming you've written the program correctly, which this chapter will explain).

If you are dormant for too long, or if too many applications are made dormant, then your application may be tombstoned. At this point all the memory variables are destroyed, and if the user returns to the application, there will be a noticeable delay (the screen will say "resuming….") while your application retrieves the memory variables from Page State and from Isolated Storage.

It is also possible that your user will not return to your application for a long time, in which case at some point you will go from tombstoned to deactivated. The next time the user comes to your application it will be as if the application started afresh, there will be (and should be) no illusion that the user is restoring a session.

Note The diagram does not show the direct return from tombstoned to closed… consider that an implicit arrow.

Fast Application Switching

When you are restored from the Dormant state you do *not* want to take the time to restore state—it is not necessary because state is preserved in the Dormant state. When you are restored from tombstoning, however, you must restore state as state is not preserved when you are tombstoned. Testing for how you are restored, and not restoring state when you don't need to is referred to as Fast Application Switching because it allows the application to resume immediately.

You can test for how you are restored in the Application_Activated event handler (in App.xaml.cs).

```
private void Application_Activated(
   object sender, ActivatedEventArgs e)
{
  if ( e.IsApplicationInstancePreserved )
  {
      // do not restore application state
  }
  else
  {
      // restore application state
  }
}
```

If you are returning from Dormant state, the IsApplicationInstancePreserved flag will be true, and you do not have to and do not *want* to restore state; your state is intact. Not restoring state under these conditions will make your application much more responsive when the user switches away and then switches back.

Managing State

It can be confusing and difficult to manage all of this state until you become comfortable with the various dictionaries available to you. The following are three key dictionaries that you can use to manage the state of the application:

> *Application State:* A key/value dictionary used for storing application-wide state.

> *Page State:* A key/value dictionary used for storing page state. Both Application and Page State dictionaries are held in memory and released if the application is closed.

> *Isolated Storage:* This is "disk"–based; the values stored in Isolated Storage are preserved even if the application is closed.

Typically, you'll use Application State to allow for the restoration of application state after being tombstoned. Similarly, you'll use Page State to allow for the restoration of the state of the current page after being tombstoned. Isolated Storage is used to restore any values that should be available not only after being tombstoned, but after the application is closed and then reopened.

Page State

You will want to manage Page State not only when the user navigates away from your application, but when the user navigates away from the page. After all, if the user fills in some fields, navigates to a second page, and then hits the back button to return to the first page, he has every reason to expect that the fields will still be filled in properly. Let's take a look at how that would work in a simple example.

Create a new Windows Phone application and on `MainPage.xaml` change ContentPanel to be a StackPanel and add a Button, a TextBlock, and a TextBox, as shown in Listing 4-1.

Listing 4-1. Changes to MainPage.xaml

```
<StackPanel
    x:Name="ContentPanel"
    Grid.Row="1"
    Margin="12,0,12,0">
    <Button
        Name="GoToPage2"
        Content="Go to page 2"
        HorizontalAlignment="Center"
        VerticalAlignment="Center" />
    <TextBlock
        HorizontalAlignment="Center"
        VerticalAlignment="Center"
        Text="Page Data:" />
    <TextBox
        HorizontalAlignment="Center"
        VerticalAlignment="Center"
        Width="350"
        Name="PageData"
        Text="" />
</StackPanel>
```

The GoToPage2 button is used to navigate to a second page. Add the event handler for the button to MainPage.xaml.cs, which is shown in Listing 4-2.

Listing 4-2. ••••••••••••••••E•••••H••••••

```
Private void GoToPage2_Click( object sender, RoutedEventArgs e )
{
    NavigationService.Navigate(
        new Uri( "/Page2.xaml", UriKind.Relative ) );
}
```

When you navigate away from MainPage.xaml, the OnNavigatedFrom method is called. If the navigation is backwards, the page will be disposed of, and there is no need to store the state. Otherwise, we'll store the state in the Page State object, which is a dictionary that will persist through being dormant and being tombstoned, but not through the application being terminated, as shown in Listing 4-3.

Listing 4-3. •••••••••••••••••

```
protected override void OnNavigatedFrom(
    System.Windows.Navigation.NavigationEventArgs e )
{
    base.OnNavigatedFrom( e );

    if ((e.NavigationMode !=
        System.Windows.Navigation.NavigationMode.Back))
    {

        State["PageData"] = PageData.Text;

    }
}
```

The important line in Listing 4-3 is shown in bold; it is when we save the text from PageData into the State dictionary under the key "PageData."

When we navigate to the page, we need to differentiate between a new page and one that is being restored after having been dormant. Earlier you saw Fast Application Switching supported by using the IsApplicationInstancePreserved flag. An alternative is to create a Boolean **flag _newPage**, which we'll initialize to false and set to true in the constructor.

The key fact is that the **flag, _newPage** will be the following:

    a.   True when we first navigate to the page

    b.   True when we return to the page by pressing the back key from Page2

    c.   True when we come back to the page after being tombstoned

    d.   False when we come back to the page after being dormant

This is exactly what we want. We want to restore state in the first three conditions, but not when we return from being dormant, because when Dormant state was not lost.

1.   You can test this by creating the second page (just create a new page named **Page2.xaml**) and then by running the application.

2.   Put a break point on the test of the flag, as follows:

```
If ( _newPage )
```

3.   Then drag the flag to the debugger watch window so you can easily see its value.

4.   Run the application and navigate to Page2, and then use the back key to return. You should observe that the flag is **true**.

5.   Next, click on the Windows button (to launch a new application) and then the back key (to resume your application).

6.   Because your application was dormant, the value is **false**, and there is no need to restore state.

7.   Finally, run your application and hit the back key to back out of and exit the application. Then restart and note that the flag is **true** again.

If you want to test the result with tombstoning, see the upcoming Debugging with Tombstoning section.

Listing 4-4 is the complete source code for Page1.xaml.cs.

Listing 4-4. Page1.xaml.cs

```
using System;
using System.Windows;
using Microsoft.Phone.Controls;

namespace PageState
{
    public partial class MainPage : PhoneApplicationPage
    {
        private bool _newPage;

        public MainPage()
        {
            InitializeComponent();
            _newPage = true;
            GoToPage2.Click += new RoutedEventHandler( GoToPage2_Click );
        }

        void GoToPage2_Click( object sender, RoutedEventArgs e )
        {
            NavigationService.Navigate(
                new Uri( "/Page2.xaml", UriKind.Relative ) );
        }

        protected override void OnNavigatedFrom(
            System.Windows.Navigation.NavigationEventArgs e )
        {
            base.OnNavigatedFrom( e );

            if ((e.NavigationMode !=
                System.Windows.Navigation.NavigationMode.Back))
            {
                State["PageData"] = PageData.Text;
            }

        }

        protected override void OnNavigatedTo(
                System.Windows.Navigation.NavigationEventArgs e )
        {
            base.OnNavigatedTo( e );

            if (_newPage)
            {
                if (String.IsNullOrEmpty( PageData.Text ))
                {
```

```
                if (State.Count > 0)
                    PageData.Text = State["PageData"].ToString();
            }
        }
        _newPage = false;
    }
  }
}
```

Support for Fast Application Switching takes little code and is painless, but the results are a dramatic improvement in the time it takes to switch back to your application. Including code for FAS should be considered "required" for every application.

Debugging with Tombstoning

Because it is important to be able to test what happens when your application returns from the Tombstoned state, and because the normal state transition is from Running to Dormant, the debugger has a special provision to ensure that your application goes into the Tombstoned state when you suspend it.

To force this, right-click on the project and choose properties. Click on the Debug tab and click the check box that says "Tombstone upon deactivation while debugging," as shown in Figure 4-2.

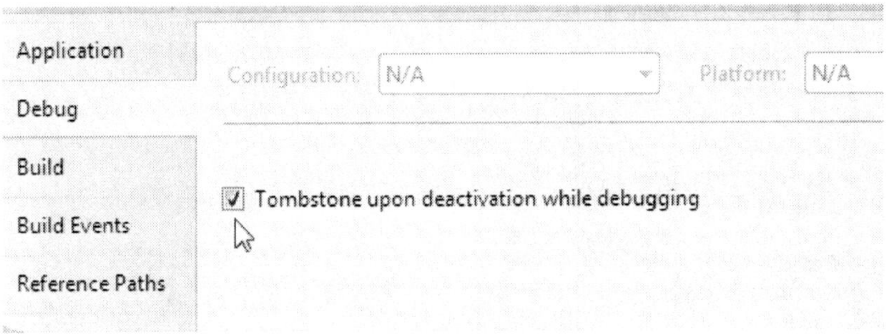

Figure 4-2. Ensure that your application is tombstoned

Once you click this checkbox, if you run the application and then click the Windows button (to launch a new app), and then click the back button to return to the application, the flag will be **true** because you'll be returning from tombstoned.

Using Background Agents

When your application is dormant, tombstoned, or closed, it stops executing. There are times, however, when you need code to continue to be executed, even if your application is not in the foreground.

Background Agents and Scheduled Tasks allow an application to execute in the background, even when the application is not running. Background agents are collectively known as Scheduled Tasks and they come in two flavors: Periodic Tasks and Resource-Intensive Tasks. The two are designed for different types of background processing scenarios and thus have different constraints.

An application may have only one background agent. The agent can be registered either as a PeriodicTask or as a ResourceIntensiveTask or both. Only one instance of an agent will run at a time and how frequently it runs is determined by what type it is and upon other constraints, such as whether the user has placed the phone in battery saving mode. See Figure 4-3 for the duration for Periodic Tasks and Figure 4-4 for the duration for Resource-Intensive Tasks.

Constraint	Description
Scheduled interval: 30 minutes	Periodic agents typically run every 30 minutes. To optimize battery life, periodic agents may be run in alignment with other background processes and therefore the execution time may drift by up to 10 minutes.
Scheduled duration: 15 seconds	Periodic agents typically run for 15 seconds. There are other constraints that may cause an agent to be terminated early.
Battery Saver mode can prevent execution	Battery Saver mode is an option that the user can enable on the device to indicate that battery life should be prioritized. If this mode is enabled, periodic agents may not run, even if the interval has elapsed.
Per-device periodic agent limit	To help maximize the battery life of the device, there is a hard limit on the number of periodic agents that can be scheduled on the phone. It varies per device configuration and can be as low as 6. There is another limit, which is lower than the hard limit, after which the user will be warned that they have multiple background agents running and may, therefore, experience faster battery consumption.

Figure 4-3 Frequency of running Periodic Tasks

Constraint	Description
Duration: 10 minutes	Resource-intensive agents typically run for 10 minutes. There are other constraints that may cause an agent to be terminated early.
External power required	Resource-intensive agents will not run unless the device is connected to an external power source.
Non-cellular connection required	Resource-intensive agents will not run unless the device has a network connection over Wi-Fi or through a connection to a PC.
Minimum battery power	Resource-intensive agents will not run unless the device's battery power is greater than 90%.
Device screen lock required	Resource-intensive agents will not run unless the device screen is locked.
No active phone call	Resource-intensive agents will not run while a phone call is active.
Cannot change network to cellular	If a resource-intensive agent attempts to call AssociateToNetworkInterface(Socket, NetworkInterfaceInfo) specifying either MobileBroadbandGSM() or MobileBroadbandCDMA(), the method call will fail.

Figure 4-4. Resource-Intensive Tasks

The code for either kind of agent is implemented in a class that inherits from BackgroundAgent. When the agent is launched, the operating system calls `OnInvoke(ScheduledTask)`. In this method, the application can determine which type of `ScheduledTask` it is being run as, and perform the appropriate actions. When the agent has completed its task, it should call `NotifyComplete()` or `Abort()` to let the operating system know that it has completed.

`NotifyComplete()` should be used if the task was successful. If the agent is unable to perform its task —such as not being able to reach a required server—the agent should call `Abort()`, which will cause the IsScheduled property to be set to `false`. The foreground application can check this property when it is running to determine whether `Abort()` was called.

To see this at work, let's create an application.

1. Begin by creating a standard Windows Phone Application. Name it Scheduled Tasks.

2. Add a new project of type *Windows Phone Scheduled Task Agent.* Your solution will now have two projects.

3. Add a reference to the new project on the original project by clicking on the project menu and selecting Add Reference... and navigating to the Projects tab. Select the agent project, and click OK.

4. In SolutionExplorer, double-click `TaskScheduler.cs` (under the agent project) to open the file. This file contains the definition for `TaskScheduler`, which inherits from `ScheduledTaskAgent`.

5. Add the two `using` directives shown in the following snippet:

```
using Microsoft.Phone.Shell
using System
```

Let's focus on the key method of the class, `OnInvoke(ScheduledTask)()`. This method is called by the operating system when the Scheduled Task is launched. This is where you should place the code you want to execute when your background agent is run.

Each application can have only one `ScheduledTaskAgent` registered at a time, but you can schedule this agent as both a resource-intensive agent and a periodic agent. If your application uses both a `ResourceIntensiveTask` and a `PeriodicTask`, you can check the type of the ScheduledTask object that is passed into the OnInvoke method to determine which task the agent is being invoked for, and branch your code execution as necessary.

If you use only one type of agent, you do not need to check the ScheduledTask object type. In this example, the agent launches a ShellToast object from `OnInvoke()`, indicating the type of scheduled task for which the agent is being called. This toast will let you see when the agent is running. However, it will not be displayed while your foreground application is running.

When your Scheduled Task code has completed, you should call `NotifyComplete()` to let the operating system know that you no longer need to execute. This allows the operating system to attempt to schedule other agents.

Listing 4-5 contains the code you need to implement `OnInvoke()`. Add it to the project.

Listing 4-5. OnInvoke(ScheduledTask) Method

```
protected override void OnInvoke(ScheduledTask task)
{
  string toastMessage = "";

  // If your application uses both PeriodicTask and ResourceIntensiveTask
  // you can branch your application code here. Otherwise, you don't need to.
  if (task is PeriodicTask)
  {
    // Execute periodic task actions here.
    toastMessage = "Periodic task running.";
  }
  else
  {
    // Execute resource-intensive task actions here.
    toastMessage = "Resource-intensive task running.";
  }

  // Launch a toast to show that the agent is running.
  // The toast will not be shown if the foreground application is running.
  ShellToast toast = new ShellToast();
```

```
  toast.Title = "Background Agent Sample";
  toast.Content = toastMessage;
  toast.Show();

  // If debugging is enabled, launch the agent again in one minute.
#if DEBUG_AGENT
  ScheduledActionService.LaunchForTest(task.Name, TimeSpan.FromSeconds(60));
#endif

  // Call NotifyComplete to let the system know the agent is done working.
  NotifyComplete();
}
```

The LaunchForTest(String, TimeSpan) method is provided so that you can run your agent on a more frequent schedule than it will run on an actual device. This method is only for application development and will not function except for in applications that are deployed using the development tools.

In this example, the method is called to launch the agent after one minute. The call is placed in an #if block to enable you to easily switch between debugging and production functionality.

To enable the call, put the following line at the *top* of the TaskScheduler.cs file:

```
#define DEBUG_AGENT
```

Let's return to the main project and set up its UI. Listing 4-6 contains the Xaml for the MainPage.xaml file.

Add the code in Listing 4-6 to MainPage.xaml.

Listing 4-6. Xaml for PeriodicStackPanel

```xml
<StackPanel>
  <StackPanel  Orientation="Vertical" Name="PeriodicStackPanel" Margin="0,0,0,40">
    <TextBlock Text="Periodic Agent" Style="{StaticResource PhoneTextTitle2Style}"/>
    <StackPanel Orientation="Horizontal">
      <TextBlock Text="name: " Style="{StaticResource PhoneTextAccentStyle}"/>
      <TextBlock Text="{Binding Name}" />
    </StackPanel>
    <StackPanel Orientation="Horizontal">
      <TextBlock Text="is enabled" VerticalAlignment="Center"  Style="{StaticResource
PhoneTextAccentStyle}"/>
      <CheckBox Name="PeriodicCheckBox" IsChecked="{Binding IsEnabled}"
Checked="PeriodicCheckBox_Checked" Unchecked="PeriodicCheckBox_Unchecked"/>
    </StackPanel>
    <StackPanel Orientation="Horizontal">
      <TextBlock Text="is scheduled: "  Style="{StaticResource PhoneTextAccentStyle}"/>
      <TextBlock Text="{Binding IsScheduled}" />
    </StackPanel>
    <StackPanel Orientation="Horizontal">
      <TextBlock Text="last scheduled time: "  Style="{StaticResource PhoneTextAccentStyle}"/>
      <TextBlock Text="{Binding LastScheduledTime}" />
    </StackPanel>
    <StackPanel Orientation="Horizontal">
      <TextBlock Text="expiration time: " Style="{StaticResource PhoneTextAccentStyle}"/>
```

```
        <TextBlock Text="{Binding ExpirationTime}" />
      </StackPanel>
      <StackPanel Orientation="Horizontal">
        <TextBlock Text="last exit reason: "  Style="{StaticResource PhoneTextAccentStyle}"/>
        <TextBlock Text="{Binding LastExitReason}" />
      </StackPanel>
    </StackPanel>
  <StackPanel  Orientation="Vertical" Name="ResourceIntensiveStackPanel" Margin="0,0,0,40">
    <TextBlock Text="Resource-intensive Agent" Style="{StaticResource PhoneTextTitle2Style}"/>
    <StackPanel Orientation="Horizontal">
      <TextBlock Text="name: " Style="{StaticResource PhoneTextAccentStyle}"/>
      <TextBlock Text="{Binding Name}" />
    </StackPanel>
    <StackPanel Orientation="Horizontal">
      <TextBlock Text="is enabled" VerticalAlignment="Center"  Style="{StaticResource
PhoneTextAccentStyle}"/>
      <CheckBox Name="ResourceIntensiveCheckBox" IsChecked="{Binding IsEnabled}"
Checked="ResourceIntensiveCheckBox_Checked" Unchecked="ResourceIntensiveCheckBox_Unchecked"/>
    </StackPanel>
    <StackPanel Orientation="Horizontal">
      <TextBlock Text="is scheduled: "  Style="{StaticResource PhoneTextAccentStyle}"/>
      <TextBlock Text="{Binding IsScheduled}" />
    </StackPanel>
    <StackPanel Orientation="Horizontal">
      <TextBlock Text="last scheduled time: "  Style="{StaticResource PhoneTextAccentStyle}"/>
      <TextBlock Text="{Binding LastScheduledTime}" />
    </StackPanel>
    <StackPanel Orientation="Horizontal">
      <TextBlock Text="expiration time: " Style="{StaticResource PhoneTextAccentStyle}"/>
      <TextBlock Text="{Binding ExpirationTime}" />
    </StackPanel>
    <StackPanel Orientation="Horizontal">
      <TextBlock Text="last exit reason: "  Style="{StaticResource PhoneTextAccentStyle}"/>
      <TextBlock Text="{Binding LastExitReason}" />
    </StackPanel>
  </StackPanel>
</StackPanel>
```

This Xaml adds two sets of controls, one for each of the agent types. Most of the controls are text blocks that will be bound to the ScheduledTask objects that represent the background agents, allowing you to view the properties of these objects.

Now we need to create two class variables to represent each of the agent types. These are the objects that will be bound to the UI. The Scheduled Action Service uniquely identifies scheduled tasks by their Name property. Create two variables containing the names that will be used for the agents.

To implement these additions, add the code in Listing 4-7 inside the class definition.

Listing 4-7. Adding the code inside the class definition

```
public partial class MainPage : PhoneApplicationPage
{
  PeriodicTask periodicTask;
  ResourceIntensiveTask resourceIntensiveTask;

  string periodicTaskName = "PeriodicAgent";
  string resourceIntensiveTaskName = "ResourceIntensiveAgent";
```

Next we need to implement a helper method named `StartPeriodicAgent`. This method uses the Find(String) method to obtain a reference to the `PeriodicTask` with the specified name. If the scheduled task object is not `null` and its `IsEnabled` property is `false`, the user has disabled background agents for this application in the device's Settings. In this case, you should alert the user and exit the method.

You cannot update agents directly. You must remove and then add. If the scheduled task object is not equal to `null`, and `IsEnabled` is `true`, then you should call `Remove(String)` to unregister the agent with the system, and then immediately create a new PeriodicTask object and assign its name in the constructor.

1. Set the Description property, which is required for Periodic agents and is used to describe the agent to the user in the background tasks Settings page on the device.

2. Call Add to register the Periodic agent with the system. Set the data context of the associated UI element to update the databinding and display the objects properties to the user.

3. To implement these changes, place the code for StartPeriodicAgent (shown in Listing 4-8) into the MainPage class definition (not the constructor).

Listing 4-8. StartPeriodicAgent

```
private void StartPeriodicAgent()
{
  periodicTask = ScheduledActionService.Find(periodicTaskName) as PeriodicTask;

  if (periodicTask != null && !periodicTask.IsEnabled)
  {
    MessageBox.Show("Background agents for this application have been disabled by the user.");
    return;
  }

  if (periodicTask != null && periodicTask.IsEnabled)
  {
    RemoveAgent(periodicTaskName);
  }

  periodicTask = new PeriodicTask(periodicTaskName);

  periodicTask.Description = "This demonstrates a periodic task.";
  ScheduledActionService.Add(periodicTask);
```

```
  PeriodicStackPanel.DataContext = periodicTask;

  // If debugging is enabled, use LaunchForTest to launch the agent in one minute.
#if(DEBUG_AGENT)
  ScheduledActionService.LaunchForTest(periodicTaskName, TimeSpan.FromSeconds(60));
#endif
}
```

You now need a start helper method for the resource-intensive task. This method is *identical* to the method for the periodic task, except it uses the ResourceIntensiveTask class to schedule the agent, and a different name is used. Note that there is an opportunity for refactoring here.

4. Add the code in Listing 4-9.

Listing 4-9. StartResourceIntensiveAgent method

```
private void StartResourceIntensiveAgent()
{
  resourceIntensiveTask = ScheduledActionService.Find(resourceIntensiveTaskName) as
ResourceIntensiveTask;

  if (resourceIntensiveTask != null && !resourceIntensiveTask.IsEnabled)
  {
    MessageBox.Show("Background agents for this application have been disabled by the user.");
    return;
  }

  if (resourceIntensiveTask != null && resourceIntensiveTask.IsEnabled)
  {
    RemoveAgent(resourceIntensiveTaskName);
  }

  resourceIntensiveTask = new ResourceIntensiveTask(resourceIntensiveTaskName);

  resourceIntensiveTask.Description = "This demonstrates a resource-intensive task.";
  ScheduledActionService.Add(resourceIntensiveTask);

  ResourceIntensiveStackPanel.DataContext = resourceIntensiveTask;

  // If debugging is enabled, use LaunchForTest to launch the agent in one minute.
#if(DEBUG_AGENT)
  ScheduledActionService.LaunchForTest(resourceIntensiveTaskName, TimeSpan.FromSeconds(60));
#endif
}
```

5. Add a Boolean class variable, ignoreCheckBoxEvents. This variable will be used to switch off the CheckBox events when initializing the page. Add event handlers for the Checked and Unchecked events for CheckBox controls. These handlers call the start and stop helper methods created in the previous steps. If ignoreCheckBoxEvents is true, the handlers return without doing anything.

6. Add the code in Listing 4-10.

Listing 4-10. ignoreCheckBoxEvents

bool ignoreCheckBoxEvents = false;

```
private void PeriodicCheckBox_Checked(object sender, RoutedEventArgs e)
{
  if (ignoreCheckBoxEvents)
    return;
  StartPeriodicAgent();
}
private void PeriodicCheckBox_Unchecked(object sender, RoutedEventArgs e)
{
  if (ignoreCheckBoxEvents)
   return;
  RemoveAgent(periodicTaskName);
}
private void ResourceIntensiveCheckBox_Checked(object sender, RoutedEventArgs e)
{
  if (ignoreCheckBoxEvents)
    return;
  StartResourceIntensiveAgent();
}
private void ResourceIntensiveCheckBox_Unchecked(object sender, RoutedEventArgs e)
{
  if (ignoreCheckBoxEvents)
    return;
  RemoveAgent(resourceIntensiveTaskName);
}
```

You need the RemoveAgent helper method to call Remove(string) in a try block (so that an exception will not cause the app to exit).

7. Add the code in Listing 4-11.

Listing 4-11. RemoveAgent method

```
private void RemoveAgent(string name)
{
  try
  {
    ScheduledActionService.Remove(name);
  }
  catch (Exception)
  {
  }
}
```

8. Finally, you need to override OnNavigatedTo() by adding the code in Listing 4-12.

Listing 4-12. OnNavigatedTo method

```
protected override void OnNavigatedTo(System.Windows.Navigation.NavigationEventArgs e)
{
    ignoreCheckBoxEvents = true;

    periodicTask = ScheduledActionService.Find(periodicTaskName) as PeriodicTask;

    if (periodicTask != null)
    {
        PeriodicStackPanel.DataContext = periodicTask;
    }

    resourceIntensiveTask = ScheduledActionService.Find(resourceIntensiveTaskName) as
ResourceIntensiveTask;
    if (resourceIntensiveTask != null)
    {
        ResourceIntensiveStackPanel.DataContext = resourceIntensiveTask;
    }

    ignoreCheckBoxEvents = false;

}
```

Summary

In this chapter, you learned how the lifecycle of a Windows Phone application works, and more important, you learned how to manage return from both the Dormant state (Fast Application Switching) and from the Tombstoned state (making use of Isolated Storage and Page State).

You also saw how to use background agents to run either periodic tasks or to run resource-intensive tasks in the background.

CHAPTER 5

■ ■ ■

Get Blended

In the dark and early days of computing, when programs were nasty, brutish and short, we used different tools for writing the code (the editor), for compiling the code (the compiler), for linking the code (the linker), and for debugging the code (the debugger). The advent of the Integrated Development Environment (IDE) had a tremendous positive impact on programmer productivity.

Thus, you may be surprised to hear that we advocate using two development tools: Visual Studio for C# code, and Expression Blend for layout, data binding, animation, and more. In fact, we each fought this two-tool solution until first we became convinced, and then overwhelmingly convinced, that the advantages far outweigh the inconvenience of working with a pair of tools rather than a single IDE.

This change in work flow was made more palatable by the fact that Visual Studio and Expression Blend work on the same files, projects, and solutions; there's no importing and exporting, and moving back and forth between them is virtually seamless.

This chapter will focus on a number of areas where Blend simply makes life enormously easier. Keep in mind, however, that everything we do in Blend can, of course, be done in Visual Studio (though not necessarily as easily) and everything we do in the design mode of Blend can also be done by hand-writing the Xaml (again, though, not as easily).

Using Styles & Templates

Every control in Windows Phone programming is *lookless.* That is, there is no official, let alone permanent appearance for any given control type. Every control has a default appearance, without which it would be very hard to get anything done, but you are free to modify that appearance, or even create a new one from scratch.

Creating a Style

To see how to create a new style with Blend, let's modify the style of a button.

1. Create a new Windows Phone application in Blend and call it `ButtonStyler`. When Blend opens, take note of its various pallets and areas. There is quite a lot to learn to become an expert in Blend and we recommend that it is more than worthwhile to pick up a book on Blend itself or to spend some serious time playing with Blend and getting to know its capabilities.

2. Click on the button control in the toolbar and then drag a button out onto the artboard, so that your application looks like the one shown Figure 5-1.

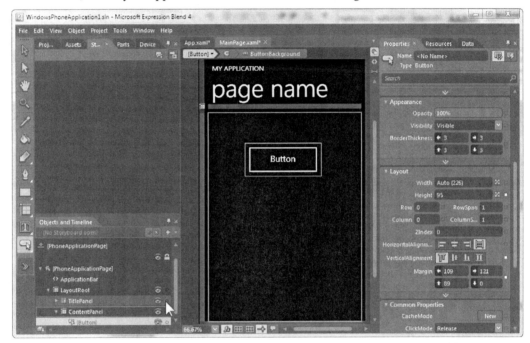

Figure 5-1. Button on the artboard

3. Type the letter "V" to change the cursor to the Selection Tool and then right-click on the Button.

4. Select Edit Template... Edit A Copy. A dialog box appears with two sets of choices. First, you can name this new style or you can check the box to indicate that the new style should be applied all buttons. In this case, name we'll name the style and call it `AccentButtonStyle`.

   Second, you can define the style in your application (in which case it can be used throughout your application) or you can define it just for this one "document," that is, this one page of the phone application.

5.   Select Application and click OK.

The artboard immediately transforms; you are now in the style editor.

Modifying Visual State

Before we go any further, you need to know a bit about *visual state.* Windows Phone supports the concept of Visual State and a Visual State Manager. Visual state allows you to dictate how a control looks (and to some degree, how it behaves!) based on the state of that control—where state is defined by the designer or programmer. For example, the Button control that we copied comes complete with the following two sets of visual states:

- *Focused states,* which can be either focused or unfocused; and

- *Common states,* as they are called: the normal state, the state of the mouse hovering over the button, the state of the button being pressed, and the state of the button being disabled.

By tying the appearance of a control to its state, you can accomplish a great deal without any programming—the button "knows" to change its appearance as it moves from one visual state to another.

Since we have made a copy of the button style, we can start off in our new style with all the "parts" of the button and all of its visual states.

1.   You can see this by clicking on the States tab, as shown in Figure 5-2.

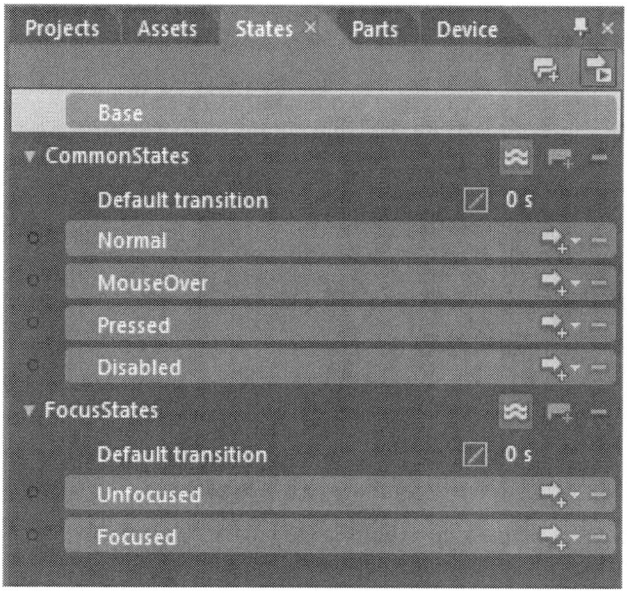

Figure 5-2. Button States

If you click on each of the `CommonStates` listed on the tab, you'll see how the standard button looks in each of them. Note particularly that when the button is `Pressed`, its background is white. We're going to change that.

2. Click on Pressed and note that a red square surrounds the artboard. You are now recording your changes.

3. Move down to the Objects and Timeline and expand the parts of the `Button` so that you can access the background, as shown in Figure 5-3.

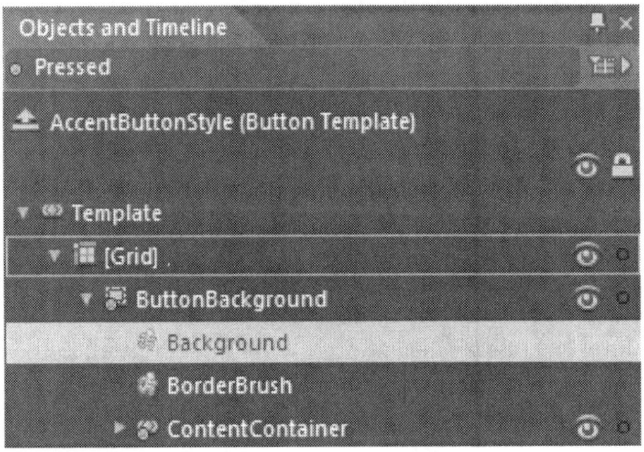

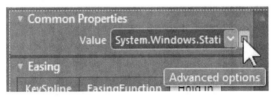

Figure 5-3. Edit the background in the Pressed state

4. With the background selected, go to the Properties window and click on the Advanced button next to the Value property for the background, as shown in Figure 5-4.

Figure 5-4. Advanced Options

5. When the menu opens, select System Resources Phone Accent Brush. This will set the background brush to the accent color the user has selected.

6. You're done editing this style, so pop back up to editing the page by clicking on the Return Scope button in the Objects and Timeline, as shown in Figure 5-5.

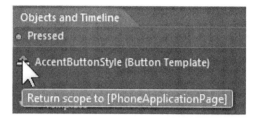

Figure 5-5. Return to the scope of the page

7.   Run the application and when you click on the button, you'll see that the
background color is now the selected accent color.

Applying a Style

If you drag a second button onto the artboard it will not have your modified style, it will have the default
style. Rather than restyling it by repeating all the steps we just took, however, you can apply the style
you created to the new button by right-clicking on it and selecting Edit Template   Apply Resource
AccentButtonStyle. Nice.

Using Behaviors

Behaviors are a gift. They were developed as a way to allow non-programmers to "make things happen"
in Blend, but they are a terrific way to write declarative (arguably, functional) programming using Xaml.
Behaviors let you drag a predetermined set of functionality onto an object and execute that functionality
without writing any C#.

Let's see this at work by creating a new application with two buttons. Our goal is that when the user
starts the application, the background will be black; but when the user clicks the first button, a penguin
image will fill the background; and when the user clicks the second button, a desert image will replace it.

1.   Create a new Windows Phone application in Blend and name it
BackgroundImages.

2.   Create a new folder in your application named Images. This also creates a
physical folder on your disk, under your project folder.

3.   Next, in the operating system, find the sample pictures that come with
Windows and copy the Penguins and the Desert images into the folder you just
created. Finally, back in Blend, right-click on the Images folder and click Add
Existing and select those two images to add them to your project.

Our background images will need to live inside a container. We'll use a grid; in fact, we'll use a
separate grid for each image.

4.   Add a new Grid to the Content Panel and name it Penguins Grid. Set its
Horizontal and Vertical alignments to stretch and its margin to 0 all around.
Set its width and height to Auto and the Grid will fill the entire Content Panel.

5. Click on the background and then click on the Image brush. In the Image Source, pick the `Penguin.jpg` file and when it appears, set the visibility to `collapsed`.

6. To hold the Desert, repeat these steps with a second grid. Name the second grid `DesertGrid`.

7. Finally, add two buttons to the Content Panel. Label one Penguins and the other Desert and set their content properties accordingly.

Defining Visual States

You certainly *could* write code to hook up the Click event handler of each button and display its image, but instead we're going to use the Visual State manager.

1. To do so, we need two new states, so click on the States tab and then click on the Add State Group button, as shown in Figure 5-6.

Figure 5-6. Adding a state group

2. Name the new State Group `BackgroundStates` and then add two new states to the Group: Penguin State and Desert State.

3. When the application enters Penguin State, we want the Penguin background to become visible. Click on that state and then while recording is on, click on the Penguin State grid in the Objects and Timeline and then click on Visible in the properties window. To stop recording, click the red button in the upper-left corner.

4. Repeat for the Desert state.

5. Make sure your states are working by clicking on Base, PenguinState and DesertState and observe that the background changes appropriately.

Look Ma, No Code

Here again, you certainly could write code so that when the Desert button is clicked, the Visual State manager switches to the Desert state, thus displaying the Desert image. We can do better than that, however, by using behaviors.

1. Switch to the Assets panel Behaviors and find the `GoToStateAction` behavior. Drag this to the Desert button. In the properties panel, use the dropdown to pick the state we want (`DesertState`). Repeat this for the Penguins button. Run the application and notice that when you click the button, the state changes and the image is displayed as the background, as shown in Figure 5-7.

Figure 5-7. Clicking the buttons to change state

All of this was accomplished without writing any C#. Be sure to take the time to examine the Xaml that Blend produces; you'll find that Xaml is not only machine-readable, it is very human-readable as well.

Creating Sample Data

Expression Blend has terrific facilities for creating sample data. The two primary ways to do so are to let Expression Blend generate the data and then to modify that data to your needs, or to have Expression Blend create the data from an existing class. We'll examine both techniques.

Sample Data Generated by Expression Blend

The simplest way to create sample data is to use Blend to do the work.

1. To create some sample data with Blend, start by clicking on the Data tab in the Blend main window (see the "Create sample data" icon shown in Figure 5-8).

   The Data tab provides three choices, but in this case select Create Sample Data. In turn, this brings up a dialog box.

2. Name your sample data `SampleInventory` and leave the remaining choices as they are.

Figure 5-8. Create sample data

Sample data is created; specifically a collection with two properties per item. The first is a string named **Property1** and the second is a **Boolean** named **Property2**.

3. To find (and change) the type of a property, click on the Property button to the right of its name.

Let's make the following changes:

a. Click on the collection and change its name to **Contacts**

b. Click on **Property1** and change its name to **Name** and use the property dropdown to change its **Format** to **Name**

c. Click on **Property2** and change its name to **Address** and its type to **string** and its format to **Address**

d. Add a third property, name it **Email** and set the type to **string** and the format to e-mail address

e. Add a final property, set its name to **Geek** and set its type to **Boolean**

Click on Edit Sample Values (as shown in Figure 5-9)…

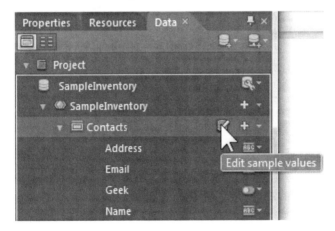

Figure 5-9. Edit Sample Values Button

…and you will be brought to a dialog box that allows you to both review and edit the number and specifics of the generated sample data, as shown in Figure 5-10.

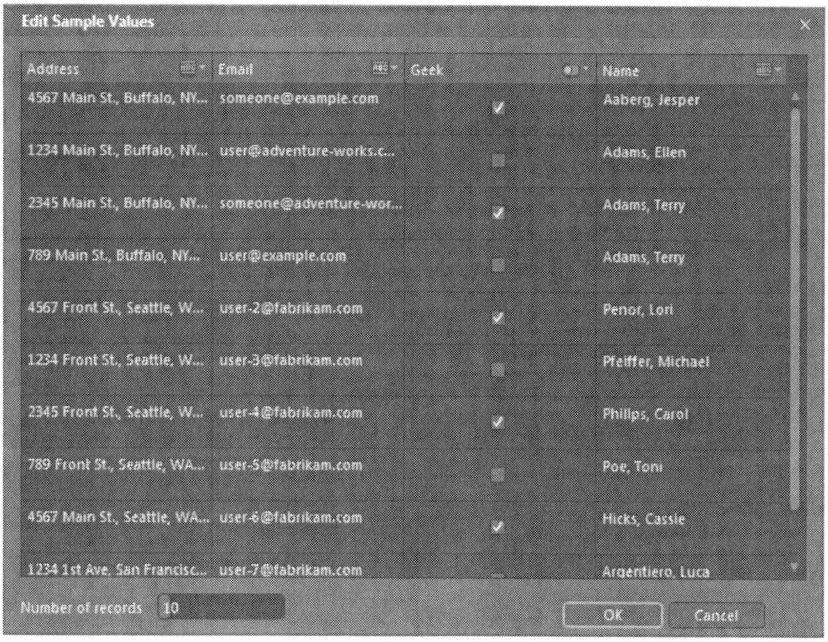

Figure 5-10. Edit Sample Values dialog

Sample Data Generated from a Class

An alternative to the process just described is to generate your sample data based on the public properties of an existing class.

1. To see this at work, create a new Windows Phone program called GeneratingSampleDataFromAClass.

2. Right-click on the project and select Edit in Visual Studio. When VS opens, right-click on the project and select Add Class and name the new class GolfCourses. Define the class as shown in Listing 5-1.

Listing 5-1. GolfCourses Class

```
public class GolfCourses
{
    public string Name { get; set; }
    public string Address { get; set; }
    public DateTime? LastPlayed { get; set; }
    public int Rating { get; set; }
}
```

99

3. Return to Blend and again choose the Create Sample Data button, but this time choose CreateSampleDataFromClass. You'll find that sample data has been generated based on the public types of your class.

Binding Data

We touched on databinding in the previous chapter, but Expression Blend makes databinding simpler, faster and generally easier.

1. To see this, create a new Windows Phone program called DataBindingToSampleCode.

In Expression Blend, create new sample code and change the type and format as shown in Table 5-1.

Table 5.1. Expression Blend

Name	Type	Format
Name	String	Name
CompanyName	String	Company Name
Phone	String	Phone Number
Picture	Image	
Rating	Number	1 digit

2. Click on the Edit Sample Values button and change all the Ratings to a value of 0 through 5. We'll use the ratings to display images of 0 through 5 stars.

3. Create a new folder named Images and copy in the files rating0.jpg through rating5.jpg (which you can download from the Apress web site).

DataItem Template

1. Click on the Customers collection in the data window and drag it onto the Content Panel. Notice that the cursor now has a tooltip that says "Create a [ListBox] and bind its ItemsSource property to Customers" (as shown in Figure 5-11).

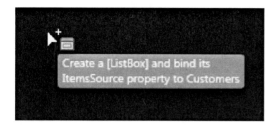

Figure 5-11. Binding in Blend

When you let go, Blend does the following:

- It binds the collection to the `ItemsSource` property

- It creates a `DataItem` template to accommodate all the various types of data

Unfortunately, the `DataItem` template it creates is blindingly ugly. But that's not a problem, as you can easily adjust the template in the template editor.

2. Turn your attention to the Objects and Timeline and open the structure all the way to the `ListBox` within the Content Panel. Right-click on the list box and select Edit Additional Templates Edit Generated Items (`ItemTemplate`) Edit Current. This puts you in the template editor, editing the template that was created for you when you bound the data.

3. Change the `StackPanel` that currently houses all the data to a data grid. Set the grid's width to Auto and its height to 150.

4. Next, we'll align and modify the `TextBlock`s. Set the font on the first `TextBlock` to 24 and set its left margin to 85, aligned top and left.

5. Set the font on the second `TextBlock` (Name) and the third `TextBlock` (phone number) to 18, and set their left margin to 85, and their top margins to 33 and 65 respectively.

6. Set the image control's margin to 8 and its top margin to 15 so that the (generated) image sits in the left column of the display.

7. Finally, add a new image control to hold the stars. Set it to align top and left, and set the width of the image to 100, its height to 24, its left margin to 275 and its top margin to 65.

We'd like to bind the rating to the stars, but the rating is an integer, and we need to convert that to the source URL for the image; to do that, we need a converter.

Data Converter

Switch over to Visual Studio and create a folder named Converters. In that folder, create a new class named `RatingToImageConverter`, which will derive from `IValueConverter`. The `IValueConverter` interface requires two methods: `Convert()` and `ConvertBack()`.

As we'll not be doing two-way databinding, we'll have `ConvertBack()` throw a not-implemented exception—it is an exception for it to be called at all in this program.

Convert's job will be to take an integer as a parameter, and return the URL (as a string) to the image we want to display. Its logic is fairly straightforward, as shown in Listing 5-2.

Listing 5-2. Rating to Image Converter Method

```
public class RatingToImageConverter : IValueConverter
{
    public object Convert(
            object value,
            Type targetType,
            object parameter,
            System.Globalization.CultureInfo culture)
    {
        string imageUrl = "/Images/rating0.jpg";
        int rating = 0;

        if(value != null && int.TryParse(value.ToString(), out rating))
        {
            imageUrl = string.Format("/Images/rating{0}.jpg", rating);
        }

        return imageUrl;
    }

    public object ConvertBack(
            object value,
            Type targetType,
            object parameter,
            System.Globalization.CultureInfo culture)
    {
        throw new NotImplementedException();
    }
}
```

Click on the new image in the Objects and Timeline panel and then in the properties window click on the Advanced Options button next to Source. Choose DataBinding. When the dialog opens, you will not see Rating because Expression Blend does not recognize it as a type that can be bound to the image source property. Click the dropdown to change from Matching Types to All Properties and Rating will appear. Make sure it is highlighted and then click on the Show Advanced Properties arrow towards the bottom of the dialog, as shown in Figure 5-12.

Figure 5-12. Show Advanced Properties button

The Advanced Properties panel opens within the dialog box. Towards the bottom, you'll find a list of Value Converters. Your value converter is not yet listed. Click the ellipses (…) button and Blend will find all implementations of `IValueConverter`. Click on `RatingToImageConverter`, then OK and then OK again to close the dialog. You've now bound the Rating to the image by way of the value converter, and you should see stars representing the appropriate ratings for each entry!

As you come to program more with Windows phone, you'll find yourself using data binding more and more. At first this seems like a simple convenience, saving you from hand-binding the data to a given control; but over time data binding becomes a central technique in decoupling your data from its representation.

Summary

We've seen that Expression Blend can make design and layout far easier, and it can make databinding a very simple process. Blend has become an important tool for all serious Windows Phone developers and it is well worth the time and effort to achieve comfort, if not expertise, with Expression Blend.

CHAPTER 6

■ ■ ■

Get Moving: Adding Animation to Your Apps

Animation is at the heart of nearly everything that happens on a Windows Phone. The most engaging Live Tiles are those that can animate, move around, and change their data dynamically. To move around the operating system, we slide from screen to screen, both vertically and horizontally. Finally, when we open an application, we get a nice page-turning animation that leads us directly into the app. Each of these animations has a purpose, and this chapter will focus on how to use this subtle, but effective, tool.

When *we* talk about animation, we're not talking about spinning buttons, or shapes streaking across the screen. Those types of actions are certainly possible, but fall squarely in the category of *gratuitous animation*. While you might use something like this for creating a game in Silverlight, this chapter is going to focus on what we call *purposeful animation* within the context of business applications.

Purposeful animation is done with a specific goal in mind. Perhaps we need to elegantly swap out some data from the screen. Or we need to compensate for a long page-load time. Maybe we just want to provide an immersive user experience. Animations make all of this possible. In this chapter, we're going to focus specifically on how to create animations, and how we can use those animations to buy ourselves some time when loading our pages.

Understanding the Lexicon of Animation

There are many words that will be used when you talk with other developers about using animations in your apps: animation, storyboard, keyframe, and tweening are the most common.

Animation is probably the most overused word of the group, and it's essentially meaningless. It doesn't refer to a specific code structure at all; instead it refers to the concept of moving some object on the screen. Anything that involves motion on an applications' screen will often be referred to as animation.

Storyboard is a bit more specific, and you'll see this in the next section. A *storyboard* is a specific code structure that holds all of the instructions for a specific set of movements or changes in our UI.

A *keyframe* is a code structure within a storyboard. Each time we want to move or change something on the screen, we need to determine what the beginning and ending states are. These beginning and ending states are keyframes; we will use these extensively in our animations.

Finally, you may hear the word *tweening* used from time to time. Tweening refers to the magic that happens between keyframes. Remember, with keyframes, we only define the starting and ending point of an animation. The best way to think about tweening is to imagine when you were younger, and you drew a small animated cartoon in the corner of one of your notebooks. On the next page, you drew the same picture, but changed by just a little. You continued through a dozen or more pages. By flipping each page of the notebook, you could piece together a simple animated scene, but you had to draw every single frame of that animation. In Silverlight animation, you basically get to draw the first and last frame of that notebook animation, and the runtime takes care of creating everything in the middle.

Creating a Simple Animation

Before we start our example, let's take a look at what defines an Animation in our Windows Phone applications. The specific Xaml structure is called a `Storyboard`, and all of the interactions can be completely defined in the Xaml markup and the code-behind. The `Storyboard` can contain multiple animation elements, which you can just think of as sets of instructions executed over time. Listing 6-1 is a simple `Storyboard` that fades the `Opacity` of the `TargetName` element to `0`, which would make it invisible.

Listing 6-1. Simple FadeOut Storyboard

```
<Storyboard x:Name="FadeOut">
        <DoubleAnimationUsingKeyFrames Storyboard.TargetProperty="(UIElement.Opacity)"
Storyboard.TargetName="TextRotator">
                <EasingDoubleKeyFrame KeyTime="0" Value="1"/>
                <EasingDoubleKeyFrame KeyTime="0:0:1" Value="0"/>
        </DoubleAnimationUsingKeyFrames>
</Storyboard>
```

As you can see in Listing 6-1, we start with a `Storyboard` element. In order to call the Storyboard from code (as with all other Xaml elements), it needs to be named. In this case, we've called it "FadeOut."

Inside that element, we have an element of type DoubleAnimationUsingKeyFrames. All this really means is that we are going to manipulate a Double value over a set of KeyFrames. We've also specified the TargetProperty of this animation, (the property we're manipulating), as well as the TargetName(the object whose property we're manipulating). In our example, we're changing the `Opacity` of the `TextBlock` named `TextRotator`.

We have defined two `KeyFrames` in our animation. They represent the starting and ending points we desire, and Silverlight takes care of the rest of it for us. The first `KeyFrame` states that at the 0th second of our animation (in other words, the beginning), the `Opacity` value should be 1, or fully opaque. At one second, however, the `Opacity` should have changed to 0, or fully transparent. The animation itself will take care of rendering the rest of the animation for us by tweening, or interpolating all the interim positions between fully visible and fully opaque, so that the text appears to fade from view over the duration of a second.

There's much to know about creating animations, all of the different animation and keyframe types, and their specific syntaxes. It would be nearly impossible to keep all of it straight in your head. Instead of typing all of this in Xaml, we recommend using Expression Blend, which can do 100 percent of the work for you using a convenient user interface.

For a simple example of an animation, let's start with a Text Rotator. Suppose we have several messages that we want to present to our user, much like a news web site (or the ticker at the bottom of the ESPN television channels.) We can manipulate the `Opacity` property of a `TextBlock` to fade the current text from the user's view, replace it with the next message, and fade it back onto the screen. We'll implement our text rotator in two steps. First, we'll create a storyboard for the animation, then we'll write the code we need to invoke it.

Using Expression Blend to Create a Storyboard

To begin work on our text rotator, we'll use Expression Blend to quickly build its storyboard. As you'll see as you work through this example, Blend simplifies the animation process, and lets you focus on the animation visually, rather than having to play a guessing game with XML values in Visual Studio.

1. In Expression Blend, create a new Windows Phone project, or just revisit one of the other projects you've created so far in this book. All we need is a page with a **TextBlock** on it. In the following example, we're going to use the **PageTitle** element that is on each page by default:

```
<TextBlock x:Name="PageTitle" Text="page name" Margin="9,-7,0,0" Style="{StaticResource
PhoneTextTitle1Style}"/>
```

2. In Blend, click on the **TextBlock** element in your design surface or Object list, as shown in Figure 6-1.

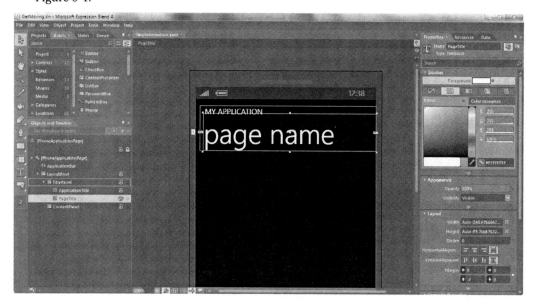

Figure 6-1. Selecting a TextBlock element

In the Objects and Timeline panel, you find a series of icons that represent our interactions with Storyboards. You can take a closer look at them in Figure 6-2, but the only button currently enabled is the + button, which we'll use to create a new Storyboard.

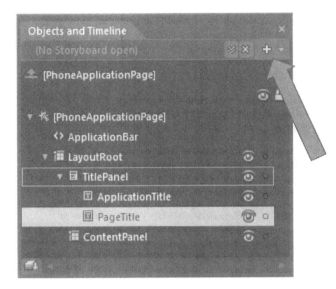

Figure 6-2. Creating a new Storyboard in Blend

3. Click the New Storyboard button, which will bring up a Create Storyboard
    Resource dialog box, shown in Figure 6-3, for you to name this Storyboard.
    Name it FadeOut and click OK.

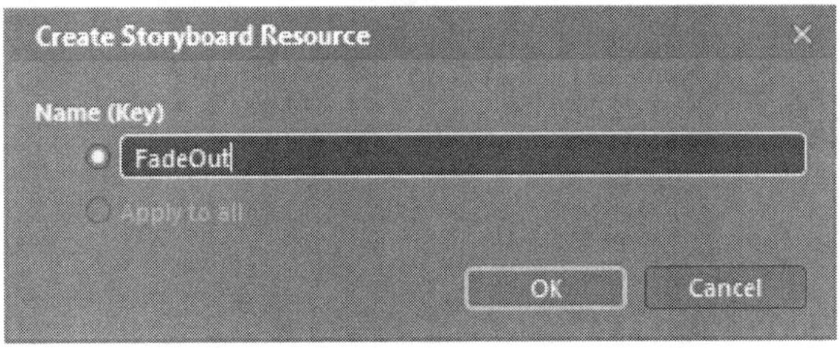

Figure 6-3. Naming a Storyboard

You should notice a few changes to the Blend environment at this point, as shown in Figure 6-4.
First, the design surface is now wrapped in a red outline, and there is text that reads "FadeOut timeline
recording is on."

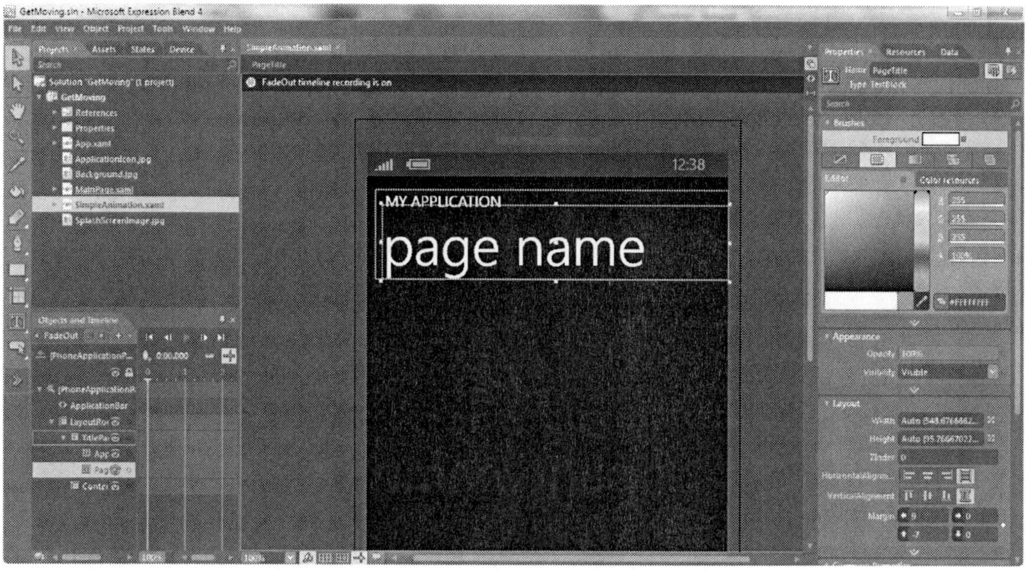
GetMoving.sln - Microsoft Expression Blend 4
FadeOut timeline recording is on
12:38
MY APPLICATION
page name

Figure 6-4. Timeline recording in Expression Blend

You should also notice, as shown in Figure 6-5, that your Objects and Timeline panel has become much more crowded. This is because we're now working directly on a Storyboard, and the timeline and playback controls are displayed.

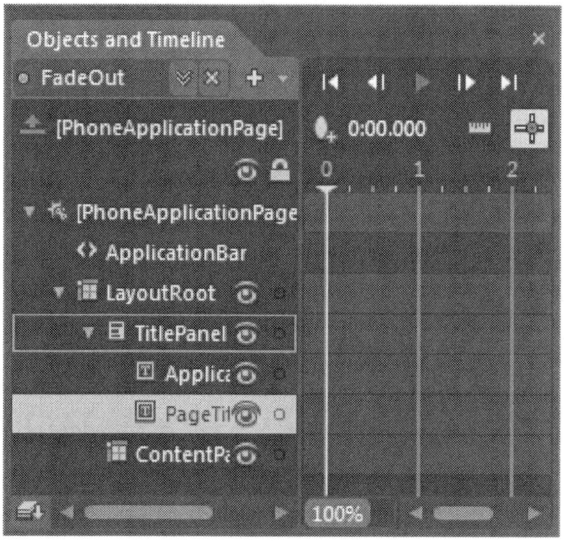
Objects and Timeline
FadeOut
[PhoneApplicationPage]
0:00.000
0
1
2
[PhoneApplicationPage
ApplicationBar
LayoutRoot
TitlePanel
Applic:
PageTi
ContentP:
100%

Figure 6-5. The Objects and Timeline Panel

4. To give yourself more room, you can press F6 to change your workspace from Design to Animation. It just moves the Objects and Timeline panel to the bottom of Blend, so that you can see the entire timeline easily (as shown in Figure 6-6). You can also do this by choosing the menu options Window ➤ Workspaces ➤ Animation.

Figure 6-6. The Animation workspace in Expression Blend

Now we are going to use this new timeline tool to manipulate the **Opacity** of our **TextBlock** over time. In Figure 6-7, there are several important features we'll be using.

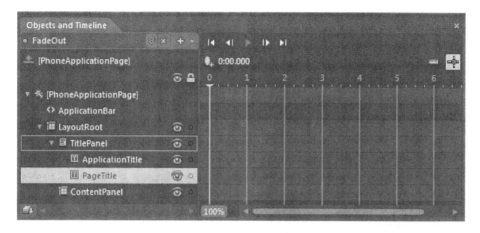

Figure 6-7. The Storyboard timeline

The first thing you should see is the yellow arrow stripe that is sitting on the zero in the timeline. This indicates the current time that you are working on in the animation. Zero means the beginning. There is a small icon above the zero that looks like an egg with a plus sign next to it. This is the New Keyframe button.

As we discussed earlier, key frames are those specific moments in your animation where you're being explicit about the position of an object, or its opacity, or whatever property you're manipulating. In the Xaml we showed you in Listing 6-1, there were two key frames defined: one at zero seconds, and one at one second. Let's do the same thing here.

5. Make sure that you've selected the PageTitle element from the list of objects on the left (like Figure 6-7), and then press the New Keyframe button. This will record that the PageTitle had opacity of 100 percent at zero seconds (as shown in Figure 6-8). Next, move that yellow line from zero seconds to one second.

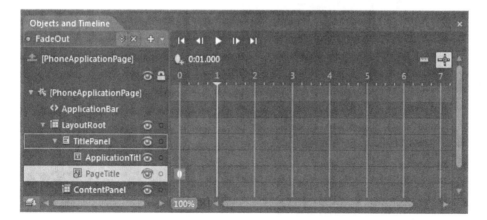

Figure 6-8. Setting keyframes in a Storyboard

Now, instead of creating another keyframe, you can just change the **Opacity** of the element, and Blend will automatically create the second keyframe for you.

6.   Look over to your Properties panel, and find the Opacity property (as shown in Figure 6-9). We need to change this value to zero.

Figure 6-9. Changing the Opacity property of a TextBlock

At this point, our FadeOut storyboard is complete. Looking back at your Objects and Timeline panel, it should now look like Figure 6-10.

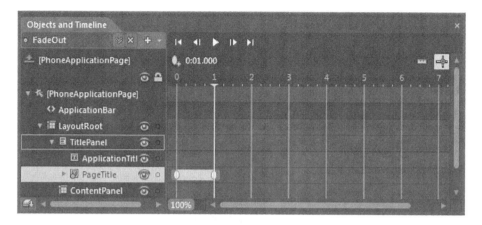

Figure 6-10. A simple, completed Storyboard in Expression Blend

7. Above the New Keyframe button, there are playback controls. If you press the Play button, you should now see your PageTitle text fade away to invisible.

In most cases, you're probably going to want to have a second animation that brings that text back to visible. While it might seem obvious to just follow these steps in Blend again, we recommend optimizing for programmer speed.

If you look at the Xaml that Blend has created for you, it should look nearly identical to Listing 6-1 from earlier. In Listing 6-2, we've simply copied and pasted that new Xaml, and changed a few values. Blend makes it very easy to create animations, but it is in your best interest to stay close to the Xaml that it generates, so you can make changes inline when necessary. If you would like, you can copy the Xaml in Listing 6-2, replacing your existing storyboard with these two.

Listing 6-2 FadeOut and FadeIn Storyboards in Xaml

```
<Storyboard x:Name="FadeOut">
        <DoubleAnimationUsingKeyFrames Storyboard.TargetProperty="(UIElement.Opacity)"
Storyboard.TargetName="PageTitle">
                <EasingDoubleKeyFrame KeyTime="0" Value="1"/>
                <EasingDoubleKeyFrame KeyTime="0:0:1" Value="0"/>
        </DoubleAnimationUsingKeyFrames>
</Storyboard>
<Storyboard x:Name="FadeIn">
    <DoubleAnimationUsingKeyFrames Storyboard.TargetProperty="(UIElement.Opacity)"
Storyboard.TargetName="PageTitle">
        <EasingDoubleKeyFrame KeyTime="0" Value="0"/>
        <EasingDoubleKeyFrame KeyTime="0:0:1" Value="1"/>
    </DoubleAnimationUsingKeyFrames>
</Storyboard>
```

You can see that all that was changed in the new FadeIn storyboard was its name, as well as the order of the Value properties of the two **KeyFrames**. Otherwise, the Xaml is identical. If you run your project (F5) in the emulator, you will notice that none of our animations actually take place. This is because we never called them from our code. Let's look at that next.

Calling Our Storyboard from Code

To kick off our Storyboard, we need to call its `Begin()` method from our code-behind file. In nearly every case, we're going to be triggering our Storyboards in response to some user interaction. Perhaps they chose to navigate to another page, or maybe they were just clicking a button. In any case, starting an animation couldn't be more straightforward.

1. To do this, open the code-behind file for your project, and add the line from Listing 6-3: `FadeOut.Begin();`. You can do this in Expression Blend or Visual Studio, so use whichever tool you are more comfortable using.

Listing 6-3. Calling a Storyboard from Code

```
namespace GetMoving
{
    public partial class SimpleAnimation : PhoneApplicationPage
    {
        public SimpleAnimation()
        {
            InitializeComponent();
            FadeOut.Begin();
        }
    }
}
```

In our example, we created two opposite storyboards. One to `FadeOut`, and one to `FadeIn`. In this example, we want to chain them together, so that the FadeIn animation starts as soon as the FadeOut animation ends. Thankfully, each storyboard also has a couple of events that we can leverage. We'll be using the `Completed` event to determine when each animation finishes. (This is also a simple way to create a delay timer. Create a storyboard that doesn't actually do anything over a specific period of time, and when it completes, you know your application has waited the appropriate amount of time.)

2. In Listing 6-4, we've created event handlers for both of our Storyboards, and they just bounce between each other. Add Listing 6-4 to the code-behind for the project.

Listing 6-4. Using the Completed Events of a Storyboard

```
public partial class SimpleAnimation : PhoneApplicationPage
{
    public SimpleAnimation()
    {
        InitializeComponent();
        FadeOut.Completed += new EventHandler(FadeOut_Completed);
        FadeIn.Completed += new EventHandler(FadeIn_Completed);
        FadeOut.Begin();
    }

    void FadeIn_Completed(object sender, EventArgs e)
    {
        FadeOut.Begin();
```

```
    }

    void FadeOut_Completed(object sender, EventArgs e)
    {
        FadeIn.Begin();
    }
}
```

As you can see, the **Completed** event handlers simply call the Begin method for the opposite Storyboard, causing our PageTitle element to fade and return from the background repeatedly. In our next step, we're going to swap the text values in PageTitle from an array of strings we have in our code-behind.

   3.   Add Listing 6-5 to the code-behind for the project.

Listing 6-5. Adding Text Swapping to Our Animations

```
public partial class SimpleAnimation : PhoneApplicationPage
{
    string[] textCollection=new string[5] {"number one!","two seconds","threeve","use the
fourth","a fifth is 20%"};
    int textCounter = 0;

    public SimpleAnimation()
    {
        InitializeComponent();
        FadeOut.Completed += new EventHandler(FadeOut_Completed);
        FadeIn.Completed += new EventHandler(FadeIn_Completed);
        FadeOut.Begin();
    }

    void FadeIn_Completed(object sender, EventArgs e)
    {
        FadeOut.Begin();
    }

    void FadeOut_Completed(object sender, EventArgs e)
    {
        FadeIn.Begin();
        PageTitle.Text = textCollection[textCounter];
        textCounter++;
        if (textCounter == 5) textCounter = 0;
    }
}
```

Because we've already identified the place where our text is invisible (The **FadeOut Completed** event handler), we can use this opportunity to swap the text in our PageTitle element while the user can't see it.

In Listing 6-5, we added an array of strings at the top of the page, and iterated through that list each time the text is invisible. We've now created a completely functional text rotator. You could use this for updating the interface with news stories, sports scores, or other relevant information that updates on a regular basis.

One of the major limitations with Storyboards that most developers find is that the name of the target element is explicitly called out in the Xaml. This means that you can't do clever tricks like the following:

```
FadeOut.Begin(SomeOtherTextBlock);
```

However, as we mentioned earlier in this book, everything that is written in Xaml can be manipulated by code. Let's take a look at how we could use the same Storyboards we just created to manipulate the other default **TextBlock** on the page, **ApplicationTitle**.

Reusing a Storyboard

To change the target of a Storyboard in code, we just need to access the **Storyboard.SetTarget** method. In our earlier example, Listing 6-5, we rotated our string values on only the **PageTitle** text block. In Listing 6-6, each time we reach the end of our string array, we switch the target of our Storyboards, resulting in our string values rotating on **PageTitle**, and then switching and rotating through **ApplicationTitle**.

Listing 6-6. Changing the Target of a Storyboard

```
    public partial class SimpleAnimation : PhoneApplicationPage
{
    string[] textCollection=new string[5]{ "number one!","two seconds","threeve","use the
fourth","a fifth is 20%"};
    int textCounter = 0;
    TextBlock currentTextBlock;

    public SimpleAnimation()
    {
        InitializeComponent();
        currentTextBlock = PageTitle;
        FadeOut.Completed += new EventHandler(FadeOut_Completed);
        FadeIn.Completed += new EventHandler(FadeIn_Completed);
        FadeOut.Begin();
    }

    void FadeIn_Completed(object sender, EventArgs e)
    {
        FadeOut.Begin();
    }

    void FadeOut_Completed(object sender, EventArgs e)
    {
        FadeOut.Stop();
        FadeIn.Stop();
        currentTextBlock.Text = textCollection[textCounter];
        textCounter++;
        if (textCounter == 5)
        {
            textCounter = 0;
```

```
        if (currentTextBlock == PageTitle) currentTextBlock = ApplicationTitle;
        else currentTextBlock = PageTitle;

        Storyboard.SetTarget(FadeIn, currentTextBlock);
        Storyboard.SetTarget(FadeOut, currentTextBlock);
    }

    FadeIn.Begin();
    }
}
```

If you use the code in Listing 6-6, you should see both of the **TextBlocks** change their values in the animation over time. It will eventually look like Figure 6-11.

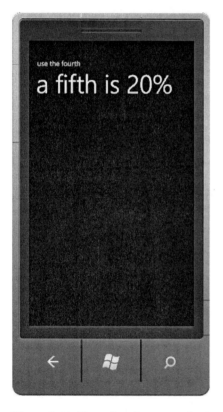

Figure 6-11. Changing the target of a Storyboard

So, at this point in the chapter, we've shown how to make a simple animation, and use it in several ways. The rest of this chapter is going to be dedicated to a noble goal: stalling your user.

Creating Custom (and Distracting) Page Transitions

There are many reasons to use animation in your applications, but none are as devious and psychological as what we're going to discuss in this section. If you've ever bought anything from a web site, you've likely seen the spinning icons and status bars that get displayed. These distractions give zero indication about how much waiting you're going to be doing, but you're content to wait because the application seems to be indicating that it's working.

We're not making spinning icons in this chapter. We can do one better. We're going to focus on creating custom page transitions that allow us to stall the user a bit. If your page loads with a transition, this means that you are giving yourself the amount of time the animation takes to load other content.

In our example for this section, we're going to create a page-turning animation that we use when a page is loaded or unloaded. The current page will fly away, and the new page will fly in. The entire transition will take under two seconds to complete, but the distraction it provides will buy you significant time to populate a `ListBox`, or bring data in from a web service. Plus, it looks very cool.

Creating the Page Turn Animation

To build this example, let's keep it very simple.

1. Add two new pages to your project. One named `PageOne.xaml`, and one named `PageTwo.xaml`. We will jump between these two pages for our entire example. On both pages, we need to start with creating an animation that rotates the entire screen like a door, both opening and closing.

In each case, we will be manipulating the `LayoutRoot` Grid element that is the root element on our pages. The earlier parts of this chapter illustrated how to create an animation using Expression Blend, so this case will focus on the Xaml that is generated, and why it is there.

2. Copy the contents of Listing 6-7 into `PageOne.xaml`, replacing the default contents of the page.

Listing 6-7. The Xaml Contents of PageOne.xaml

```
<phone:PhoneApplicationPage
    x:Class="GetMoving.PageOne"
    xmlns="http://schemas.microsoft.com/winfx/2006/xaml/presentation"
    xmlns:x="http://schemas.microsoft.com/winfx/2006/xaml"
    xmlns:phone="clr-namespace:Microsoft.Phone.Controls;assembly=Microsoft.Phone"
    xmlns:shell="clr-namespace:Microsoft.Phone.Shell;assembly=Microsoft.Phone"
    xmlns:d="http://schemas.microsoft.com/expression/blend/2008"
    xmlns:mc="http://schemas.openxmlformats.org/markup-compatibility/2006"
    FontFamily="{StaticResource PhoneFontFamilyNormal}"
    FontSize="{StaticResource PhoneFontSizeNormal}"
    Foreground="{StaticResource PhoneForegroundBrush}"
    SupportedOrientations="Portrait" Orientation="Portrait"
    mc:Ignorable="d" d:DesignHeight="768" d:DesignWidth="480"
    shell:SystemTray.IsVisible="True">

    <phone:PhoneApplicationPage.Resources>
        <Storyboard x:Name="FlipIn">
```

```xml
                    <DoubleAnimationUsingKeyFrames
Storyboard.TargetProperty="(UIElement.Projection).(PlaneProjection.RotationY)"
Storyboard.TargetName="LayoutRoot">
                        <EasingDoubleKeyFrame KeyTime="0" Value="-120"/>
                        <EasingDoubleKeyFrame KeyTime="0:0:0.8" Value="0"/>
                    </DoubleAnimationUsingKeyFrames>
            </Storyboard>
            <Storyboard x:Name="FlipOut">
                    <DoubleAnimationUsingKeyFrames
Storyboard.TargetProperty="(UIElement.Projection).(PlaneProjection.RotationY)"
Storyboard.TargetName="LayoutRoot">
                        <EasingDoubleKeyFrame KeyTime="0" Value="0"/>
                        <EasingDoubleKeyFrame KeyTime="0:0:0.5" Value="90"/>
                    </DoubleAnimationUsingKeyFrames>
            </Storyboard>
    </phone:PhoneApplicationPage.Resources>

    <Grid x:Name="LayoutRoot" Background="Transparent" RenderTransformOrigin="0,0">
        <Grid.Projection>
            <PlaneProjection CenterOfRotationX="0" RotationY="-120"/>
        </Grid.Projection>
        <Grid.RowDefinitions>
            <RowDefinition Height="Auto"/>
            <RowDefinition Height="*"/>
        </Grid.RowDefinitions>
        <StackPanel x:Name="TitlePanel" Grid.Row="0" Margin="12,17,0,28">
            <TextBlock x:Name="ApplicationTitle" Text="MY APPLICATION" Style="{StaticResource
PhoneTextNormalStyle}"/>
            <TextBlock x:Name="PageTitle" Text="page one" Margin="9,-7,0,0"
Style="{StaticResource PhoneTextTitle1Style}"/>
        </StackPanel>
        <Grid x:Name="ContentPanel" Grid.Row="1" Margin="12,0,12,0">
            <Button Content="Button" Height="72" HorizontalAlignment="Left"
Margin="137,153,0,0" Name="button1" VerticalAlignment="Top" Width="160" Click="button1_Click"
/>
        </Grid>
    </Grid>
</phone:PhoneApplicationPage>
```

As you can see, we've created two separate **Storyboards**, **FlipIn** and **FlipOut**. They rotate the entire page of our application like a door swinging inwards and outwards. We can do this by manipulating the RotationY property of its PlaneProjection. Another important change to note is the **RenderTransformOrigin** on the **LayoutRoot** Grid element. It is set to "0,0"—which means that all of our calculations on the x and y-axis will happen from their respective zero values, not from the middle of the element, which is the default. Finally, you should see that we have rotated our LayoutRoot element by the amount of -120 degrees on its Y axis. This is the starting position that all of our pages will contain, because in order to rotate it in, it can't already be displayed on screen. Much like our previous example, however, we need to call these storyboards from code. Let's take a look at that in the next section.

Adding the Animation to Your Page Events

Initially, it might seem to make sense to attach our animations to the page lifecycle events:
OnNavigatedTo and OnNavigatedFrom. What you'll find, however, is that both OnNavigatedFrom and
OnNavigatingFrom will terminate your page before the animation completes. This means that we've
got to handle the animation and page navigation ourselves, using a combination of event handlers and
the OnNavigatedTo event.

1. Copy the code from Listing 6-8 into your **PageOne.xaml.cs** file, replacing the
    default code.

Listing 6-8. Code Contents of PageOne.xaml.cs

```
using System;
using System.Windows;
using Microsoft.Phone.Controls;

namespace GetMoving
{
    public partial class PageOne : PhoneApplicationPage
    {
                public PageOne()
        {
            InitializeComponent();
        }

                protected override void
OnNavigatedTo(System.Windows.Navigation.NavigationEventArgs e)
                {
                    base.OnNavigatedTo(e);
                    FlipOut.Completed += new EventHandler(FlipOut_Completed);
                    FlipIn.Begin();
                }

        void FlipOut_Completed(object sender, EventArgs e)
        {
                    NavigationService.Navigate(new Uri("/PageTwo.xaml",
UriKind.Relative));
        }

        private void button1_Click(object sender, RoutedEventArgs e)
        {
                    FlipOut.Begin();
        }
    }
}
```

In Listing 6-8, we have three methods that we are using to manage both the FlipIn and FlipOut
animations. The first, and most important, is the **OnNavigatedTo** method. This is fired each time that
your page is navigated to (vs. the Loaded method, which is only called when the page is actually loaded),
so kicking off the FlipIn storyboard makes perfect sense here. We also want to define a **Completed** event

handler for the FlipOut storyboard, because we'll need to know when it's done in order to navigate to the appropriate page.

In our **button1_Click** event, we are handling for when the user clicks the button in our interface. Since the button is designed for navigation to another page, we call the FlipOut storyboard, to show the final animation for our page.

When **FlipOut** completes, we can run the code that is in the **FlipOut_Completed** event handler. In our simple example, we've hard-coded the navigation method here, which navigates to **PageTwo.xaml**.

The code for **PageTwo.xaml** (Listing 6-9) and **PageTwo.xaml.cs** is in Listing 6-10. You'll notice that they're nearly identical to PageOne's files in every way, except where the pages refer to themselves or each other.

2. Copy the contents of Listing 6-9 and Listing 6-10 to their appropriate pages in your project.

Listing 6-9. Code Contents of PageTwo.xaml

```
<phone:PhoneApplicationPage
    x:Class="GetMoving.PageTwo"
    xmlns="http://schemas.microsoft.com/winfx/2006/xaml/presentation"
    xmlns:x="http://schemas.microsoft.com/winfx/2006/xaml"
    xmlns:phone="clr-namespace:Microsoft.Phone.Controls;assembly=Microsoft.Phone"
    xmlns:shell="clr-namespace:Microsoft.Phone.Shell;assembly=Microsoft.Phone"
    xmlns:d="http://schemas.microsoft.com/expression/blend/2008"
    xmlns:mc="http://schemas.openxmlformats.org/markup-compatibility/2006"
    FontFamily="{StaticResource PhoneFontFamilyNormal}"
    FontSize="{StaticResource PhoneFontSizeNormal}"
    Foreground="{StaticResource PhoneForegroundBrush}"
    SupportedOrientations="Portrait" Orientation="Portrait"
    mc:Ignorable="d" d:DesignHeight="768" d:DesignWidth="480"
    shell:SystemTray.IsVisible="True">

    <phone:PhoneApplicationPage.Resources>
        <Storyboard x:Name="FlipIn">
            <DoubleAnimationUsingKeyFrames
Storyboard.TargetProperty="(UIElement.Projection).(PlaneProjection.RotationY)"
Storyboard.TargetName="LayoutRoot">
                <EasingDoubleKeyFrame KeyTime="0" Value="-120"/>
                <EasingDoubleKeyFrame KeyTime="0:0:0.8" Value="0"/>
            </DoubleAnimationUsingKeyFrames>
        </Storyboard>
        <Storyboard x:Name="FlipOut">
            <DoubleAnimationUsingKeyFrames
Storyboard.TargetProperty="(UIElement.Projection).(PlaneProjection.RotationY)"
Storyboard.TargetName="LayoutRoot">
                <EasingDoubleKeyFrame KeyTime="0" Value="0"/>
                <EasingDoubleKeyFrame KeyTime="0:0:0.5" Value="90"/>
            </DoubleAnimationUsingKeyFrames>
        </Storyboard>
    </phone:PhoneApplicationPage.Resources>
    <Grid x:Name="LayoutRoot" Background="Transparent" RenderTransformOrigin="0,0">
        <Grid.Projection>
```

```xml
                <PlaneProjection CenterOfRotationX="0" RotationY="-120"/>
            </Grid.Projection>
            <Grid.RowDefinitions>
                <RowDefinition Height="Auto"/>
                <RowDefinition Height="*"/>
            </Grid.RowDefinitions>
            <StackPanel x:Name="TitlePanel" Grid.Row="0" Margin="12,17,0,28">
                <TextBlock x:Name="ApplicationTitle" Text="MY APPLICATION" Style="{StaticResource
PhoneTextNormalStyle}"/>
                <TextBlock x:Name="PageTitle" Text="page two" Margin="9,-7,0,0"
Style="{StaticResource PhoneTextTitle1Style}"/>
            </StackPanel>
            <Grid x:Name="ContentPanel" Grid.Row="1" Margin="12,0,12,0">
                <Button Content="Button" Height="72" HorizontalAlignment="Left"
Margin="145,153,0,0" Name="button1" VerticalAlignment="Top" Width="160" Click="button1_Click"
/>
            </Grid>
        </Grid>
</phone:PhoneApplicationPage>
```

Listing 6-10. Code Contents of PageTwo.xaml.cs

```csharp
using System;
using System.Windows;
using Microsoft.Phone.Controls;

namespace GetMoving
{
    public partial class PageTwo : PhoneApplicationPage
    {
        public PageTwo()
        {
            InitializeComponent();
        }

        protected override void
OnNavigatedTo(System.Windows.Navigation.NavigationEventArgs e)
        {
            base.OnNavigatedTo(e);
            FlipOut.Completed += new EventHandler(FlipOut_Completed);
            FlipIn.Begin();
        }

        void FlipOut_Completed(object sender, EventArgs e)
        {
            NavigationService.Navigate(new Uri("/PageOne.xaml",
UriKind.Relative));
        }

        private void button1_Click(object sender, RoutedEventArgs e)
        {
```

```
                    FlipOut.Begin();
            }
    }
}
```

In each case, you can see that the pages have practically the same contents. This straightforward approach to page navigation with animation will ultimately save you from the perceived load times that each of your pages take.

Run your project. You should see that when you click on the buttons of the pages, they neatly transition to each other. The time that elapses during that transition is *free* time that you have to load data, or get other processing out of the way. You've probably already noticed that you wait until the page transition completes before you attempt to the click the button again.

Regarding page transitions, there's another great set of tools and code that you can use that includes several different page transitions and controls that are not included with the default Windows Phone tools. You can use these additional page transitions and controls instead of trying to build them yourself from scratch. There is a free download from Microsoft on CodePlex (`http://codeplex.com`), an open source software repository. It is called the Silverlight Toolkit for Windows Phone, and we will be covering it in more depth in Chapter 11 of this book. To get the code and find out more about this collection of controls, you can download it at `http://silverlight.codeplex.com`.

Summary

Every time you add an animation to your app, it should be done with purpose. This chapter showed you how we can use animations both for swapping content from the screen in an elegant way, as well as a way to create page transitions (also known as distractions) that buy you time to load the contents of a page. In either case, they were done with a goal in mind, and not just for the gratuitous sake of moving elements on the screen. Animations are also a great way to create simple Silverlight games, and the event model that we used makes game development a fun way to interact with our users.

In the next chapter, we are going to walk through an extensive set of tools that make it easy for us, as developers, to interact with many of the default apps and user data that live on the phone. You'll learn how to make the phone dial a phone number, send a text message, and even how to retrieve a user's contact list. These mechanisms, called Tasks, will make your app much more interesting with only a few lines of code.

CHAPTER 7

■ ■ ■

Get a Job: Interacting with User Data

In nearly every application that you build, you're going to have that moment when you wish you had access to the users' data. Maybe it's contacts or phone numbers, or maybe you want to save a ringtone to their devices. In any case, Windows Phone makes it easy to interact with all sorts of user data, both retrieving and saving back to the phone.

This chapter will cover the Microsoft.Phone.Tasks namespace, which provides the APIs that you will use to access user data. We'll discuss the importance of each available task, and how and when you should use it. We'll also provide sample code to get you started. At the end of this chapter, we'll introduce the Microsoft.Phone.UserData namespace, which is new with Windows phone 7.5. The APIs in this namespace require more work, but they provide more robust access to your user's most valuable data.

Distinguishing Launchers and Choosers

Windows Phone provides two types of task APIs for interacting with user data: launchers and choosers. Both are tasks, but differ in the type of work they perform. *Launchers* start a task but do not return data to your application, while *choosers* start a task and allow the user to choose data that is returned to your application.

For example, the `PhoneCallTask`, a launcher, allows you to prompt the user to dial a specific number. After they confirm the choice, the launcher will start the phone application and your application will end. You are "launching" the phone from your app.

In contrast, the `EmailAddressChooserTask`, a chooser, as the name implies, allows you to take the user to his list of contacts on the phone, choose one from the list, and the selected contact's e-mail address will be returned to your application as data that you can use. Tables 7-1 and 7-2 list all of the tasks available to us in the Windows Phone 7.1 SDK. We will spend the majority of this chapter walking through each one.

This chapter is not meant to be a reference. There are plenty of online resources for that, including the Microsoft Launchers and Choosers Overview (`http://msdn.microsoft.com/en-us/library/ff769542(v=VS.92).aspx`). The web will be far more recently updated (that is, until we can figure out how to push updates to this paper book you're holding). Instead, this chapter is an examination of how and when to use each of the Tasks that were available when this book was published, and includes all through the Windows Phone 7.1 SDK.

Table 7-1. Launchers

Name	Use	SDK Version
BingMapsDirectionsTask	Launches the Maps application and immediately provides directions from a start to an end point.	7.1
BingMapsTask	Launches the Maps application, centering the map on the location specified.	7.0, 7.1
ConnectionSettingsTask	Allows you to launch the user into different parts of the Settings on the device.	7.1
EmailComposeTask	Launches the Mail client on the device, allowing you to populate a message before a user sends it.	7.0, 7.1
MarketplaceDetailTask	Launches the Marketplace app, directing the user to an app that you specify.	7.0, 7.1
MarketplaceHubTask	Launches the Marketplace app.	7.0, 7.1
MarketplaceReviewTask	Launches the Marketplace app, directing the user to review your application.	7.0, 7.1
MarketplaceSearchTask	Launches a Marketplace search based on the criteria you provide.	7.0, 7.1
MediaPlayerLauncher	Launches an audio or video file in the default media player on the device.	7.0, 7.1
PhoneCallTask	Prompts the user to make a phone call to a number you specify.	7.0, 7.1
SaveContactTask	Allows you to save an entire contact record to the user's device.	7.1
SaveEmailAddressTask	Allows you to save an e-mail address to a contact on the user's device.	7.1
SavePhoneNumberTask	Allows you to save a phone number to a contact on the user's device.	7.1
SaveRingtoneTask	Allows you to save a ringtone to the user's device.	7.1
SearchTask	Launches a Bing search based on your search criteria.	7.0, 7.1

Table 7-1 cont.

ShareLinkTask	Allows a user to post a link to his social networks.	7.1
ShareStatusTask	Allows a user to post a status to her social networks.	7.1
SmsComposeTask	Prompts the user to send a text message based on your specific data.	7.0, 7.1
WebBrowserTask	Launches Internet Explorer and navigates to a page that you specify.	7.0, 7.1

Table 7-2. Choosers

Name	Use	SDK Version
AddressChooserTask	Prompts the user to select a contact from his device and returns the physical address of that contact to your application.	7.1
CameraCaptureTask	Prompts the user to take a picture with her device and returns the photo to your app.	7.0, 7.1
EmailAddressChooserTask	Prompts the user to select a contact from his device and returns the e-mail address of that contact to your app.	7.1
PhoneNumberChooserTask	Prompts the user to select a contact from her device and returns the phone number of that contact to your app.	7.1
PhotoChooserTask	Prompts the user to select a photo from his device and returns that image to your app.	7.0, 7.1

A complete code project that incorporates all of the Launchers and Choosers (as well as the UserData namespace as discussed later in this chapter) is provided at the end of the chapter, and referenced throughout.

Setting up a Launcher

Launchers, as mentioned earlier, are what we call a "fire and forget" mechanism. We launch a browser, or a text message, but we don't get any data back to our app. In fact, we might not even get our user back to our app! We are sending them away to perform a task, and it will be up to the user to return to our application. As an example of this, let's look briefly at the PhoneCallTask in Listing 7-1.

Listing 7-1. Setting up a Launcher

```
PhoneCallTask pct = new PhoneCallTask();
pct.DisplayName = "Rick Astley";
pct.PhoneNumber = "(772) 257-4501";
pct.Show();
```

As the code in Listing 7-1 shows, using a launcher consists of creating a new task object, adding some properties (like `DisplayName` and `PhoneNumber`), and finally calling a `Show()` method that launches the task. Figure 7-1 shows the user interface that your user will see when this task is used:

Figure 7-1 An example of the PhoneCallTask user interface

Setting up a Chooser

Choosers, unlike Launchers, are designed to return data to your application. Photos, e-mail addresses, phone numbers—these are all valuable pieces of data that you will want to get from your users. This means that Choosers require a bit more code to be effective, because we need a setup code (like the Launchers), but we also need an event handler that grabs the data when it is returned. Listing 7-2 shows the code necessary to use the `AddressChooserTask`. You'll see that we initialize the task in our `MainPage()` constructor method, and then get the `AddressResult` in our event handler.

Listing 7-2. Setting up a Chooser

```
public MainPage()
{
    InitializeComponent();

    act = new AddressChooserTask();
    act.Completed += new EventHandler<AddressResult>(act_Completed);
    act.Show();
}

void act_Completed(object sender, AddressResult e)
{
    if (e.TaskResult == TaskResult.OK)
    {
        string address = e.Address;
        string name = e.DisplayName;
    }
}
```

As we show in the event handler, you can make sure that the user completed the task by checking the `TaskResult` object. Once we know we have received a result, we can grab the Properties of the `AddressResult` object, `Address` and `DisplayName`.

As we move through the tasks in this chapter, you will find that the tasks follow the model of the Launcher or the Chooser. We have categorized them by the way they are used, Bing Tasks, Camera Tasks, Communication Tasks, Contact Tasks, Marketplace Tasks, and a Miscellaneous Tasks category for those few that don't fit in another group.

Bing Tasks

Each of the tasks in this category uses either Bing Search or Bing Maps to provide its functionality. There is also an entire suite of Bing APIs available on the web at `www.bing.com/toolbox/bingdeveloper`, but for the purposes of this chapter, we will focus on three tasks: `BingMapsDirectionsTask`, `BingMapsTask`, and `SearchTask`.

BingMapsDirectionsTask

The `BingMapsDirectionsTask` is a new task in the Windows Phone 7.1 SDK release, and allows you pass a start and end point to the Maps application on the phone, and it will generate directions for the user.

In Listing 7-3, we show the code you need to make this task performs its action.

Listing 7-3. Using the BingMapsDirectionsTask

```
using System.Device.Location;

BingMapsDirectionsTask bmdt = new BingMapsDirectionsTask();
bmdt.Start = new LabeledMapLocation("8800 Lyra Ave, Columbus, OH  43240", new
GeoCoordinate());
bmdt.End = new LabeledMapLocation("Thurman's Cafe, Columbus, OH", new GeoCoordinate());
bmdt.Show();
```

A great feature about this Task, however, is that almost none of the data is required. In fact, if you don't include a Start location, it will assume you want the user's current location. If you haven't used a `GeoCoordinate` object before, think a latitude/longitude position. In order to use these objects, we need to make sure that you add a reference to the `System.Device` assembly to your project. If you don't include actual `GeoCoordinate` values, it will use the Label attribute as a search term. (Note that we provided empty `GeoCoordinate` values in our start and end points.) This means you don't have to do any geocoding to an address to get the converted latitude and longitude values, because if you type an address into the Label property, it will use that instead. Figure 7-2 shows the user interface your user will see when the `BingMapsDirectionsTask` is launched.

Figure 7-2 .The BingMapsDirectionsTask user interface

You will definitely want to test the addresses you are using before publishing your app. If you provide a partial address to the task, it will do its best to determine what you are talking about. This is because it's not using the raw values you provide, but using those values to perform a search for the best result. If you want your users to be able to find their way to your offices, you're going to want to be certain that the task understands your commands.

BingMapsTask

This launcher has been around since the beginning, but the first release of Windows Phone required geocoordinates in order to function properly. In the Windows Phone 7.1 SDK, you can now specify a SearchTerm property that allows you to use a location, address, or even a company's name as your criteria. If you are using the SearchTerm property, we recommend that you be very specific. Vague searches might end up giving you a different location than you expected. Listing 7-4 shows how we use the BingMapsTask.

Listing 7-4. Using the BingMapsTask

```
BingMapsTask bmt = new BingMapsTask();
bmt.SearchTerm = "Progressive Field, Cleveland, OH";
bmt.Show();
```

If you're already prepared to generate the latitude and longitude for addresses, you can still use those for the best accuracy. Just use the Center property (as shown in Listing 7-5) and pass the coordinates in as a GeoCoordinate object. The challenge with using Center is that you are truly only centering the map on that location. No labels will appear on the map, so unless you're trying to show your user a general area, we'd recommend using the search term with an address every time. Even with the highest ZoomLevel of 20, you're still likely to be looking at a larger area than you intended. Listing 7-5 shows what the Center and ZoomLevel properties look like (you can use this *instead* of the SearchTerm).

Listing 7-5. Using GeoCoordinates with the BingMapsTask

```
BingMapsTask bmt = new BingMapsTask();
bmt.Center = new GeoCoordinate(41.42322600, -81.920683);
bmt.ZoomLevel = 20;
bmt.Show();
```

If you're absolutely determined to use lat/long values (and don't already have a way to determine them), there's an outstanding geocoding service that will convert addresses to lat/long, and will even convert lat/long to potential addresses if you're feeling adventurous; it's found at http://msdn.microsoft.com/en-us/library/cc966793.aspx. Our recommendation is to rely on the SearchTerm property with a specific address or location. This should be a can't-miss option every time, and you should end up with a result that looks like Figure 7-3.

Figure 7-3. The BingMapsTask user interface, using the SearchTerm property

SearchTask

There are plenty of APIs out there to retrieve search engine results from, but for a simpler and easier solution to doing a web search in your application, you should use the SearchTask. As with all Launchers, please remember that this is not something that happens within your app, but is instead handled by the Windows Phone operating system. You're not going to have access to the results of this SearchTask, but if you need to let your user search the web, there's no easier way to do it on Windows Phone. Listing 7-6 shows how to use the SearchTask.

Listing 7-6

```
SearchTask st = new SearchTask();
st.SearchQuery = "Migrating To Windows Phone";
st.Show();
```

This will take the user to the default search application on the phone, which now contains tabs for web, local, and images. Figure 7-4 shows the user interface for the Search application this task uses.

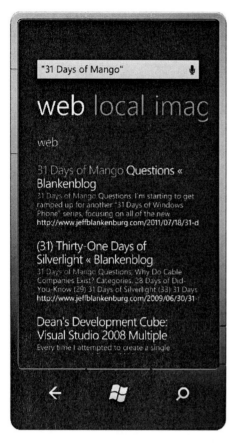

Figure 7-4. The user interface for the SearchTask

Camera Tasks

There are only two tasks in this category, but they serve the two purposes we have for the camera: taking a photo and selecting a previously selected photo. These are the CameraCaptureTask and the PhotoChooserTask.

CameraCaptureTask

There are many similarities between the CameraCaptureTask and the PhotoChooserTask, specifically that both tasks return a PhotoResult object, which we will look at shortly. With the CameraCaptureTask, the expectation is that the user is going to be taking a new photo. With the PhotoChooserTask, the user is taken to the photo library on her phone and she is expected to select an existing photo.

In the CameraCaptureTask, the user will immediately be taken to the camera application. Once she has taken a picture, she will be prompted to "Accept" the image before it is returned to your application.

Working with images is obviously a little trickier than working with text, and we'll need another namespace, System.Windows.Media.Imaging. In Listing 7-7, we create a new CameraCaptureTask, as well as a new event handler for the result. In order to capture the result as a BitmapImage, you will need this namespace.

Listing 7-7

```
CameraCaptureTask cct;

public MainPage()
{
    InitializeComponent();
    cct = new CameraCaptureTask();
    cct.Completed += new EventHandler<PhotoResult>(cct_Completed);
    cct.Show();
}

void cct_Completed(object sender, PhotoResult e)
{
    if (e.TaskResult == TaskResult.OK)
    {
        string imagename = e.OriginalFileName;
        BitmapImage image = new BitmapImage();
    }
}
```

When you try to use this Chooser in the Windows Phone emulator, you'll find that it doesn't actually have access to a camera. Instead, you'll see a screen similar to the one shown in Figure 7-5.

Figure 7-5. The user interface for the CameraCaptureTask in the emulator

Notice that although there's not an image shown, there's a Capture button in the top-right corner. You will only see this button in the emulator, as Windows Phones all have a dedicated camera shutter button as part of the hardware specification. When you click the button, you'll end up with a screen that looks something like Figure 7-6.

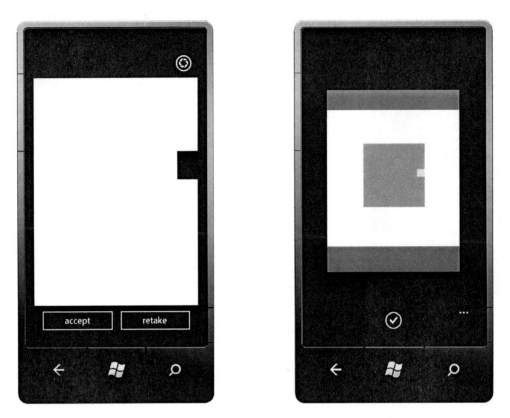

Figure 7-6. The "fake" images you see in the Windows Phone emulator

The primary difference between yours and the one in Figure 7-6 will be the location of the small black box in the white field. It rotates clockwise around the outside of the white field, so each picture you "take" on the emulator should result in the box being in a different location. When you get the final image returned to you, the emulator adds a hint of flashy color to the image, making the white box red and the black box green. On an actual device, you'd use the camera just as you normally do, and the image would be the image you took.

PhotoChooserTask

Similar to the CameraCaptureTask, this Chooser allows your user to select an image from their photo library. Unlike the CameraCaptureTask, you can allow your user to select an image or take a new one with the camera. You can enable this feature, as well as a cropping feature, before you launch this task. Ultimately, you will treat the data you receive from the PhotoChooserTask the same way that you did with the CameraCaptureTask.

You'll need the System.Windows.Media.Imaging namespace, and you'll be receiving the image, as well as its location, on the device in the Completed event handler's return data, as shown in Listing 7-8.

Listing 7-8. Using the PhotoChooserTask

```
PhotoChooserTask pct;

public MainPage()
{
    InitializeComponent();

    pct = new PhotoChooserTask();
    pct.Completed += new EventHandler<PhotoResult>(pct_Completed);
    pct.ShowCamera = true;
    pct.PixelWidth = 100;
    pct.PixelHeight = 100;
    pct.Show();
}

void pct_Completed(object sender, PhotoResult e)
{
    if (e.TaskResult == TaskResult.OK)
    {
        string imagename = e.OriginalFileName;
        BitmapImage image = new BitmapImage();
    }
}
```

You'll notice that we define a PixelWidth and PixelHeight property before we launch the Chooser. This is actually defining the aspect ratio of the cropping box that your user will be presented. This box allows you, as the developer, to get an image that is the appropriate shape for your purposes. The user gets to decide which part of the image they would like to select, and then the image is returned to you at the dimensions you specified, as shown in Figure 7-7.

Figure 7-7 .The optional cropping box from the PhotoChooserTask

This makes selecting images for headshots, where you need a consistent size for every user, incredibly simple to manage. You don't have to worry about sizing down the images to save file space or that the user is uploading an image that is 5 MB in file size. You get exactly what you want, and nothing more.

You also get to specify whether the user can take a new photo with the `ShowCamera` property. We can't think of a good reason to ever exclude this, but if you only want your user to be able to select from an existing photo, it's certainly an option. This was enabled by the `pct.ShowCamera = true;` code in Listing 7-8.

In most cases where you need your user to provide an image, we would recommend using this Chooser rather than the `CameraCaptureTask`, which requires a new photo to be taken.

Communication Tasks

The tasks covered in this section relate to communicating with someone else via a Windows Phone. This covers sending e-mail and text messages, but also making phone calls and posting information to social networks.

EmailComposeTask

Every single Windows Phone application should be using this Launcher. To clarify, every single
Windows Phone application should have a way to contact the developer that created it. There are
thousands of applications in the marketplace that don't do this, and they're missing an opportunity to
improve their applications and engage with their customers. Figure 7-8 demonstrates how this could be
used in an application.

Figure 7-8. Showing a contact e-mail address in your application

When your users tap on the e-mail address shown in Figure 7-8, you can completely fill in the e-mail
details for them, so that in many cases, all they need to do is write their message and press the Send
button. None of the fields are required, but you can specify Subject, Body, To, Cc, and Bcc. Listing 7-9
shows the syntax for using the `ComposeEmailTask`.

Listing 7-9. Using the EmailComposeTask

```
EmailComposeTask ect = new EmailComposeTask();
ect.Subject = "This is a test message";
ect.Body = "I am sending you a message from the Launchers and Choosers app.";
ect.To = "windowsphone@jeffblankenburg.com";
ect.Cc = "windowsphone@jesseliberty.com";
ect.Bcc = "blindcopy@jeffblankenburg.com";
ect.Show();
```

You can see that all of the values are strings. This means that you still need to validate that the values you use are appropriate. Because we are launching a separate application to handle sending an e-mail, any issues or errors in your values will only be visible to the user. For example, if you accidentally have an e-mail address with an invalid character, the user won't even notice until they try to click the Send button (shown in Figure 7-9). It's incredibly important to make sure you have valid values for these properties because all of the issues will have to be handled by your users. You'll also notice that you can't attach files to this message. This is one of the current limitations of the `EmailComposeTask`, but the interface does allow the user to attach a file, so they still have that ability if they need it.

Figure 7-9. The e-mail interface for the EmailComposeTask

Another important note to remember about this Launcher is that the Windows Phone emulator does not have the ability to set up e-mail accounts, and because of this, when you launch the `EmailComposeTask` in the emulator, you'll get an error that looks like the message shown in Figure 7-10.

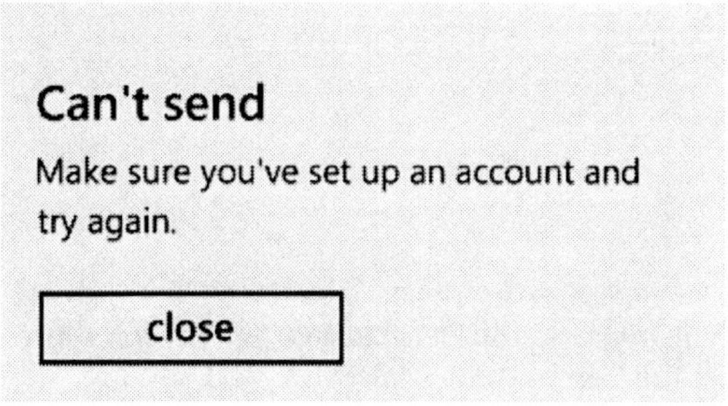

Can't send

Make sure you've set up an account and try again.

close

Figure 7-10. An expected error message from the Windows Phone emulator

If you get this error in the emulator, you're doing it right. When you try it on an actual phone, however, you should be taken to a screen that allows you to send the e-mail message. It is very important that you test your entire application on a real phone before pushing it to the Windows Phone Marketplace. You don't want little issues like this to sneak through, because the Marketplace Test Team will definitely find them.

PhoneCallTask

The `PhoneCallTask` is another great tool for allowing your users to contact you, however, we wouldn't recommend it. If your application gets really popular (as you hope it does), you're not going to want those millions of users to have your direct number. Instead, the `PhoneCallTask` is an essential tool for letting your user call other people. For example, in combination with the `PhoneNumberChooserTask`, you can provide a simple mechanism for someone to pick one of their existing contacts and call them from your application. Again, they'll be using the built-in phone dialer on their phone, so your application will be in the background while they make their call.

You do have the ability to provide two pieces of data to the dialer: the `PhoneNumber` and a `DisplayName` to show along with the number (shown in Listing 7-10). We recommend providing both values every time, because without the context of a display name, dialing a random phone number might be unsettling to your user. Figures 7-11 and 7-12 show the difference in what they'll see.

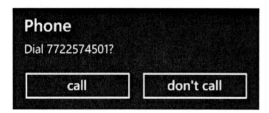

Phone
Dial 7722574501?

call   don't call

Figure 7-11. Without display name

Figure 7-12. With display name

Another recommendation we suggest is to format the PhoneNumber property. You'll notice in Figures 7-11 and 7-12 that it's just a random string of ten digits. By formatting the PhoneNumber, it will look more familiar to your user, and give them the confidence to press the Call button. Make sure that you are providing a number that is relevant to your user. For example, inside the United States, we don't need to use the +1 international code. But if your user is in Ireland, or Bulgaria, or China, they're absolutely going to need that calling code. You can either choose to include it always, or detect the region of the device and add it when necessary. Figure 7-13 shows the prompt you'll see when you format the number.

Figure 7-13. The fully-formatted PhoneCallTask user interface

Finally, Listing 7-10 show the actual code you need to make it happen. Nothing surprising here; just a string for PhoneNumber and a string for DisplayName.

Listing 7-10

```
PhoneCallTask pct = new PhoneCallTask();
pct.DisplayName = "Rick Astley";
pct.PhoneNumber = "(772) 257-4501";
pct.Show();
```

Ultimately, as with all of our tasks, the user has to press the "call" button. All we can do with these tasks is prompt the user to make the choice, but if they don't want to make the call, they will always have the option to decline.

ShareLinkTask

In short, the ShareLinkTask allows you to help your user share links with their social networks. For example, let's say you that you have created a news app, and when a user finds an article that they want to share with their friends, you would use the **ShareLinkTask** to do it. Listing 7-11 shows how to use the **ShareLinkTask**.

Listing 7-11. Using the ShareLinkTask

```
ShareLinkTask slt = new ShareLinkTask();
slt.LinkUri = new Uri("http://jeffblankenburg.com");
slt.Message = "This is an awesome website.";
slt.Title = "The Blankenblog";


slt.Show();
```

In this example, we get to specify a **LinkURI** (this is the actual link we're sharing), as well as a message and a title. These values become a little more apparent when we look at the user interface, as shown in Figure 7-14.

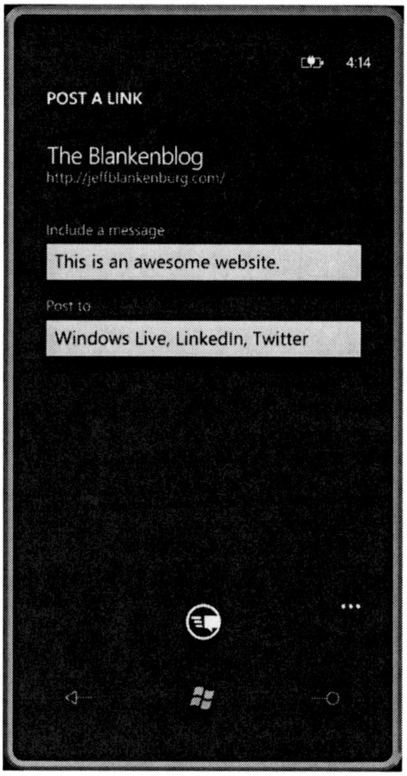

Figure 7-14. The ShareLinkTask user interface

Depending on which social networks the user selects, the link will be used in different ways. Figures 7-15, 7-16, and 7-17 show examples of how the data is used on Twitter, Facebook, and Windows Live, respectively.

 @jeffblankenburg
Jeff Blankenburg

This is an awesome website.
jeffblankenburg.com

Figure 7-15. Twitter using the data from the ShareLinkTask

Jeff Blankenburg
This is an awesome website.

The Blankenblog

 Like · Comment · 47 seconds ago via Windows Phone

Figure 7-16. Facebook using the data from the ShareLinkTask

Jeff Blankenburg This is an awesome website. - via Windows Phone
· 2 minutes ago

Comment

The Blankenblog

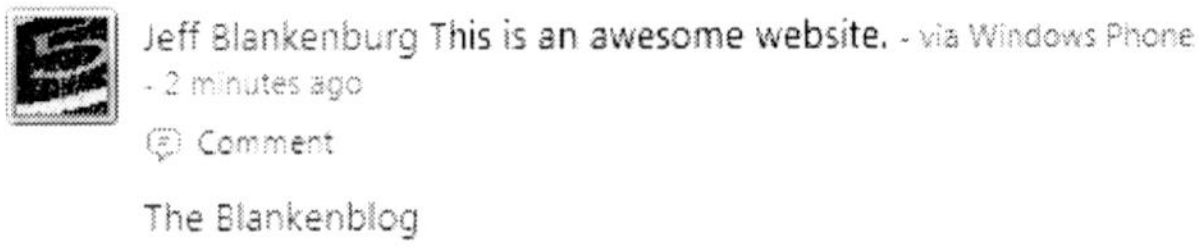

Figure 7-17. Windows Live using the data from the ShareLinkTask

As we show in the Figures 7-15, 7-16, and 7-17, each social network will use the data differently; but the idea is the same: share a link with a community of people. The next task, ShareStatusTask, performs a similar job, but with status messages instead of links.

ShareStatusTask

Similar to the ShareLinkTask that we just discussed, the ShareStatusTask allows you to prompt a user to post a status message to their social networks. This is incredibly handy when you're running a promotion that you want your users to mention. Perhaps you've seen something on Twitter like "RT this message to win a $100 gift card!" The ShareStatusTask would be a way to encourage your users to post those messages (not that we encourage that kind of spammy behavior, mind you).

To use the ShareStatusTask, take a look at the code in Listing 7-12.

Listing 7-12. Using the ShareStatusTask

```
ShareStatusTask sst = new ShareStatusTask();
sst.Status = "This is my status message.";
sst.Show();
```

In this example, we only get the Status property (a string) to use, but most social networks will automatically link URLs that you place in the text automatically, so feel free to include them in your text. The interface the user will see is shown in Figure 7-18.

Figure 7-18. The user interface for the ShareStatusTask

SmsComposeTask

At its core, this task makes it simple for your users to send a text message. We've often referred to this Launcher as the "poor man's Twitter API." For those of you unfamiliar with Twitter, you can execute most of their functionality via text messages (`http://support.twitter.com/groups/34-apps-sms-and-mobile/topics/153-twitter-via-sms/articles/14020-twitter-sms-commands`). In most cases, however, this will be used as an application promotion tool: "For 500 Mooby points, text your friends to tell them about this application!"

It's also a great tool for fundraising. You may have seen the commercials that say "Send a text to 90999 to donate $10!" If your application can bring up the text message, fully filled out, users are much more likely to press Send. The SmsComposeTask is how you do it, and you can see that in Listing 7-13.

Listing 7-13. Using the SmsComposeTask

```
SmsComposeTask sct = new SmsComposeTask();
sct.To = "40404";
sct.Body = "Sign me up for Twitter!";
sct.Show();
```

We get two properties in the SmsComposeTask: To and Body. Much like the EmailComposeTask we used earlier, it is up to you to make sure that the To value is valid; otherwise your user will be stuck trying to determine what is wrong. Figure 7-19 shows the interface your user will see.

Figure 7-19. The user interface for the SmsComposeTask

SMS messages are sent the same way a user normally does it, through their Messaging application. The SmsComposeTask does not have access to any responses or any future messages that are part of the conversation, but it's a great way to get a user to send that initial text message that so many services are hungry for.

Contacts Tasks

Each of the tasks covered in this section relate to contact data. Getting e-mail addresses, phone numbers, and physical addresses in and out of a user's contact records is what we can accomplish using these six tasks: AddressChooserTask, EmailAddressChooserTask, PhoneNumberChooserTask, SaveContactTask, SaveEmailAddressTask, and SavePhoneNumberTask.

AddressChooserTask

As straightforward as it sounds, the AddressChooserTask allows your user to select the address of one of the contacts on his phone. The downside is that you're on your own to parse the result. You'll get an AddressResult object, which does not separate the individual elements of an address into child properties. Your address data will look like this:

```
789, 1st Ave\r\nNew York, NY  96001
```

On the plus side, you'll also be given the contact's name with the DisplayName property. This allows you to use both pieces of information when you leverage this data. For example, you could use the BingMapsDirectionTask that we covered in the Launchers section, passing in these two values as the Label and Location. In Listing 7-14, we build a new AddressChooserTask with a Completed event handler.

Listing 7-14

```
private AddressChooserTask act;

public MainPage()
{
    InitializeComponent();

    act = new AddressChooserTask();
    act.Completed += new EventHandler<AddressResult>(act_Completed);
    act.Show();
}

void act_Completed(object sender, AddressResult e)
{
    if (e.TaskResult == TaskResult.OK)
    {
        string address = e.Address;
        string name = e.DisplayName;
    }
}
```

As you can see, we have a Completed event handler that handles the result of that Task. Each of the Choosers will operate this way, with an event handler method receiving the results of the task. An `AddressChooserTask` returns two values to us, the `Address` and the `DisplayName`.

The user will be shown a very familiar contact list on their screen, and selecting a contact will be how the data is triggered to return to us. Figure 7-20 shows the interface that the Windows Phone emulator will show.

Figure 7-20. The Choose A Contact dialog that the AddressChooserTask uses

A *very* important thing to note about this task (as well as the `EmailAddressChooserTask` and `PhoneNumberChooserTask`) is that the contact list that is shown (like Figure 7-20) is a *filtered* list. What this means is that it will only display the contacts that actually have the data you've indicated. In this example, only three of the seven contacts on the Windows Phone emulator have any address data.

We feel that this is a *major* shortcoming of these tasks because it will likely confuse your users. If I have 100 contacts on my phone, and you launch this task, and my contact list only has three records (I don't usually keep physical addresses in this example), I'm going to freak out. My concern is no longer about selecting a contact to use in this application; it has shifted to "Why isn't my mom in my contacts anymore?"

This is why we generally recommend taking one of two approaches with these tasks, as follows:

1. Alert the user that the list will only contain the contacts that have a physical address in their record.

2. Use the Contacts API that we will cover at the end of this chapter.

Ultimately, using an AddressChooserTask is going to be much easier to use, but it does present the opportunity to confuse your users.

EmailAddressChooserTask

There are many situations in which you, as the application developer, will want your users to contact their friends. Perhaps you are writing a social networking application. Maybe you want them to share some data with another contact. In any case, e-mail is often the medium of choice.

By combining the EmailAddressChooserTask with the EmailComposeTask we discussed earlier, you can make sending an e-mail a trivial task for the user.

The EmailAddressChooserTask is very similar to the AddressChooserTask, except that we'll be retrieving an EmailResult object this time. Listing 7-15 shows a new EmailAddressChooserTask and the necessary event handler to gather the data it returns.

Listing 7-15

```
EmailAddressChooserTask eact;

public MainPage()
{
    InitializeComponent();

    eact = new EmailAddressChooserTask();
    eact.Completed += new EventHandler<EmailResult>(eact_Completed);
    eact.Show();
}

void eact_Completed(object sender, EmailResult e)
{
    if (e.TaskResult == TaskResult.OK)
    {
        string emailaddress = e.Email;
        string displayname = e.DisplayName;
    }
}
```

As with the AddressChooserTask, we have the new DisplayName property. Before this was introduced in Windows Phone 7.5, we only received the e-mail address and nothing else. When collecting contacts in your application, having the contact's name is a big bonus.

PhoneNumberChooserTask

At this point, you've probably noticed that there are several choosers that do practically the same thing (EmailAddressChooserTask, AddressChooserTask), but differ in the type of contact data they expose. This is done to limit the overhead of the request. If you only need a phone number, there's no reason to get the entire contact record. At the end of this chapter, we'll cover UserData, and how you can retrieve the entire contact record, as well as calendar information.

With the PhoneNumberChooserTask we're able to access a contact's phone number, which, in combination with the SmsComposeTask, would allow you to compose a text message for the user's contact. This becomes more important for applications that have invitations or a social aspect, like Foursquare. Creating a text message that users can send to their contacts makes it easy for them to spread the word about your application or the user's accomplishments. Listing 7-16 shows how you grab the phone number of a contact.

Listing 7-16. Using the PhoneNumberChooserTask

```
PhoneNumberChooserTask pnct;

// Constructor
public MainPage()
{
    InitializeComponent();
    pnct = new PhoneNumberChooserTask();
    pnct.Completed += new EventHandler<PhoneNumberResult>(pnct_Completed);
    pnct.Show();
}

void pnct_Completed(object sender, PhoneNumberResult e)
{
    if (e.TaskResult == TaskResult.OK)
    {
        string phonenumber = e.PhoneNumber;
        string displayname = e.DisplayName;
    }
    else if (e.TaskResult == TaskResult.Cancel)
    {
        //USER CANCELLED THE TASK.
    }
}
```

As with any of the tasks in this category (and also including the PhotoChooserTask and the CameraCaptureTask), you need to make sure that you are validating that you received a TaskResult of OK before you proceed. Without that check, you may not be receiving the values you expect because the user cancelled the action. If you would like to also detect the cancellation, you can add an else if statement to your event handler, like the one in Listing 7-16.

SaveEmailAddressTask

The SaveEmailAddressTask allows you to prompt your user to save an e-mail address to their contacts. They will be given the option to add it to an existing contact or to create a new contact. Because they are editing a contact profile, they'll actually be able to edit the entire contact record.

This task (and the ones that follow it in this section) doesn't have the feel of the other tasks, primarily because there *is* an event handler, but there isn't any data returned to you.

In Listing 7-17, you'll also notice that we must specify the e-mail address (as a String) before we call the Show() method. Without it, this Chooser will only prompt the user to add a new e-mail address to their selected contact.

Listing 7-17. Using SaveEmailAddressTask

```
SaveEmailAddressTask seat;

public MainPage()
{
    InitializeComponent();

    seat = new SaveEmailAddressTask();
    seat.Completed += new EventHandler<TaskEventArgs>(seat_Completed);
    seat.Email = "windowsphone@jeffblankenburg.com";
    seat.Show();
}


void seat_Completed(object sender, TaskEventArgs e)
{
    if (e.TaskResult == TaskResult.OK)
    {
        //Save was successful!
    }
    else (e.TaskResult == TaskResult.Cancel)
    {
        //Save was cancelled!
    }
}
```

As you can see, when saving data to a contact record, you'll have the confidence of knowing that the user completed the action, or that they cancelled it.

SavePhoneNumberTask

The SavePhoneNumberTask gives our users the ability to save a specific phone number to their contact list, much like the previous task, the SaveEmailAddressTask. It is up to them where they save it, or if they save it at all, but this tool certainly makes it easy and is particularly convenient when you have a phone number likely to be called in the future (like customer service or technical support).

Figure 7-21 shows the interface your user will see when the SavePhoneNumberTask is launched and after he has selected a specific contact.

Figure 7-21. The user interface for the SaveEmailAddressTask

To make this task work, take a look at the code sample in Listing 7-18.

Listing 7-18. Using the SavePhoneNumberTask

```
SavePhoneNumberTask spnt;

public MainPage()
{
    InitializeComponent();

    spnt = new SavePhoneNumberTask();
    spnt.Completed += new EventHandler<TaskEventArgs>(spnt_Completed);
    spnt.PhoneNumber = "(772) 257-4501";
    spnt.Show();

}

void spnt_Completed(object sender, TaskEventArgs e)
{
```

```
    if (e.TaskResult == TaskResult.OK)
    {
        //Save was successful!
    }
}
```

As with the SaveEmailAddressTask, the PhoneNumber property is required or the task will simply prompt the user to add a new phone number to his selected contact record.

SaveContactTask

The SaveContactTask is certainly the most robust of the tasks in this category, and perhaps this entire chapter. It allows you to create and save an entire Contact record on the user's device. This is obviously incredibly beneficial for businesses, salesmen, or anyone else that wants to provide an easy way to be contacted. To do this, we'll follow the same patterns we introduced in the previous two tasks, but you'll see in Listing 7-19 that there are significantly more properties that we can provide.

Listing 7-19. Using the SaveContactTask

```
SaveContactTask spnt;

public MainPage()
{
    InitializeComponent();

        sct = new SaveContactTask();
    sct.Completed += new EventHandler<SaveContactResult>(sct_Completed);
        sct.FirstName = "Jeff"
    sct.LastName = "Blankenburg";
    sct.Company = "Microsoft";
    sct.WorkAddressStreet = "8800 Lyra Ave. #400";
    sct.WorkAddressCity = "Columbus";
    sct.WorkAddressState = "OH";
    sct.WorkAddressZipCode = "43240";
    sct.WorkEmail = "jeblank@microsoft.com";
    sct.WorkPhone = "(614) 719-5900";
    sct.PersonalEmail = "windowsphone@jeffblankenburg.com";
    sct.Website = "http://jeffblankenburg.com";
    sct.Show();
}

void sct_Completed(object sender, SaveContactResult e)

{
    if (e.TaskResult == TaskResult.OK)
    {
        //Save was successful!
    }
}
```

There are numerous properties available in `SaveContactTask`, above and beyond what is shown in Listing 7-19, including `JobTitle` and `MiddleName` if you need those values. As before, we have an event handler to determine whether or not your user completed the save.

Marketplace Tasks

Each of the tasks in this section relate specifically to the Windows Phone Marketplace. You'll see how to get your app reviewed, as well as a simple mechanism to show a user your other applications (think cross-selling!). This section will cover the `MarketplaceDetailTask`, `MarketplaceHubTask`, `MarketplaceReviewTask`, and the `MarketplaceSearchTask`.

MarketplaceDetailTask

The `MarketplaceDetailTask` allows you to send users to the Marketplace for a specific application. Left to its default values, it will automatically take them to the details of the application they're using. In many cases, however, you have more than one application, and you'd like to let your users know about them. We recommend making this a part of all your applications. It's an incredibly easy way to direct your fans to your other great apps. To do this, you'll need a very specific piece of information about that app: the application ID. You may also see this listed as Product ID in your AppHub account. If you don't already have an application in the Windows Phone Marketplace, you might not be familiar with this ID value. Every application that successfully gets accepted to the Marketplace is assigned a unique GUID value. This is the ID number that we are looking for. Figure 7-22 is an example from one of Jeff's apps.

Product ID: f08521cd-1cff-df11-9264-00237de2db9e

Deep link example: http://social.zune.net/redirect?type=phoneApp&id=f08521cd-1cff-df11-9264-00237de2db9e

Figure 7-22. The product ID and deep link for your application in the marketplace.

So, to use this Launcher, all we need to do is create a new `MarketplaceDetailTask`, and specify this Product ID as the content identifier, as shown in Listing 7-20.

Listing 7-20. Using the MarketplaceDetailTask

```
MarketplaceDetailTask mdt = new MarketplaceDetailTask();
mdt.ContentIdentifier = "f08521cd-1cff-df11-9264-00237de2db9e";
mdt.Show();
```

Again, this is another case where you really need to verify that the value you use for `ContentIdentifier` is an appropriate value, because you will get an error from the Marketplace otherwise. If you are using the `MarketplaceDetailTask` to take the user to the details for the current app he's using, you do not need to use the `ContentIdentifier` property. It will use the current app's value by default. Figure 7-23 shows an example of the Marketplace Detail screen and Figure 7-24 shows the error screen you'll see if you're testing an unpublished app.

Figure 7-23. The user interface for the MarketplaceDetailTask

Figure 7-24. An expected error from an unpublished application that you are testing

You will primarily use this task to recommend other applications to your user, but it's also a great way to convert a trial user to a full purchase. (We cover Trial Mode in Chapter 10, but in short, Trial Mode enables you to provide your app for free with limited functionality, with the option for the user to buy the full version at a future time.)

MarketplaceHubTask

This might be the simplest of the current Launchers, as all you can do is send the user to the Marketplace app. No search terms, so specific apps, just the Marketplace Hub. We're not exactly clear on why you would want to do this (as opposed to using the next few Launchers), but we suppose it's always good to know that you can. You do have the ability to specify Applications or Music, but that's it. When you search for Applications, you're actually searching for apps and games, so be aware of that as you use this. Listing 7-21 shows how to implement this task.

Listing 7-21. Using the MarketplaceHubTask

```
MarketplaceHubTask mht = new MarketplaceHubTask();
mht.ContentType = MarketplaceContentType.Applications;
mht.Show();
```

There's nothing especially fancy about this task, but if you need to direct the user to the Marketplace, there isn't another way to do it.

MarketplaceReviewTask

Of all the marketplace Launchers, this is certainly one you're going to want to use frequently. Once a user has installed your application, it's up to you to drive them to review the app. They won't be prompted to review the app otherwise. By providing a reminder to your users to review your application, you'll get far more reviews, which should translate to more users. Unlike the MarketplaceDetailTask, you can't send your users to any other app but the one they are currently using, so there's no way to specify an Application ID in this Launcher. This takes them directly to the review page for your application.

```
MarketplaceReviewTask mrt = new MarketplaceReviewTask();
mrt.Show();
```

While you're building your application, this is another one of the Launchers that doesn't work in the emulator. In fact, it won't work if you deploy it to a phone either. That's because it's looking for an application that doesn't yet exist in the Marketplace. If you're doing it properly, you should see an error that looks like the one displayed in Figure 7-24. The page that the user will see is shown in Figure 7-25.

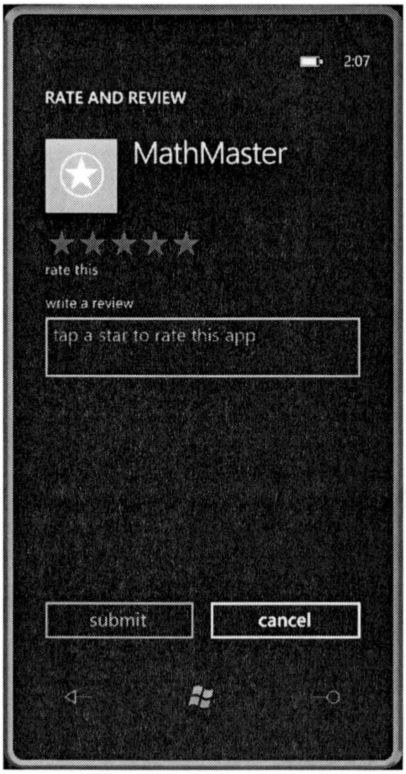

Figure 7-25. The Rate and Review screen the MarketplaceReviewTask uses

MarketplaceSearchTask

Another marketplace Launcher, this allows you to perform a search of the marketplace, and you can even specify applications or music again, like you did with the `MarketplaceHubTask`. In Listing 7-22, we're searching for the song "Code Monkey" by Jonathan Coulton. You'll also notice in Listing 7-22 that we can just pack all of the search terms into one string, and the Marketplace does an astonishing job of finding what we're looking for.

Listing 7-22. Using the MarketplaceSearchTask

```
MarketplaceSearchTask mst = new MarketplaceSearchTask();
mst.ContentType = MarketplaceContentType.Music;
mst.SearchTerms = "Code Monkey Coulton";
mst.Show();
```

There's not significantly more to say about this task, but this is another great way to show a user to your other applications. By searching the name of the app (or in Jeff's case, his name is unique enough), you can present the user with a list of content he might be interested in buying.

Miscellaneous Tasks

As with any collection of things, there's always a few that just don't fit into a specific category. The next four tasks that we'll cover definitely fit that classification. The ConnectionSettings task gives us links to specific parts of the user's phone settings. The MediaPlayerLauncher, aside from being the only task without the word "task" in its name, launches the default media player on the phone. The SaveRingtoneTask allows you to save audio files to the user's ringtone collection. The WebBrowserTask launches Internet Explorer, loading a page you specify.

ConnectionSettingsTask

This task was a late addition to the Windows Phone 7.1 SDK, as it wasn't even available until the final release of the tools. The ConnectionSettingsTask allows you to direct the user to four different sections of her phone's settings: AirplaneMode, Bluetooth, Cellular, and Wi-Fi. To do this, we can use the simple code example shown in Listing 7-23.

Listing 7-23. Using the ConnectionSettingsTask

```
ConnectionSettingsTask cst = new ConnectionSettingsTask();
cst.ConnectionSettingsType = ConnectionSettingsType.AirplaneMode;
cst.Show();
```

Using the example in Listing 7-23, the user would automatically be redirected to the Airplane Mode settings screen on her phone, as shown in Figure 7-26.

Figure 7-26. The user interface for the ConnectionSettingsTask using AirplaneMode.

You can use the `ConnectionSettingsTask` inside of your application, but we see this as a significant way to provide Home Screen functionality to your user. By creating secondary tiles for your application (we cover this in Chapter 8), you can provide the ability for the user to access her settings directly from her Home Screen.

MediaPlayerLauncher

This is *not* like the `MediaElement` you may have become familiar with. A `MediaElement` allows you to embed a video on your page in your application. The `MediaPlayerLauncher` does just what its title describes: it launches the Media Player on the phone and leaves your application. Having said that, this is a simple way to launch a video or song from your application, but it's not an effective way to play that music while the user continues to use your application or game.

You also get the ability to specify the controls that are used on the MediaPlayer using the Controls property, as shown in Listing 7-24. Maybe you only want to offer the ability to pause or stop. You can do that by specifying each control separately by using the `MediaPlaybackControls` enumeration, as shown in Listing 7-25. The available controls are Pause, Stop, FastForward, Rewind, and Skip. All uses all of the controls and None uses none of them.

Listing 7-24. Using the MediaPlayerLauncher with All Controls Enabled

```
MediaPlayerLauncher mpl = new MediaPlayerLauncher();
mpl.Controls = MediaPlaybackControls.All;
mpl.Location = MediaLocationType.Install;
mpl.Media = new Uri("video/DramaticChipmunk.mp4", UriKind.Relative);
mpl.Show();
```

Listing 7-25. Specifying the Controls the MediaPlayerLauncher Will Use

```
MediaPlayerLauncher mpl = new MediaPlayerLauncher();
mpl.Controls = MediaPlaybackControls.Pause | MediaPlaybackControls.Stop;
mpl.Location = MediaLocationType.Install;
mpl.Media = new Uri("video/DramaticChipmunk.mp4", UriKind.Relative);
mpl.Show();
```

Notice the Location property in Listing 7-25. This is required to tell the control where the media file resides. If you've included the media file in your XAP, you want to choose the `MediaLocationType.Install`. If your application stored the media file in `IsolatedStorage`, you'll want to choose the `MediaLocationType.Data`.

The MediaPlayer is capable of playing several different formats of media, including WAV, MP3, WMA, MP4, AAC, M4A, and WMV. For a complete and up-to-date listing of available formats, please check out `http://msdn.microsoft.com/en-us/library/ff462087(v=VS.92).aspx`.

SaveRingtoneTask

The `SaveRingtoneTask`, as you'll see, is the most code-intensive example in this chapter, but this is for a specific reason: in order to save a ringtone to a user's phone, you must first save it to `IsolatedStorage`. So, in this section, our code sample will not only show you how to use the `SaveRingtoneTask`, but also how to save an MP3 file to `IsolatedStorage`, so that you can use it with this task. Listing 7-26 shows the code that is specific to using the `SaveRingtoneTask`.

Listing 7-26. Using the SaveRingtoneTask

```
SaveRingtoneTask srt;

// Constructor
public MainPage()
{
    InitializeComponent();
        srt = new SaveRingtoneTask();
    srt.Completed += new EventHandler<TaskEventArgs>(srt_Completed);
    srt.DisplayName = "Scotch";
    srt.IsShareable = true;
    srt.Source = new Uri("isostore:/Scotch.mp3");
    srt.Show();
}

void srt_Completed(object sender, TaskEventArgs e)
{
```

```
    if (e.TaskResult == TaskResult.OK)
    {
        //RINGTONE SAVED SUCCESSFULLY!
    }
    else if (e.TaskResult == TaskResult.Cancel)
    {
        //USER CANCELLED THE SAVE.
    }
}
```

At this point in the chapter, most of this code should look really familiar. We create a new SaveRingtoneTask and a Completed event handler. The DisplayName property is what the user will see when the ringtone is installed on the user's device, as shown in Figure 7-27. IsShareable indicates whether other applications can use your ringtone file, which you'd want to prevent with DRM'd audio files.

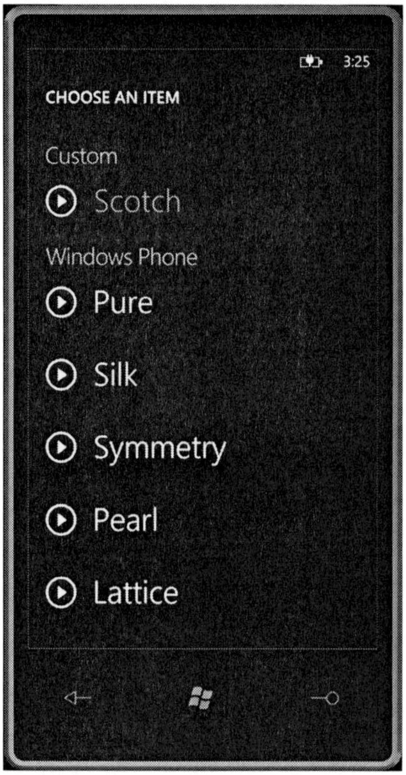

Figure 7-27. The ringtone selection screen with our custom ringtone listed

Finally, if you refer back to Listing 7-26, we have the Source property. This uses a Uri format that may look unfamiliar; this is because it is referring to a file that was previously saved in IsolatedStorage.

We covered IsolatedStorage in Chapter 3, but Listing 7-27 shows a simple example of saving an MP3 file from our application into IsolatedStorage. We referred to the saved location of this file in Listing 7-26.

Listing 7-27. Saving an MP3 File to IsolatedStorage

```
var s = Application.GetResourceStream(new Uri("audio/Scotch.mp3", UriKind.Relative));
{
    using (var f = IsolatedStorageFile.GetUserStoreForApplication().CreateFile("Scotch.mp3"))
    {
        var buffer = new byte[2048];
        int bytesRead = 0;

        do
        {
            bytesRead = s.Stream.Read(buffer, 0, 1024);
            f.Write(buffer, 0, bytesRead);
        }
        while (bytesRead > 0);

        f.Close();
    }
}
```

This example in Listing 7-27 will save your file to IsolatedStorage, allowing you to then use the code in Listing 7-26 to save the ringtone to your user's device. When the task executes, the user will see the screen shown in Figure 7-28.

Figure 7-28. The Save Ringtone dialog that the SaveRingtoneTask uses

If the user checks the "Make this my ringtone" box, it will also assign this ringtone to be his default ringtone for the entire device.

WebBrowserTask

The WebBrowserTask is often confused with the WebBrowserControl. The WebBrowserControl is used inside an application, where the WebBrowserTask launches the Internet Explorer application on the user's phone. The primary distinction we like to make is this: if you have a mobile web site that could supplement as part of your application (think the current ESPN application), then you should be using the WebBrowserControl. However, if you are just providing a link to a web site as a reference (or maybe just to your home page), we would recommend using the WebBrowserTask.

The WebBrowserTask gives you some additional pieces of functionality that you would have no access to (like Favorites), or would have to build yourself (like the address bar). You should also pay attention to the fact that in the Windows Phone 7.5 release, the URL property was exchanged for the more common Uri property. It is still there is in the code, but you should definitely avoid using it. Listing 7-28 shows how to use the WebBrowserTask.

Listing 7-28

```
WebBrowserTask wbt = new WebBrowserTask();
wbt.Uri = new Uri("http://JesseLiberty.com");
wbt.Show();
```

Much like the `EmailComposeTask` that we showed earlier in this chapter, if you have a web site that relates to your applications, you should provide a way for your users to check it out *from* your applications; allowing them to click a link that launches the `WebBrowserTask` is the perfect way to accomplish this.

Using the Microsoft.Phone.UserData Namespace

There's a new namespace in Windows Phone 7.5 that provides programmatic access to more of the user data on the phone than we have had previously. We can access all Contacts and Appointments, as well as specific details in each.

Contacts

At first, this API appears to give you the ability to search through the contacts and appointments on the user's device. In reality, you have full access to this data. In the contacts example, we start by creating a new reference to the user's contacts, and then setting up an asynchronous search. We've also set up an event handler to get the data when the search is completed, as shown in Listing 7-29.

Listing 7-29. Setting up an Asynchronous Search of Contacts

```
Contacts c = new Contacts();
c.SearchCompleted += new EventHandler<ContactsSearchEventArgs>(c_SearchCompleted);
c.SearchAsync("Jeff", FilterKind.DisplayName, null);
```

In Listing 7-29, you can see that we're searching for any contact that matches the term "Jeff" in the `DisplayName` property of the Contact record. This will bring you back an `IEnumerable` list of Contact objects, with the entire contact's record included. This means you have access to multiple e-mail addresses, phone numbers, street addresses, birthdates, companies, and all of the other data available in the People Hub.

However, if you change some of your search criteria, you can get a complete list of the user's entire contact list. This is especially handy when you want to compare their contacts to the members you have on your service (think Twitter, Facebook, Google+, etc.). To do this, just exchange the last line of the Listing 7-29 for the one in Listing 7-30.

Listing 7-30. Using an Empty Search String to Retrieve All Contacts

```
c.SearchAsync(string.Empty, FilterKind.None, null);
```

Peter Parker's Uncle Ben reminded him, "with great power comes great responsibility" (a reference from the 2002 film *Spider-Man*). Just because you have access to a user's contact list does not mean you should exploit that privilege. Getting your app installed on a user's phone requires a high level of trust. If you violate that trust by spamming all of his friends and contacts with e-mail and other junk, not only will you be uninstalled, but your user's frustration will also be reflected in negative reviews in the marketplace.

In our example, we're going to show how to use the EmailAddressChooserTask in combination with this new namespace to allow our user to select an entire contact record without much effort on our part. Since we've done part of this earlier in this chapter, the AddressChooserTask code is in Listing 7-31.

Listing 7-31. Using the EmailAddressChooserTask to Provide a Contact List

```
EmailAddressChooserTask emailAddressChooserTask = new EmailAddressChooserTask();
emailAddressChooserTask.Completed += new
EventHandler<EmailResult>(emailAddressChooserTask_Completed);
emailAddressChooserTask.Show();
```

In our Completed event handler, we're going to perform a search on that contact similar to Listing 7-31, except that we're going to use the DisplayName property that was returned to us from our Chooser (shown in Listing 7-32).

Listing 7-32. Using the EmailAddressChooserTask

```
private void emailAddressChooserTask_Completed(object sender, EmailResult e)
{
    if (e.TaskResult == TaskResult.OK)
    {
        Contacts c = new Contacts();
        c.SearchCompleted += new EventHandler<ContactsSearchEventArgs>(c_SearchCompleted);
        c.SearchAsync(e.DisplayName, FilterKind.DisplayName, null);
    }
}
```

When the search completes, we are returned a list of matching contacts. Because it's possible we will get more than one record when matching on any of the search criteria, you should always be certain that you're only selecting one record. This applies both to the contact record itself, as well as the data contained inside. You can have multiple phone numbers, e-mail addresses, even birthdates! We will use the FirstOrDefault() option when selecting all of these items, but you should be cautious of two things when working with this data:

1. Don't assume that every contact has every piece of data. You will get a NullReferenceException if data is missing. This means that you should check before just assigning values to your code. While it's frustrating to have to check each value for actual data, it's the only way to prevent your application from crashing with missing data. The only exception to this rule is the DisplayName property, for which there will always be a value.

2. There are actually ContactPhoneNumber, ContactEmailAddress, ContactAddress and several other specific classes that contain the data you want, and some additional metadata like "(Mobile)" for a phone number. These are important pieces of additional data that are buried within the Contact class.

Listing 7-33 is an example of how to gather the DisplayName, e-mail address, and phone number of the contact we just retrieved and assign them variables, with an eye on the two lessons we just covered.

Listing 7-33. Working with a Contact List

```
private void c_SearchCompleted(object sender, ContactsSearchEventArgs e)
{
    Contact c = e.Results.FirstOrDefault();
    if (c.DisplayName != null)
    {
        contactName.Text = c.DisplayName;
    }

    if (c.EmailAddresses != null)
    {
        string contactEmail = c.EmailAddresses.FirstOrDefault().EmailAddress;
    }

    if (c.PhoneNumbers != null)
    {
        string contactPhone = c.PhoneNumbers.FirstOrDefault().PhoneNumber;
    }

    if (c.Addresses   != null)
    {
        string contactAddress = c.Addresses.FirstOrDefault().PhysicalAddress.AddressLine1 +
"\n" + c.Addresses.FirstOrDefault().PhysicalAddress.City + ", " +
c.Addresses.FirstOrDefault().PhysicalAddress.StateProvince + "   " +
c.Addresses.FirstOrDefault().PhysicalAddress.PostalCode;
    }
}
```

As you can see, we combined the street address into one value, but you can retrieve each of these values separately. It would be very interesting, for example, to gather up the zip codes of all of the user's contacts, and place each of them on a map. We will cover something similar to this in Chapter 9 when we discuss the Map control.

Appointments

In many ways, working with the Appointments API is very similar to the Contacts API. We're going to search for a range of appointments (by time), and a collection of Appointment objects will be returned to us. We search for events by time, as shown in Listing 7-34.

Listing 7-34 Searching for Appointments

```
private void getAppointments()
{
    Appointments a = new Appointments();
    a.SearchCompleted += new EventHandler<AppointmentsSearchEventArgs>(a_SearchCompleted);
    a.SearchAsync(DateTime.Now, DateTime.Now.AddDays(7), null);
}
```

In our Completed event handler (shown in Listing 7-35), we can start gathering up all of this rich data.

Listing 7-35. SearchCompleted Event Handler

```
private void a_SearchCompleted(object sender, AppointmentsSearchEventArgs e)
{
    Appointment a = e.Results.Skip(10).FirstOrDefault();
    string startDate = a.StartTime.ToLongDateString();
    string startTime = a.StartTime.ToShortTimeString();
    string subject = a.Subject;
    string details = a.Details;
}
```

One of the key ways we can see this being used (aside from something simple and obvious like a calendaring application) is calendar replication. As an example, I have all of my work appointments in my corporate Exchange/Outlook account. I don't have an effective way to share those appointments with my wife, however (at least not without breaking the rules and giving her my credentials). So, with two children that have an array of summer activities, we've found a burning need to replicate parts of my work calendar to a Windows Live Calendar that we can share. Right now, it's a manual process. By using this API, we could easily grab my calendar events from my Outlook calendar, and using the Windows Live API, duplicate all of those events to a more public calendar.

Summary

There are many ways to access rich, useful data from your user's device. From calendar data, to contacts and photos, we can make our applications feel customized to the user. The Windows Phone tasks described in this chapter give you an opportunity to provide immersive phone experiences without having to write all of the code yourself. We can make phone calls, take photos, recommend a user review our application, or even provide turn-by-turn directions.

It's also important to note that Section 5.6 of the Windows Phone Technical Certification Requirements states: "An application must include the application name, version information, and technical support contact information that are easily discoverable."

This means that in nearly every application, there's an opportunity to use the EmailComposeTask (so that the user can send you a support message), the MarketplaceReviewTask (so the user can leave public feedback about your app), the PhoneCallTask (so that the user can call your customer service number), and the WebBrowserTask (so that the user can visit your web site). Your application has a web site, right?

In the next chapter, we're going to discuss how we can make our applications receive updates, even when the app isn't currently running. We'll do this through using push notifications, toast messages, and Live Tile updates. These technologies facilitate a level of interaction with your user that is not possible in any other way.

■ ■ ■

CHAPTER 8

Get Pushy: Using Push Notifications to Keep Your Users Up-to-Date

This chapter will focus on keeping your users up-to-date. Push Notifications are certainly one way to do that, but we're also going to focus on Live Tile updates from your application.

For those of you that aren't familiar with Push Notifications, how they work, or the purpose they serve, we have a story for you about the US Postal Service.

Understanding Push Notifications (and the US Postal Service)

Let's pretend that Microsoft's Push Notification Service is the Post Office. Everyone has gotten mail in the past, and this seems to work as a great analogy. The Microsoft Push Notification Service is central to how notifications are handled in Windows Phone apps, much like the US Post Office is central to how mail is delivered in the United States.

Tomorrow, you are going to finish building a brand-new home for you and your family. One of the first things this house is going to need is a street address. So, you call the post office, and register your home with them, and they give you back a street address that people can use to send housewarming gifts and credit card offers.

The home, in this analogy, is your application installed on a user's phone. The first time a user runs your application, it must call the Push Notification Service and request an address. This address is a URI that your web service can use to send messages (think housewarming gifts) to the app.

As the person living in the house, knowing your address is valuable, but not exactly the point. You want your friends, family, and the companies that you interact with to know the address, so that they can send you things via the postal service. Once we have an address we call our friends and give it to them so the next time they need to send us something, they know where to send it.

Your friends, in this story, are your own personal web services. Perhaps they're running in Windows Azure, or maybe they're a smaller set of services on your own shared hosting plan. In any case, these web services are going to be the "friends" that are sending you "packages."

Your birthday rolls around, and your friends want to send you a card with an Applebee's gift card inside. Rarely will they drive across town (or across the country) to hand it to you in person. Instead, they take it to their local post office. That local post office takes the card and drives/flies/warps it to the post office that is nearest to your address. Your local post office then takes that card to your house.

When an event happens on your web service, like a new message, or photo, or a weather update, you want to notify your users. Your web service will create a package of data, and send it to the address that you received at the beginning of this story. The Push Notification Service takes that package, identifies the users that need to receive it, and delivers it to the phones on your behalf. This package of data can take one of three forms: a tile update, a toast notification, or a raw notification. We will cover how to create each of these packages in this chapter, and how they interact with your user's device. Figure 8-1 illustrates the relationship between the phone, your web service, and the push notification service.

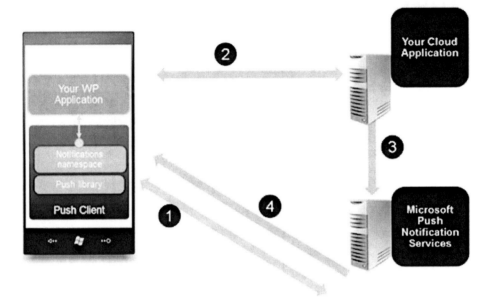

Figure 8-1. A representation of the relationships in a Push Notification

Using the Push Notification Service does not require any registration, and its use is free. If, however, you're app is sending more than 500 notifications per phone per day (which is about one message every 3 minutes, 24 hours a day), Microsoft will require you to send your messages using an authenticated web service. Much more on this topic can be found at `http://msdn.microsoft.com/en-us/library/ff941099.aspx`.

Creating a Notification App

Enabling a Windows Phone application to receive Push Notifications is actually the easy part of this process. As in our analogy, our application needs to call to the Push Notification service and get an address. Once we have this address, we can use it to push all of the different types of notifications to that device. An example will make this clear.

1. To get started, create a new Windows Phone application, and complete the New Project dialogue in similar fashion to what's shown in Figure 8-2.

Figure 8-2. Creating a new Windows Phone application

In the `MainPage.xaml.cs` file, we need to create that call to the Push Notification service. To start, we need to add a new namespace: `Microsoft.Phone.Notification`. This allows us to use objects like the HttpNotificationChannel. This does all of the work for us behind the scenes, so that we don't have to manage the call and connection on our own.

2. Add the code in Listing 8-1 to `MainPage.xaml.cs`. This is the minimum code you'll need in order to make the call to the Notification Service in your application.

Listing 8-1. The Windows Phone Code to Register with the Push Notification Service

```
using System;
using Microsoft.Phone.Controls;
using Microsoft.Phone.Notification;

namespace NotificationApp
{
    public partial class MainPage : PhoneApplicationPage
    {
```

```csharp
// Constructor
public MainPage()
{
        InitializeComponent();

HttpNotificationChannel pushChannel;
        string channelName = "myPushChannel";


        pushChannel = HttpNotificationChannel.Find(channelName);

        if (pushChannel == null)
        {
                pushChannel = new HttpNotificationChannel(channelName);
                pushChannel.ChannelUriUpdated += new
EventHandler<NotificationChannelUriEventArgs>(pushChannel_ChannelUriUpdated);
                pushChannel.Open();
                pushChannel.BindToShellToast();
                pushChannel.BindToShellTile();
        }
        else
        {
                pushChannel.ChannelUriUpdated += new
EventHandler<NotificationChannelUriEventArgs>(pushChannel_ChannelUriUpdated);
        }
}

        void pushChannel_ChannelUriUpdated(object sender,
NotificationChannelUriEventArgs e)
        {
                Dispatcher.BeginInvoke(() =>
                {
                        System.Diagnostics.Debug.WriteLine(e.ChannelUri.ToString());
                });
        }
    }
}
```

As you can see in Listing 8-1, we start by naming a new HttpNotificationChannel. We also create a string that we will use to name our notification channel when it is opened. Before anything else, we need to check to make sure that our application hasn't already created a notification channel. If we have, we just register an event handler for notifications.

In the case of a first time call, we create the new HttpNotificationChannel, using the channelName string that we created earlier. We also want to create an event handler so that we receive notification for when we have a new channel URI. Finally, we open the new push channel, and bind it to the operating system for both toast and tile notifications.

It is these BindToShellToast and BindToShellTile method calls that allow us to alert the system with notifications from our web services or other applications. If you don't need Toast or Tile updates for your application, you can skip the ones you don't want to use.

Notice that in our pushChannel_ChannelUriUpdated event handler, we spin up a separate thread and write the new ChannelUri value to our Output window in Visual Studio. This will make it simple to copy and paste the channel address that the Push Notification service assigns to our application on our test device, be it an actual Windows Phone or the emulator.

3. Run your project. In the Output window, copy the ChannelURI once it has been retrieved. It should appear similar to Figure 8-3.

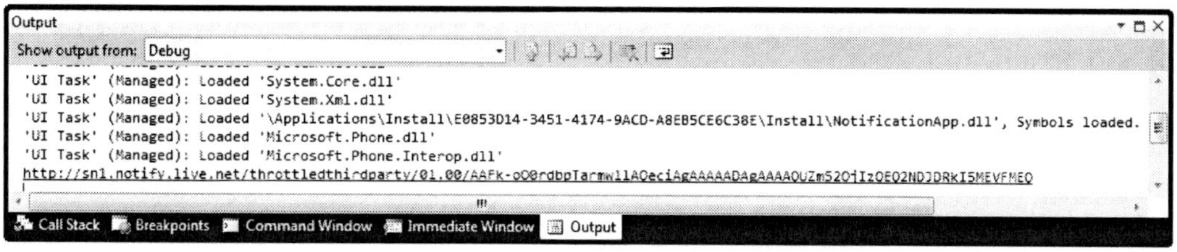

Figure 8-3. The Output panel of our Windows Phone application

This ChannelURI is retrieved from the Push Notification Service, and returned asynchronously to our application. When it arrives, our pushChannel_ChannelUriUpdated event handler fires, which allows us to capture the value and write it to the screen. In a more realistic example, we would take this ChannelURI value and pass it to our web service to be stored until we need to use it.

Creating a Toast Notification

In our first example of Push Notifications, we are going to send a toast message to our Windows Phone application. This can be done a variety of ways, using a web service, creating a client application, or even from a simple Web Form. For the following examples, we are going to use the web form approach because it illustrates concepts without adding the complexity that web services can create.

For our Toast notification example, you will need to create a new ASP.NET Empty Web Application project.

If you are using the version of Visual Studio 2010 that came with the Windows Phone Tools, you will need to get Visual Web Developer 2010 Express, which can be downloaded for free, or a full, paid version of Visual Studio 2010. Visual Web Developer 2010 Express can be downloaded at www.microsoft.com/visualstudio/en-us/products/2010-editions/visual-web-developer-express.

You will need to run these applications side-by-side, one for building your phone app, and one for building the web site we'll use to send our notifications. If you have a full license of Visual Studio 2010, you can use the same tool for both projects.

Figure 8-4 shows what the New Project dialog will look like.

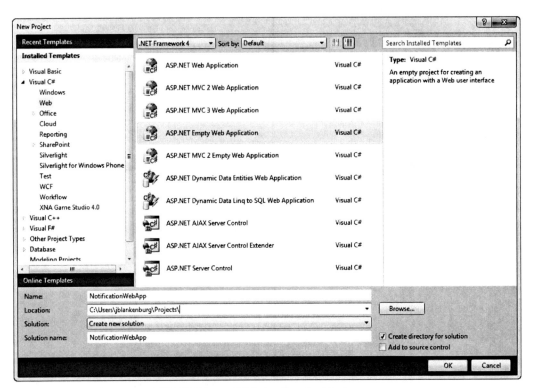

Figure 8-4. Creating a new ASP.NET Empty Web Application Project

1. Create a new ASP.NET Empty Web Application Project.

2. Next, create a new Web Form, as shown in Figure 8-5.

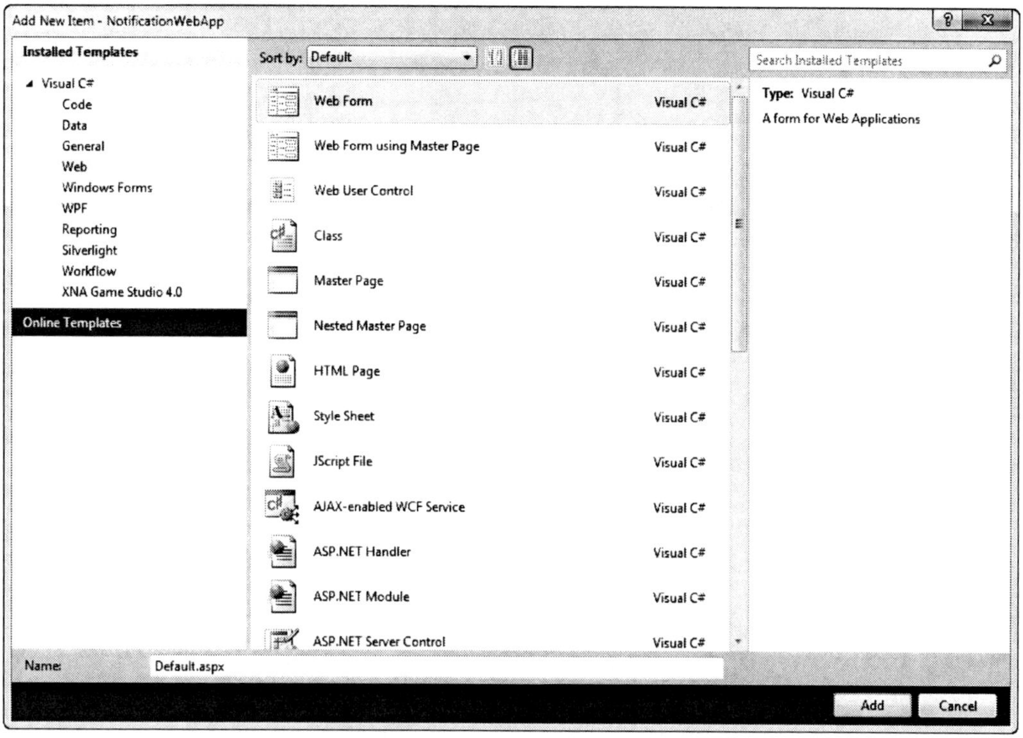

Figure 8-5. Adding a new Web Form to our project

Our Web Form requires almost no user interface, except for a button. We are going to use that button to send the toast notifications.

3. Add the button to the Default.aspx file that you created, and title it "Toast," using the code in Listing 8-2.

Listing 8-2. Adding Three Buttons to Our HTML Web Interface

```
<%@ Page Language="C#" AutoEventWireup="true" CodeBehind="Default.aspx.cs"
Inherits="NotificationWebApp.Default" %>

<!DOCTYPE html PUBLIC "-//W3C//DTD XHTML 1.0 Transitional//EN"
"http://www.w3.org/TR/xhtml1/DTD/xhtml1-transitional.dtd">

<html xmlns="http://www.w3.org/1999/xhtml">
<head runat="server">
    <title></title>
</head>
<body>
    <form id="form1" runat="server">
    <div>
```

175

```
                <asp:Button ID="ToastButton" runat="server" Text="Toast"
OnClick="ToastButton_Click" />
   </div>
    </form>
</body>
</html>
```

As you can see in Listing 8-2, we are using an asp:Button control because we will be calling a method in our code-behind file. Before you try to run this project, we also need to create that event handler method, as shown in Listing 8-3.

4.   Add the code in Listing 8-3 to your Default.aspx.cs file.

Listing 8-3. Adding the Button Event Handlers to the Code-Behind File

```
using System;
using System.Collections.Generic;
using System.Linq;
using System.Web;
using System.Web.UI;
using System.Web.UI.WebControls;

namespace NotificationWebApp
{
        public partial class Default : System.Web.UI.Page
        {
                protected void Page_Load(object sender, EventArgs e)
                {

                }

                protected void ToastButton_Click(object sender, EventArgs e)
                {

                }
        }
}
```

In each of these event handlers, we will be creating a package of data to be sent to the phone client. In order for this simple example to work, we will need that ChannelURI that was created when we ran and deployed our NotificationApp to the Windows Phone emulator.

Using that URI, we will need to create a string value that we can use in our web application. Listing 8-4 shows how we will store that value.

ListiNg 8-4. Storing the Channel URI in Our Web Application

```
string channelURI = "http://sn1.notify.live.net/throttledthirdparty/01.00/AAFk-
oOOrdbpTarmw1lAQeciAgAAAAADAgAAAAQUZm52OjIzOEQ2NDJDRkI5MEVFMEQ";
```

5. Add the code from Listing 8-4 directly above our Page_Load method, remembering to use your own channelURI value, not the one shown in Listing 8-4.

Finally, we need to create the Toast package that we will send to our application. To do this, we will be creating a HTTP POST request to the Push Notification service. (This is actually the only type of request allowed.) We are going to POST an XML message to the service, with a very specific format. Listing 8-5 shows the entire ToastButton_Click method code.

6. Use the code from Listing 8-5 as your ToastButton_Click event handler code.

Listing 8-5. Sending a Toast Notification

```
protected void ToastButton_Click(object sender, EventArgs e)
{
        HttpWebRequest notification = (HttpWebRequest)WebRequest.Create(channelURI);
        notification.Method = "POST";

        string toast = "<?xml version=\"1.0\" encoding=\"utf-8\"?>" +
        "<wp:Notification xmlns:wp=\"WPNotification\">" +
                "<wp:Toast>" +
                        "<wp:Text1>Houston...</wp:Text1>" +
                        "<wp:Text2>The eagle has landed.</wp:Text2>" +
                "</wp:Toast> " +
        "</wp:Notification>";

        byte[] notificationMessage = Encoding.Default.GetBytes(toast);

        notification.ContentLength = notificationMessage.Length;
        notification.ContentType = "text/xml";
        notification.Headers.Add("X-WindowsPhone-Target", "toast");
        notification.Headers.Add("X-NotificationClass", "2");
        notification.Headers.Add("X-MessageID", "b1711c5a-a6c1-4998-b160-c24ffd79ddc1");

        using (Stream requestStream = notification.GetRequestStream())
        {
                requestStream.Write(notificationMessage, 0, notificationMessage.Length);
        }

        HttpWebResponse response = (HttpWebResponse)notification.GetResponse();
        string notificationStatus = response.Headers["X-NotificationStatus"];
        string subscriptionStatus = response.Headers["X-SubscriptionStatus"];
        string deviceConnectionStatus = response.Headers["X-DeviceConnectionStatus"];
        string messageID = response.Headers["X-MessageID"];

        System.Diagnostics.Debug.WriteLine("NOTIFICATION STATUS:" + notificationStatus);
        System.Diagnostics.Debug.WriteLine("DEVICE CONNECTION STATUS:" +
deviceConnectionStatus);
        System.Diagnostics.Debug.WriteLine("SUBSCRIPTION STATUS:" + subscriptionStatus);
        System.Diagnostics.Debug.WriteLine("MESSAGE ID:" + messageID);
}
```

As you can see in the code from Listing 8-5, sending a Toast notification is not a lengthy process, but there are some very specific things that you need to do in order for it to work properly.

We create a new string, toast, that contains our XML message. The <wp:Text1> node is the title of our message, and the <wp:Text2> node is our message. We then convert that XML string into a byte array (`notificationByteArray`) before adding some message headers. Each message header has a specific meaning, and as we look at the other notification types in this chapter, they will become more obvious. The following is a quick look at each of those message headers, and their values:

> `X-WindowsPhone-Target`: We specify a value of "toast" to indicate that this is going to be a toast notification to the phone. This tells the target phone that the message should be used as a toast notification.

> `X-NotificationClass`: We use a value of 2 to specify a toast message, again. This value is used by the Push Notification Service to batch messages so that you don't get 3 or 4 at exactly the same time.

> `X-MessageID`: This is actually an optional value that you can use to identify your messages in the response. You must specify a GUID value, and it will be returned to you in the response, identifying the specific message. Without this, you won't be able to match your responses to your messages accurately.

Finally, we send the stream of data to the Push Notification service. The GetResponse() method that is called on our HttpWebRequest object (notification) actually passes the data to the Push Notification service, and the four string values that follow it are really for our own bookkeeping more than anything else. They provide us with the following few valuable pieces of information about our message:

> `X-NotificationStatus`: Was the message received?

> `X-SubscriptionStatus`: Is the user's phone accepting Toast notifications?

> `X-DeviceConnectionStatus`: Is the user's phone accepting data at all?

> `X-MessageID`: The unique identifier we gave the message when we sent it.

Finally, we use `System.Diagnostics.Debug.Writeline()` to write those messages to our Output window so that we can easily see what happened to our message. In your "real" application, you would probably commit these header values to a database, or even use them to re-queue messages that weren't received at a future time.

7. Finally, run your web application and your phone application at the same time, making sure you have an accurate channelURI. When you click the "Toast" button, you should see the result in your emulator, which looks like Figure 8-6.

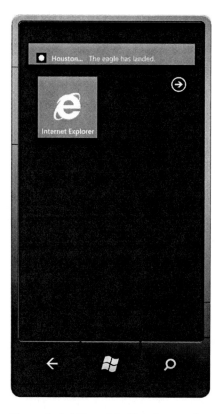

Figure 8-6. A Toast Notification on the Windows Phone emulator

The icon that you see in the toast message (in Figure 8-6) is actually the icon of your application. It is used automatically, to make the user aware of which application sent them the message.

So that's all it takes to send a Toast message to a Windows Phone. It was a long journey, but we've actually laid most of the framework for the next two notification types. Let's take a look at what we need to do for Raw Notifications next.

Creating a Raw Notification

This section, as well as the Tile Notification section that follow it, assumes that you have gone through the Toast notification section of this chapter already. There's a significant amount of overlap between these three processes, and it seemed incredibly redundant to repeat most of the work in each section. For Raw Notifications, we will need to change the Windows Phone application slightly, so that we can receive the data.

8. Open the same Windows Phone application we've been working on, and add one new event handler to our `MainPage.xaml.cs` file, as shown in Listing 8-6. The entire contents of `MainPage.xaml.cs` are shown for reference, but we have only added the new HttpNotificationReceived event handler, and its method, shown in bold.

Listing 8-6. Adding the HttpNotificationReceived Event Handler

```
using System;
using System.Windows;
using Microsoft.Phone.Controls;
using Microsoft.Phone.Notification;
using System.Text;

namespace NotificationApp
{
        public partial class MainPage : PhoneApplicationPage
        {
                // Constructor
                public MainPage()
                {
                        InitializeComponent();

HttpNotificationChannel pushChannel;
                        string channelName = "myPushChannel";

                                        pushChannel =
HttpNotificationChannel.Find(channelName);

                        if (pushChannel == null)
                        {
                                pushChannel = new HttpNotificationChannel(channelName);
                                pushChannel.ChannelUriUpdated += new
EventHandler<NotificationChannelUriEventArgs>(pushChannel_ChannelUriUpdated);
                                pushChannel.HttpNotificationReceived += new
EventHandler<HttpNotificationEventArgs>(pushChannel_HttpNotificationReceived);
                                pushChannel.Open();
                                pushChannel.BindToShellToast();
                                pushChannel.BindToShellTile();
                        }
                        else
                        {
                                pushChannel.ChannelUriUpdated += new
EventHandler<NotificationChannelUriEventArgs>(pushChannel_ChannelUriUpdated);
                        }
                }

                void pushChannel_HttpNotificationReceived(object sender,
HttpNotificationEventArgs e)
                {
                        string rawData;
```

```
                        using (System.IO.StreamReader streamReader = new
System.IO.StreamReader(e.Notification.Body))
                        {
                                rawData = streamReader.ReadToEnd();
                        }

                        Dispatcher.BeginInvoke(() =>
                                MessageBox.Show(String.Format("New XML Data {0}:\n{1}",
                                        DateTime.Now.ToShortTimeString(), rawData))
                                        );

                }

                void pushChannel_ChannelUriUpdated(object sender,
NotificationChannelUriEventArgs e)
                        {
                                Dispatcher.BeginInvoke(() =>
                                {
                                        System.Diagnostics.Debug.WriteLine(e.ChannelUri.ToString());
                                });
                        }
                }
        }
}
```

An important thing to remember about Raw Notifications is that you are just sending raw data. If you prefer XML, send XML. If you would rather use JSON, send yourself JSON. If you're just sending plain text, you can send that as well. The only real restriction is that your data is sent as text (XML and JSON are just text all gussied up).

You'll see that in our simple example in Listing 8-6, we use a StreamReader to grab the data when it arrives, and then publish it to the phone's screen in a MessageBox. Generally, you're going to do something more interesting with your data, but for the purposes of our illustration, this certainly achieves the goal.

Now we need to modify our web application to send a Raw Notification message.

9. Update your code in Default.aspx to look like Listing 8-7. We have only added a new Button to the page, but the entire code is shown as a reference.

Listing 8-7. Adding the Raw Button to the HTML Interface

```
<%@ Page Language="C#" AutoEventWireup="true" CodeBehind="Default.aspx.cs"
Inherits="NotificationWebApp.Default" %>

<!DOCTYPE html PUBLIC "-//W3C//DTD XHTML 1.0 Transitional//EN"
"http://www.w3.org/TR/xhtml1/DTD/xhtml1-transitional.dtd">

<html xmlns="http://www.w3.org/1999/xhtml">
<head runat="server">
    <title></title>
</head>
<body>
```

```
        <form id="form1" runat="server">
        <div>
            <asp:Button ID="ToastButton" runat="server" Text="Toast" OnClick="ToastButton_Click"
/>
            <asp:Button ID="RawButton" runat="server" Text="Raw" OnClick="RawButton_Click" />
        </div>
        </form>
</body>
</html>
```

In our code-behind, we will need another event handler method, `RawButton_Click`. There are really only three differences between the `RawButton_Click` event handler and the `ToastButton_Click` event handler that we looked at in Listing 8-5.

- Toast messages require a very specific XML format. Raw messages do not.

- We do not need the X-WindowsPhone-Target Header on our notification.

- We change the X-NotificationClass header value from 2 to 3.

Listing 8-8 shows the entire RawButton_Click event handler method, but the lines that differ from those in a Toast message are **bolded**.

10. Add the code from Listing 8-8 to your Default.aspx.cs file.

Listing 8-8. The Raw Notification Event Handler

```
protected void RawButton_Click(object sender, EventArgs e)
{
        HttpWebRequest notification = (HttpWebRequest)WebRequest.Create(channelURI);
        notification.Method = "POST";

        string rawMessage = "<?xml version=\"1.0\" encoding=\"utf-8\"?>" +
        "<root>" +
                "<FirstName>Jeff</FirstName>" +
                "<LastName>Blankenburg</LastName>" +
        "</root>";

        byte[] notificationMessage = Encoding.Default.GetBytes(rawMessage);

        notification.ContentLength = notificationMessage.Length;
        notification.ContentType = "text/xml";
        notification.Headers.Add("X-NotificationClass", "3");
        notification.Headers.Add("X-MessageID", "b1711c5a-a6c1-4998-b160-c24ffd79ddc1");


        using (Stream requestStream = notification.GetRequestStream())
        {
                requestStream.Write(notificationMessage, 0, notificationMessage.Length);
        }

        HttpWebResponse response = (HttpWebResponse)notification.GetResponse();
        string notificationStatus = response.Headers["X-NotificationStatus"];
```

```
        string subscriptionStatus = response.Headers["X-SubscriptionStatus"];
        string deviceConnectionStatus = response.Headers["X-DeviceConnectionStatus"];
        string messageID = response.Headers["X-MessageID"];

        System.Diagnostics.Debug.WriteLine("NOTIFICATION STATUS:" + notificationStatus);
        System.Diagnostics.Debug.WriteLine("DEVICE CONNECTION STATUS:" +
deviceConnectionStatus);
        System.Diagnostics.Debug.WriteLine("SUBSCRIPTION STATUS:" + subscriptionStatus);
        System.Diagnostics.Debug.WriteLine("MESSAGE ID:" + messageID);
}
```

As you can see from Listing 8-8, sending Toast and Raw Notifications are nearly identical. Our final example using Push Notification services is a Tile Update, and you'll find that in this example, we use much of the same code again.

Creating a Tile Notification

Creating a tile notification is very similar to the previous two examples, Toast and Raw notifications. In fact, our Windows Phone application doesn't need any additional code to make this work. If you are starting on this section of the chapter without having read the beginning of it, you'll want to reference Listing 8-1 to create your Windows Phone application.

To actually send a tile update, we need yet another button in our HTML interface, so let's start there, in Listing 8-9.

11. Add the code for the Button in Listing 8-9 to your Default.aspx file.

Listing 8-9 Adding a Tile Button to Our HTML Interface

```
<%@ Page Language="C#" AutoEventWireup="true" CodeBehind="Default.aspx.cs"
Inherits="NotificationWebApp.Default" %>

<!DOCTYPE html PUBLIC "-//W3C//DTD XHTML 1.0 Transitional//EN"
"http://www.w3.org/TR/xhtml1/DTD/xhtml1-transitional.dtd">

<html xmlns="http://www.w3.org/1999/xhtml">
<head runat="server">
    <title></title>
</head>
<body>
    <form id="form1" runat="server">
    <div>
        <asp:Button ID="ToastButton" runat="server" Text="Toast" OnClick="ToastButton_Click"
/>
        <asp:Button ID="RawButton" runat="server" Text="Raw" OnClick="RawButton_Click" />
        <asp:Button ID="TileButton" runat="server" Text="Tile" OnClick="TileButton_Click" />
    </div>
    </form>
</body>
</html>
```

In our code-behind, we will create a third and final event handler method for the new button, and again, most of the code will be redundant from our previous Toast and Raw examples. The unique pieces of code for Tile notifications are shown in bold in Listing 8-10.

12. Add the TileButton_Click event handler from Listing 8-10 to your Default.aspx.cs file.

Listing 8-10. The Tile Event Handler Code for Our Web Code-Behind
protected void TileButton_Click(object sender, EventArgs e)

```
{
        HttpWebRequest notification = (HttpWebRequest)WebRequest.Create(channelURI);
        notification.Method = "POST";

        string tile = "<?xml version=\"1.0\" encoding=\"utf-8\"?>" +
        "<wp:Notification xmlns:wp=\"WPNotification\">" +
                "<wp:Tile>" +
                        "<wp:BackgroundImage></wp:BackgroundImage>" +
                        "<wp:Count>23</wp:Count>" +
                        "<wp:Title>Notify!</wp:Title>" +
                        "<wp:BackBackgroundImage></wp:BackBackgroundImage>" +
                        "<wp:BackTitle>!Yfiton</wp:BackTitle>" +
                        "<wp:BackContent>Back that tile up.</wp:BackContent>" +
                "</wp:Tile> " +
        "</wp:Notification>";

        byte[] notificationByteArray = Encoding.Default.GetBytes(tile);

        notification.ContentLength = notificationByteArray.Length;
        notification.ContentType = "text/xml";
        notification.Headers.Add("X-WindowsPhone-Target", "token");
        notification.Headers.Add("X-NotificationClass", "1");


        using (Stream requestStream = notification.GetRequestStream())
        {
                requestStream.Write(notificationByteArray, 0, notificationByteArray.Length);
        }

        HttpWebResponse response = (HttpWebResponse)notification.GetResponse();
        string notificationStatus = response.Headers["X-NotificationStatus"];
        string subscriptionStatus = response.Headers["X-SubscriptionStatus"];
        string deviceConnectionStatus = response.Headers["X-DeviceConnectionStatus"];
        string messageID = response.Headers["X-MessageID"];

        System.Diagnostics.Debug.WriteLine("NOTIFICATION STATUS:" + notificationStatus);
        System.Diagnostics.Debug.WriteLine("DEVICE CONNECTION STATUS:" +
deviceConnectionStatus);
        System.Diagnostics.Debug.WriteLine("SUBSCRIPTION STATUS:" + subscriptionStatus);
        System.Diagnostics.Debug.WriteLine("MESSAGE ID:" + messageID);
}
```

You should notice that there are six pieces of information that we can dynamically change in our application's Live Tile. They are part of the new XML string that we've created named tile. Illustrations of these values can be seen in Figure 8-7. The following describes the six pieces of information:

BackgroundImage: An image that is already part of your Windows Phone app that can be used as a background for your tile. An example would be a weather application. You might have a rainy tile, a sunny tile, and a snowy tile.

Count: The number that shows up in the small circle in the top right corner. This can range from zero to 99. Any number greater than 99 will only show 99 as the value.

Title: The text shown on the bottom of the tile. You have no control over font size, color, or family, and you get approximately 20 characters.

BackBackgroundImage: Exactly like the background image on the front side of the tile, except we are specifying the one on the back of the tile, when it flips over. Without an image specified, the back of the tile will always be red.

BackTitle: Text in the same position as the front title. Same restrictions.

BackContent: The large text on the back of the tile.

Figure 8-7. A Live Tile in default, updated, and flipped states

The other differences in the code for our TileButton_Click event handler method are semantics more than anything else. We need to add the X-WindowsPhone-Target header back in (we used it for the Tile messages), using "token" as our value. The X-NotificationClass header needs a "1" value to indicate that it is a Tile notification as well. Otherwise, all of your code should look identical to the previous two examples.

Live Tile Updates

At this point, you might be wishing for a way to update your Live Tile from your application, rather than from a web service (or our fancy web application). The good news is: you can. For this example, we'll continue working on our NotificationApp that we've been working on over this entire chapter.

13. Add two buttons to our MainPage.xaml page in our Windows Phone project, as shown in Listing 8-11.

Listing 8-11. Adding Buttons to Our XAML Interface

```
<Button Content="Primary" Height="72" HorizontalAlignment="Left" Margin="130,152,0,0"
Name="PrimaryButton" VerticalAlignment="Top" Width="214" Click="PrimaryButton_Click" />
<Button Content="Secondary" Height="72" HorizontalAlignment="Left" Margin="130,299,0,0"
Name="SecondaryButton" VerticalAlignment="Top" Width="214" Click="SecondaryButton_Click" />
```

As you can see, we've created a Click event for each of these buttons, and we will be implementing the code to change these tiles in those event handler methods.

SECONDARY LIVE TILES

You may have noticed that the second button is titled "Secondary." This is because in the Windows Phone 7.5 release, you can now create additional tiles (in addition to your primary one) on your user's home screen. This becomes especially important when you want to expose specific functionality from your application without forcing the user to launch it from the beginning and navigate to that action. Imagine your specific flights being exposed by an airline app, or being able to launch into specific areas of a game, right from your home screen. That's what secondary tiles provide us as developers.

Now that we have added those buttons to our Xaml interface, we need to write some code in the event handler methods in `MainPage.xaml.cs`. To update a primary tile, we need to dive into the collection of `ShellTiles` that our application has, and grab the first one. This will always be our primary tile.

14. Listing 8-12 shows our PrimaryButton_Click method and its contents. Add this to your `MainPage.xaml.cs` file. Make sure that you also add a using statement for System.Linq, or the example code won't work for you.

Listing 8-12. Updating a Primary Tile

```
private void PrimaryButton_Click(object sender, RoutedEventArgs e)
{
        ShellTile PrimaryTile = ShellTile.ActiveTiles.First();

        if (PrimaryTile != null)
        {
                StandardTileData TileUpdate = new StandardTileData
                {
                        Title = "Yoda Tile",
                        BackgroundImage = new Uri("", UriKind.Relative),
                        Count = 1,
                        BackTitle = "The Dark Side",
                        BackBackgroundImage = new Uri("", UriKind.Relative),
                        BackContent = "Beware, this side you should."
                };

                PrimaryTile.Update(TileUpdate);
        }
}
```

As we show you in Listing 8-12, we grab the first ShellTile object as the primary tile, and then we can update the tile's information using the StandardTileData class. The code in this example is also how you will update Secondary Tiles after they have been created. The primary difference is in which tile in the ActiveTiles collection you select.

In the next code example, Listing 8-13, we will create a new Secondary Tile. We'll do this inside the SecondaryButton_Click event handler method that we already created. An important thing to remember about creating Secondary Tiles is that as soon as you create the tile, your user will be whisked away to their Home screen to see the tile in its new location. This means that you will have to create each tile individually, and there's no real mechanism for creating several Secondary Tiles at a time.

    15. Add the event handler in Listing 8-13 to your `MainPage.xaml.cs` file.

Listing 8-13. Creating a Secondary Tile

```
private void SecondaryButton_Click(object sender, RoutedEventArgs e)
{
        ShellTile SecondaryTile = ShellTile.ActiveTiles.FirstOrDefault(x =>
x.NavigationUri.ToString().Contains("Tile=2"));

        if (SecondaryTile == null)
        {
                StandardTileData NewTile = new StandardTileData
                {
                        BackgroundImage = new Uri("", UriKind.Relative),
                        Title = "Cautionary Tile",
                        Count = 42,
                        BackTitle = "Baby Got Back",
                        BackContent = "L.A. Face with an open data feed.",
                        BackBackgroundImage = new Uri("", UriKind.Relative)
```

```
        };

        ShellTile.Create(new Uri("/AlternatePage.xaml?Tile=2", UriKind.Relative),
NewTile);
        }
```

Much of the code in Listing 8-13 should look similar to that of the Primary Tile update we did in Listing 8-12. The specific difference is in how we determine which tile we're working with. You can search through the NavigationUri property of the **ActiveTiles**, so it is recommended that you add unique query string variables to the end of your Navigation URI values. In our example, we used "Tile=2" as our unique value, and we were searching to make sure that our Secondary Tile didn't already exist.

To update a Secondary Tile, we perform the same search, but we want to make sure that the value *isn't* null, and we call an Update() method on our existing tile instead of the .Create() method on the ShellTile class.

16.   Use the code in Listing 8-14 to create our third event handler in our MainPage.xaml.cs file.

Listing 8-14. Updating a Secondary Tile

```
private void UpdateButton_Click(object sender, RoutedEventArgs e)
{
        ShellTile UpdateTile = ShellTile.ActiveTiles.FirstOrDefault(x =>
x.NavigationUri.ToString().Contains("Tile=2"));

        if (UpdateTile != null)
        {
                StandardTileData UpdateData = new StandardTileData
                {
                        BackgroundImage = new Uri("", UriKind.Relative),
                        Title = "Tile E. Coyote",
                        Count = 8,
                        BackTitle = "AC/DC",
                        BackContent = "Back in Black",
                        BackBackgroundImage = new Uri("", UriKind.Relative)
                };

                UpdateTile.Update(UpdateData);
        }
}
```

As described in Listing 8-14, the code structure is almost exactly the same, with the exception of the null if statement and the Update call. This should make it very easy to create "tile factories" in your code, reducing the redundancy in your application.

Summary

You can see that we have the ability to add and update any of our tiles directly from our application, or from a web service using the Push Notification Service. This provides us with an incredible opportunity to keep our users up to date, engaged, and interested in what our application is doing. Some of the best applications, going forward, will be those that you potentially never even need to open. All of the information and data you need is found directly on your home screen, with no need to spin up the actual application. We look forward to seeing how you take advantage of these powerful tools.

■ ■ ■

CHAPTER 9

Get Oriented: Interacting with the Phone, Camera, GPS, and More

When you hold a modern mobile phone in your hands, you are a holding a sophisticated and complex system of sensors, hardware, and software—all working in harmony. It's easy to forget that just a few short years ago, each of these "parts" had its own API, and that it was up to the developer to figure out how to make it work.

With Windows Phone, the operating system provides a rich set of integrated APIs for you to use in your application when you want to know the device's location (GPS), orientation (compass, accelerometer and gyroscope), or surroundings (the camera). In this chapter, we'll cover how to use these sensors in your applications, as well as the best situations in which to use each of them.

Prior to the release of the 7.1 SDK, some of these sensors were unavailable. The first is access to the raw data feed from the camera. This enables key scenarios like image manipulation and augmented reality applications. Newer phones may also contain a gyroscope, and there's now an API for the compass that has been in every Windows Phone 7 since the beginning.

Tracking the Position of Your Device

There is much to be learned about a user's device from the data its sensors provide. Location is an obvious one, and it's important to know where the device is in order to give the user more information about where they currently are. Orientation of the device can be equally, if not more important, however. Using the compass, the accelerometer and the gyroscope, we can determine exactly which direction the phone is facing, its physical orientation in space, and rate at which it is rotating.

What makes the orientation sensors exceptional, however, is the Microsoft is also provides us with the Motion class, which aggregates the data from all three of those sensors into one robust class that does a bunch of really complicated math on our behalf. We will cover each of these sensors, as well as the Motion class in this chapter.

Using Location Services

Windows Phone provides three ways to determine the location—the latitude and longitude—of a phone: GPS, mobile phone triangulation, and Wi-Fi. The first and most obvious choice is GPS. Every Windows Phone has a GPS chip, and for most purposes, it works incredibly well. That is, until you go inside a building.

Second, there's mobile phone triangulation. There are cell towers all over the place in metro areas, and by measuring the signal latency from the surrounding towers (and knowing their locations), you can make an educated estimation as to where the phone is, sometimes within as few as 50 feet.

Finally, there's Wi-Fi lookups. By connecting to a Wi-Fi access point, you have an IP address, and that IP address can be located with a reverse-IP lookup. This is not the most accurate process, but if you're trying to find the nearest McDonalds, it's almost certainly sufficient.

Each of these methods has its advantages and disadvantages, as shown in Table 9-1. GPS doesn't work well inside a building, it's relatively slow to get a signal, and it uses a lot of power, but it's extremely accurate. Triangulation is fast and low-power, but less accurate and really only works in populated areas. (There are not many cell towers in Antarctica or North Dakota, for example.) Wi-Fi is probably the least accurate, but again, it's fast.

Table 9-1. Location Services Sensors, and Their Ratings (1 = Best, 3 = Worst)

	GPS	Triangulation	Wi-Fi
Accuracy	1	2	3
Power Use	3	1	2
Speed	3	1	2
Signal Limitation	Indoors	Wilderness	Wilderness

Thankfully, for Windows Phone, we don't have to determine which service to use. In fact, we can't. Microsoft provides a single object for all of this data in Location Services. To show a device's location, you need a small bit of code in both your Xaml and C# files. Listing 9-1 shows the Xaml you'll need. We are adding three TextBlock values.

Listing 9-1. The Xaml Elements to Add to Your Location Services Project

```
<TextBlock Height="30" HorizontalAlignment="Left" Margin="12,101,0,0" Text="Latitude"
VerticalAlignment="Top" />
<TextBlock Height="30" HorizontalAlignment="Left" Margin="12,239,0,0" Text="Longitude"
VerticalAlignment="Top" />
<TextBlock Height="30" HorizontalAlignment="Left" Margin="12,376,0,0" Text="Status"
VerticalAlignment="Top" />
<TextBlock Height="101" HorizontalAlignment="Left" Margin="12,137,0,0" x:Name="Latitude"
Text="" VerticalAlignment="Top" Width="438" FontSize="72" />
<TextBlock Height="101" HorizontalAlignment="Left" Margin="12,275,0,0" x:Name="Longitude"
Text="" VerticalAlignment="Top" Width="438" FontSize="72" />
<TextBlock Height="101" HorizontalAlignment="Left" Margin="12,406,0,0" x:Name="Accuracy"
Text="" VerticalAlignment="Top" Width="438" FontSize="72" />
<TextBlock Height="30" HorizontalAlignment="Left" Margin="73,34,0,0" x:Name="Status"
Text="Stopped" VerticalAlignment="Top" Width="306" TextAlignment="Center" />
```

1. Create a new Windows Phone Application project named "LocationSample."

2. In MainPage.xaml, use the code from Listing 9-1 inside the default Grid named "ContentPanel."

Now that we have a simple interface to work with, we can dive into the code to get our actual Location data. Listing 9-2 assumes that you want to get a new location every time the device moves, which is why we are using event handlers to get the data.

Listing 9-2. Detecting Location in Our Code-Behind File

```
using System;
using System.Device.Location;
using Microsoft.Phone.Controls;

namespace LocationSample
{
    public partial class MainPage : PhoneApplicationPage
    {
        GeoCoordinateWatcher gcw = new GeoCoordinateWatcher();

        public MainPage()
        {
            InitializeComponent();

            gcw.StatusChanged += new
EventHandler<GeoPositionStatusChangedEventArgs>(gcw_StatusChanged);
            gcw.PositionChanged += new
EventHandler<GeoPositionChangedEventArgs<GeoCoordinate>>(gcw_PositionChanged);
            gcw.Start();
        }

        void gcw_StatusChanged(object sender, GeoPositionStatusChangedEventArgs e)
        {
            Status.Text = e.Status.ToString();
        }

        void gcw_PositionChanged(object sender, GeoPositionChangedEventArgs<GeoCoordinate> e)
        {
            Latitude.Text = e.Position.Location.Latitude.ToString();
            Longitude.Text = e.Position.Location.Longitude.ToString();
            Accuracy.Text = e.Position.Location.HorizontalAccuracy.ToString();
        }

    }
}
```

In Listing 9-2, you can see that we instantiate a new GeoCoordinateWatcher object, and in our constructor method, MainPage(), we add two event handlers to that GeoCoordinateWatcher before we start it up. The GeoCoordinateWatcher class exposes the Location Services that we discussed earlier. Follow the next steps to use this in your project:

1. Replace the code in your MainPage.xaml.cs file with the code in Listing 9-2.

2. Run the application (F5).

The first event handler in Listing 9-2, StatusChanged, is more for our purposes as a developer than for the end user. It gives us information about what the GeoCoordinateWatcher is doing. This is important because we need to know if it is looking for data, unable to find data, or actively returning data. The values it will return are shown in Table 9-2.

Table 9-2. Possible StatusChanged Values from the GeoCoordinateWatcher

Value	Meaning
Initializing	The GeoCoordinateWatcher is currently trying to acquire a location.
Ready	The GeoCoordinateWatcher has determined a location and is returning the data through the PositionChanged event.
NoData	The GeoCoordinateWatcher was unable to determine a location; this typically occurs because it could not receive a signal from all three data sources.
Disabled	The GeoCoordinateWatcher was unable to determine a location because the Location Settings on the user's phone have been disabled.

The second event handler, PositionChanged, is where the important data is kept. Each time that the GeoCoordinateWatcher detects that the user's position has changed, this event will fire again, returning a GeoCoordinate object for us to manipulate. The two primary properties of the GeoCoordinate object are a Timestamp object, so we know *when* we got the information from the device, and a Location object, which contains all of the specifics about the location of the device.

In our example, we retrieved the three most common Location values you'll use: Latitude, Longitude, and HorizontalAccuracy. While Latitude and Longitude are measures with which we're all familiar, HorizontalAccuracy is less so. It measures the GeoCoordinateWatcher's margin of error. HorizontalAccuracy is returned to you in a length of meters, and is meant to specify the radius of a circle that could be drawn around the lat/long point that was provided. This information should be conveyed to the user so that they're aware you're not 100 percent confident in their location. You should never expect a HorizontalAccuracy less than 4 to 5 meters, as commercial GPS devices are generally prevented from greater accuracy than that.

▨**Note**: An important point to remember about Location Services is that there are specific rules about when you can and cannot use them in an application. This refers to Section 2.7 of the Application Certification Requirements for Windows Phone (http://msdn.microsoft.com/library/hh184843.aspx). You should take the time and care to read the entire document from start to finish.

It's also important to remember that your user must always be confident that Location services are only being used when they authorize them to be. This means that you need to provide a mechanism for them to turn Location services off (if applicable), or at the very least, the ability to opt-in every time you're going to gather that kind of data. You will fail Marketplace registration without adhering to these rules, so it's very important that you are aware of them.

You will discover that the emulator always defaults to Seattle, Washington, no matter where your computer is actually located. There is, however, a new tool in the emulator that makes it simple to change where the emulator thinks it is. To access it, open your Windows Phone emulator and press the chevron (>>) button that appears next to the emulator. Clicking the Location tab will take you to this feature, as shown in Figure 9-1.

Figure 9-1. Windows Phone emulator location add-on

With this emulator add-on, you can use Bing Maps to specify your location, enter custom latitude and longitude values, or even record a trip to emulate data as the user drives across town or the country. To accomplish the trip emulation, you can click on the map in multiple places, and the individual locations will be added to a list in the Current Location panel of the tool. Once you have a list of locations, you click the Live button at the top of the map, which will enable the "Fire every 1 second" button to its right. You may change the duration to any number of seconds, and pressing the Play button will trigger the emulator to move through the list of locations you created, pausing for the duration of time you specified.

3. Click on the map a few times to add some locations to your map.

4. Click the Live button at the top of the tool.

5. Press the Play icon to have the tool feed each of your locations into your app on a one-second interval.

Now that you know how to determine the location of your device, the next piece of information we can use is the direction the device is heading *from* that location. We can accomplish this with the Compass sensor.

Using the Compass

The term compass is somewhat of a misnomer in mobile devices. There's not a little magnetic needle pointing north within your phone; instead we're actually accessing a device called a *magnetometer* (mag-neh-TOM-eh-ter). A magnetometer measures the strength and direction of a magnetic field, and it is the sensor we will use to determine the direction a device is pointing.

There are two primary values that we are interested in when we use the Compass API, MagneticHeading and TrueHeading. MagneticHeading contains the current heading of the device, measured in clockwise degrees, from the Earth's *magnetic* north. TrueHeading is measured in clockwise degrees from the Earth's *geographic* north (also referred to as True North). There are many publications dedicated to more specifics on these two locations, but the short explanation is that the true North Pole is a specific location where the Earth's axis of rotation meets Earth's surface. The magnetic north pole is the point on Earth's surface where Earth's magnetic field points vertically downwards. For real compass functionality, you'll want to use the MagneticHeading property.

To get started, we need to create a Xaml interface that shows compass data effectively. Listing 9-3 shows the elements you'll need to use.

Listing 9-3. The Xaml We Will Use to Show the Compass Data in an App

```
<TextBlock Height="30" HorizontalAlignment="Left"  Margin="20,73,0,0" Text="MAGNETIC"
VerticalAlignment="Top" Foreground="White" FontSize="28" FontWeight="Bold"/>
<TextBlock Height="30" HorizontalAlignment="Right"  Margin="0,74,47,0" Text="TRUE"
VerticalAlignment="Top" Foreground="Gray" FontSize="28" FontWeight="Bold"/>
<TextBlock Height="30" HorizontalAlignment="Left"  Margin="20,100,0,0" Name="magneticValue"
Text="1.0" VerticalAlignment="Top" Foreground="White" FontSize="28" FontWeight="Bold"
Width="147" TextAlignment="Center" />
<TextBlock Height="30" HorizontalAlignment="Right"  Margin="0,100,20,0" Name="trueValue"
Text="1.0" VerticalAlignment="Top" Foreground="Gray" FontSize="28" FontWeight="Bold"
Width="123" TextAlignment="Center" />
<TextBlock Height="30" HorizontalAlignment="Left"  Margin="20,140,0,0" Name="xBlock" Text="X:
1.0" VerticalAlignment="Top" Foreground="Red" FontSize="28" FontWeight="Bold"/>
<TextBlock Height="30" HorizontalAlignment="Center"  Margin="0,140,0,0" Name="yBlock" Text="Y:
1.0" VerticalAlignment="Top" Foreground="Green" FontSize="28" FontWeight="Bold"/>
<TextBlock Height="30" HorizontalAlignment="Right"  Margin="0,140,20,0" Name="zBlock" Text="Z:
1.0" VerticalAlignment="Top"  Foreground="Blue" FontSize="28" FontWeight="Bold"/>
<Line x:Name="magneticLine" X1="240" Y1="350" X2="240" Y2="270" Stroke="White"
StrokeThickness="4"></Line>
```

Figure 9-2 shows what this interface will look like. To add this code to your application, take the following steps:

6. Create a new Windows Phone Application project named "CompassSample."

7. Like our Location example earlier, add the contents of Listing 9-3 to the ContentPanel Grid that Visual Studio created by default.

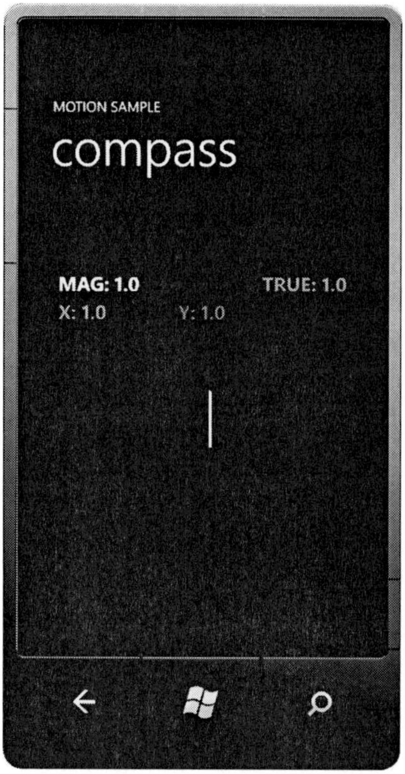

Figure 9-2. The user interface for our compass application

To access `MagneticHeading` and `TrueHeading` values on a Windows Phone device, we need to create and start a new Compass object, and then monitor an event handler for the values we need. Every Windows Phone has a compass, but only those that have been upgraded to Windows Phone 7.5 actually have the Compass API. Because of this, we'll also need to check to make sure we have access to this data. The code to do this is shown in Listing 9-4. Please note that we need a using statement for `Microsoft.Devices.Sensors` to access this sensor.

Listing 9-4. The C# We Will Use in Our MainPage.xaml.cs File for the Compass

```
using System;
using Microsoft.Phone.Controls;
using Microsoft.Devices.Sensors;
using Microsoft.Xna.Framework;

namespace CompassSample
{
        public partial class MainPage : PhoneApplicationPage
        {
                Compass compass;
```

```
        public MainPage()
        {
            InitializeComponent();

            if (Compass.IsSupported)
            {
                compass = new Compass();
                compass.TimeBetweenUpdates = TimeSpan.FromMilliseconds(1);
                compass.CurrentValueChanged += new
EventHandler<SensorReadingEventArgs<CompassReading>>(compass_CurrentValueChanged);
                compass.Start();
            }
        }

        void compass_CurrentValueChanged(object sender, SensorReadingEventArgs<CompassReading>
e)
        {
            Dispatcher.BeginInvoke(() => UpdateUI(e.SensorReading));
        }

        private void UpdateUI(CompassReading compassReading)
        {
            magneticValue.Text = compassReading.MagneticHeading.ToString("0.00");
            trueValue.Text = compassReading.TrueHeading.ToString("0.00");

            magneticLine.X2 = magneticLine.X1 - (200 *
Math.Sin(MathHelper.ToRadians((float)compassReading.MagneticHeading)));
            magneticLine.Y2 = magneticLine.Y1 - (200 *
Math.Cos(MathHelper.ToRadians((float)compassReading.MagneticHeading)));

            xBlock.Text = "X: " + compassReading.MagnetometerReading.X.ToString("0.00");
            yBlock.Text = "Y: " + compassReading.MagnetometerReading.Y.ToString("0.00");
            zBlock.Text = "Z: " + compassReading.MagnetometerReading.Z.ToString("0.00");
        }
    }
}
```

Much like the Location example in Listing 9-2, you will need a new Compass object created at the top of your code. In the initialization method this time, we need to check to make sure that the Compass sensor is supported. We do this with the `Compass.IsSupported` boolean check. Windows Phones running the original operating system do not have the ability to access the Compass sensor, and will result in an error if we try. To get this code into your project, the following are the next steps:

8. Replace the code in your `MainPage.xaml.cs` file with the contents of Listing 9-4.

9. Run your project in the emulator (F5).

10. Be disappointed that the emulator doesn't support the Compass.

Yes, step 5 is utter disappointment. The emulator does not support the compass sensor. It is our hope that in the future, there will be a gyroscope and compass tool (like the Accelerometer and Location tools we have now), but for now, you will need to test this application on a real device.

There is one event handler that we will use regularly with the Compass, `CurrentValueChanged`. As with the other sensors we'll cover in this chapter, you should notice that we actually pass our `CompassReading` data to a separate thread so that we don't freeze or interrupt the user interface thread. This is done using the `Dispatcher.BeginInvoke()` method, which moves the processing of our data to a separate thread.

In our `CompassReading` data, we get a great number of data points, but the most common ones are used in our example. `MagneticHeading` and `TrueHeading` are covered earlier in this section, but you can see that we also have access to an X, Y, and Z value. These are the raw Magnetometer readings, measured in microteslas (mT), which are a measurement of magnetic field strength. As an example, a common refrigerator magnet is around 5 mT, while a MRI (magnetic resonance imaging) generally measures around 3,000 mT. The values you will get from the earth's magnetic poles can vary greatly depending on the device's location, so make sure that you understand these variances as you use this sensor. Wikipedia has an excellent article on this topic; you can find it at `http://en.wikipedia.org/wiki/Earth%27s_magnetic_field`.

We have also created a Line as part of our user interface, and in the code in Listing 9-4, you can see that we are using the `MagneticHeading` to give that line a direction to point.

As we mentioned earlier, make sure you are aware of the possibility that other magnetic fields can and will interfere with the readings of the compass and its magnetometer, which shouldn't be trusted as 100 percent accurate all of the time. If you are building a true compass application, it might be best to verify your readings against a recent set of GPS locations, to verify that the user is actually traveling the direction that your compass is suggesting. Otherwise, you are going to be getting your customers lost, and that's probably not a great user experience.

At this point, we've covered how to determine the location and heading of our user's device. The rest of this section will focus on the orientation and rotation of a Windows Phone, starting with the accelerometer.

Using the Accelerometer

An accelerometer in Windows Phone is a sensor that measures the acceleration of the device on three axes (X, Y, Z) relative to freefall perpendicular to the earth, as illustrated by Figure 9-3. .In addition to a timestamp, the values are expressed in G-forces (1G = 9.81 m/s^2 or as you may have learned in school, 32 feet per second per second). What this means is that if the phone is laying face-up on a perfectly flat surface, the Z axis would read -1.0, and the other two axes would read zero. To help illustrate this concept, take a look at Figure 9-3. If the phone is sitting still on a flat table, the force of Earth's gravity is pulling the accelerometer downwards on the Z axis, resulting in a -1.0 value. Turning the phone face down would turn the Z axis reading to a positive value. The important lesson here is that the "positive" directions for the phone are when it is being pulled forward, up, or right. Backward, left, and down will all result in a negative value.

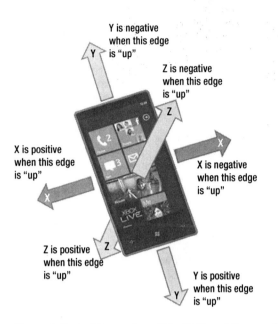

Figure 9-3. An illustration of the X, Y, and Z axes of the accelerometer

Thankfully, getting data from this sensor is very straightforward. The only real challenge we face with this is that we want to keep the process thread-safe. This means passing our accelerometer actions to a separate thread, so that we don't impact the UI thread and lock it up while we acquire the data.

Listing 9-5 shows the Xaml we will need for this simple example. We have a few TextBlock elements that will display the X, Y, and Z axis values from the accelerometer. Figure 9-4 shows what this interface will look like.

Listing 9-5. A Simple Xaml Interface for Our Accelerometer Application

```
<TextBlock Text="X = " FontSize="60" Margin="0,0,0,0" />
<TextBlock Text="Y = " FontSize="60" Margin="0,100,0,0" />
<TextBlock Text="Z = " FontSize="60" Margin="0,200,0,0" />
<TextBlock x:Name="xValue" FontSize="60" Margin="110,0,0,0" />
<TextBlock x:Name="yValue" FontSize="60" Margin="110,100,0,0" />
<TextBlock x:Name="zValue" FontSize="60" Margin="110,200,0,0" />
```

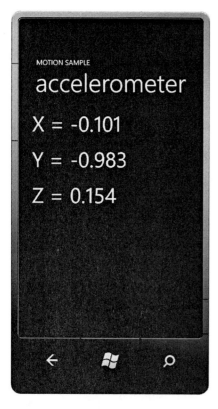

Figure 9-4. Our simple accelerometer application interface

To build this application, start with the following:

11. Create a new Windows Phone Application called "AccelerometerSample."

12. Add the Xaml found in Listing 9-5 to the `ContentPanel Grid` in your `MainPage.xaml` file.

Listing 9-6 shows the entirety of our `MainPage.xaml.cs` file for this example. Also notice that we had to add a new reference to `Microsoft.Devices.Sensors` to get access to the accelerometer.

Listing 9-6. Using C# to Access the Accelerometer

```
using System;
using Microsoft.Phone.Controls;
using Microsoft.Devices.Sensors;

namespace AccelerometerSample
{
    public partial class MainPage : PhoneApplicationPage
    {
```

```
        Accelerometer accelerometer;

        public MainPage()
        {
            InitializeComponent();

            accelerometer = new Accelerometer();
            accelerometer.CurrentValueChanged += new
EventHandler<SensorReadingEventArgs<AccelerometerReading>>(accelerometer_CurrentValueChanged);
            accelerometer.Start();
        }

        void accelerometer_CurrentValueChanged(object sender,
SensorReadingEventArgs<AccelerometerReading> e)
        {
            Dispatcher.BeginInvoke(() => UpdateUI(e));
        }

        void UpdateUI(SensorReadingEventArgs<AccelerometerReading> e)
        {
            xValue.Text = e.SensorReading.Acceleration.X.ToString("0.000");
            yValue.Text = e.SensorReading.Acceleration.Y.ToString("0.000");
            zValue.Text = e.SensorReading.Acceleration.Z.ToString("0.000");
        }
    }
}
```

In order to use this in your project, follow the remaining steps.

13. Replace the code in your `MainPage.xaml.cs` file with the C# in Listing 9-6.

14. Run your project in the emulator (F5).

When you try to run the code in Listing 9-6 in the emulator, you'll notice that you get a value of -1.0 from the Y axis, and zeroes on the others. This is the default value for the emulator, and indicates that the "device" is sitting perfectly vertical. To get actual values in the emulator, pick up your computer and shake it. Okay, don't actually do that.

You have the following options for getting real data while you're debugging:

- Deploy your app to an actual Windows Phone device

- Use the new emulator add-on

- Use one of many third-party libraries that provide ways to simulate accelerometer data

We're going to cover the simplest of those solutions, the emulator add-on. To access it, you can open the Additional Tools from the emulator again, and click the Accelerometer tab (it is selected by default.) It costs nothing to get and is surprisingly fun to use. All you need to do is move the small circle around inside the tool, and the phone emulator will appear to rotate in 3D space. It also provides the ability to feed in random shake data, as well as reset the device to standard orientations like "Portrait Standing" and "Landscape Flat," as shown in Figure 9-5.

Figure 9-5. Using the Accelerometer tool in the Windows Phone emulator

The accelerometer gives us a great deal of information about the gravitational forces that are being exerted on the device. In the next section, we're going to look at its sister, the gyroscope, which gives us information about rotational velocity of the device.

Using the Gyroscope

The gyroscope sensor is as easy to use as the accelerometer, but we don't get the benefit of any the additional tools in the emulator. A gyroscope measures rotational velocity of the device on the same three axes as the accelerometer: X, Y, and Z. The data you receive measures this velocity in radians per second.

This means that you can more accurately, and more smoothly measure the current orientation of the device. This will become especially handy when you build applications that perform augmented reality. In most cases, however, you're probably not going to be accessing the gyroscope by itself. There are a couple of reasons for this:

- Not all Windows Phones will have a gyroscope. In fact, only phones that come out after the Mango release will be capable of having a gyroscope, and it is still an optional piece of hardware.

- Microsoft has created a Motion API that combines the data from the Accelerometer, the Compass, and the Gyroscope into one class that we can use more effectively.

.However, in case you do need to use the gyroscope independent of the Motion API, you can use the sample code in Listings 9-7 and 9-8.user interface

Listing 9-7. A Xaml Interface to View Our Gyroscope Data

```
<TextBlock Height="30" HorizontalAlignment="Left"  Margin="20,100,0,0" Name="xTextBlock"
Text="X: 1.0" VerticalAlignment="Top" Foreground="Red" FontSize="28" FontWeight="Bold"/>
<TextBlock Height="30" HorizontalAlignment="Center"  Margin="0,100,0,0" Name="yTextBlock"
Text="Y: 1.0" VerticalAlignment="Top" Foreground="Yellow" FontSize="28" FontWeight="Bold"/>
<TextBlock Height="30" HorizontalAlignment="Right"  Margin="0,100,20,0" Name="zTextBlock"
Text="Z: 1.0" VerticalAlignment="Top"  Foreground="Blue" FontSize="28" FontWeight="Bold"/>
<Line x:Name="xLine" X1="240" Y1="350" X2="340" Y2="350" Stroke="Red"
StrokeThickness="4"></Line>
<Line x:Name="yLine" X1="240" Y1="350" X2="240" Y2="270" Stroke="Yellow"
StrokeThickness="4"></Line>
<Line x:Name="zLine" X1="240" Y1="350" X2="190" Y2="400" Stroke="Blue"
StrokeThickness="4"></Line>
<TextBlock Height="30" HorizontalAlignment="Center" Margin="6,571,6,0" Name="statusTextBlock"
Text="TextBlock" VerticalAlignment="Top" Width="444" />
```

In order to use the code in Listing 9-7, follow these next steps.

15. Create a new Windows Phone Application project called "GyroscopeSample."

16. Add the code in Listing 9-6 into the `ContentPanel` Grid in your `MainPage.xaml` file.

The interface we are building will look like the image in Figure 9-6.

Figure 9-6. The user interface for our gyroscope application

In order to access the gyroscope directly, you should always wrap your code with a check to determine that the device supports the gyroscope sensor. As we did with the Accelerometer, we set up an event handler for when the values of the Gyroscope change, pass that data to a separate thread, and then update the data in our user interface as shown in Listing 9-8.

Listing 9-8. Using C# to Access the Gyroscope Sensor

```csharp
using System;
using Microsoft.Phone.Controls;
using Microsoft.Devices.Sensors;
using Microsoft.Xna.Framework;

namespace GyroscopeSample
{
    public partial class MainPage : PhoneApplicationPage
    {
        Gyroscope g;

        public MainPage()
```

```
        {
            InitializeComponent();

            if (Gyroscope.IsSupported)
            {
                g = new Gyroscope();
                g.TimeBetweenUpdates = TimeSpan.FromMilliseconds(20);
                g.CurrentValueChanged += new
EventHandler<SensorReadingEventArgs<GyroscopeReading>>(g_CurrentValueChanged);
                g.Start();
            }
        }

        void g_CurrentValueChanged(object sender, SensorReadingEventArgs<GyroscopeReading> e)
        {
            Dispatcher.BeginInvoke(() => UpdateUI(e.SensorReading));
        }

        private void UpdateUI(GyroscopeReading gyroscopeReading)
        {
            statusTextBlock.Text = "getting data";

            Vector3 rotationRate = gyroscopeReading.RotationRate;

            // Show the numeric values.
            xTextBlock.Text = "X: " + rotationRate.X.ToString("0.00");
            yTextBlock.Text = "Y: " + rotationRate.Y.ToString("0.00");
            zTextBlock.Text = "Z: " + rotationRate.Z.ToString("0.00");

            // Show the values graphically.
            xLine.X2 = xLine.X1 + rotationRate.X * 200;
            yLine.Y2 = yLine.Y1 - rotationRate.Y * 200;
            zLine.X2 = zLine.X1 - rotationRate.Z * 100;
            zLine.Y2 = zLine.Y1 + rotationRate.Z * 100;
        }
    }
}
```

To use the code from Listing 9-8 in your sample application, take the following steps:

17. Replace the contents of your `MainPage.xaml.cs` file with the code in Listing 9-8.

18. Run your application (F5).

19. Realize that the gyroscope is also not supported by the emulator.

To explain Listing 9-8 clearly, we create a new `Gyroscope` object first. After checking to make sure that the `Gyroscope` is supported with the `Gyroscope.IsSupported` boolean value, we create an event handler for `CurrentValueChanged`. The `Gyroscope`, like the `Compass`, allows our event handler method to fire every time the Gyroscope detects a new value, keeping the `TimeBetweenUpdates` value in consideration. In our example, we will get updates no faster than every 20 milliseconds. We gather each of the X, Y, and Z values from the Vector3 value `RotationRate`. We are just displaying the data values in

TextBlocks, but not doing anything useful with the data. To do something more interesting, we created an interface that visually represents that data (shown in Figure 9-7).

Figure 9-7. A closer look at the data visualization of the Gyroscope

If you imagine each line segment to represent a different data point (the horizontal line is X, the vertical line is Y, and the diagonal line is the Z axis. You could then manipulate the lengths of these lines to represent the rotational velocity of the device. Each of these calculations will extend the length of their respective lines, giving you a very illustrative example of what types of rotation your device is experiencing. While this is handy, you'll find that using the Motion API will give you this information as well, in addition to several other calculations.

Using the Motion API

Bringing the Accelerometer, Gyroscope, and Compass together, the Motion class allows you to detect a great number of motion values, like pitch, yaw, and roll. In flight dynamics, these are the three critical parameters used to determine the orientation of an aircraft in relation to its center of gravity. Each term refers to rotation about their respective axes. Figure 9-8 is a simple illustration, in relation to an airplane.

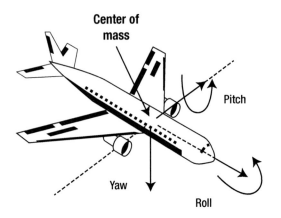

Figure 9-8..An illustration of pitch, yaw, and roll in aviation.

Simplistically, roll will move a given wing up or down, pitch will move the nose up or down, and yaw will move the nose right or left, as shown in Figure 9-8.

You can see that the arrows that extend from the center of the airplane are exactly the same lines that we created when we were looking at the gyroscope, X, Y, and Z. In this case, however, we also have the ability to measure the rotation *around* those axes, not just in relation to the center of the phone.

In our code example for the Motion class, you can use the code in Listing 9-9 to place a star in the middle of our page, and have it rotate as the Motion object detects changes to the orientation of the device. We will have it move in relation to the yaw value, which will make the star appear to remain stationary as we rotate the device. By rotating it on a flat plane, you will be able to see the orientation of the star remain static at all times. To build this interface, use the code in Listing 9-9. In previous examples, we have only included the Xaml that you need to add to your `ContentPanel Grid` control. This sample shows the contents of the `MainPage.xaml` file to show a new namespace we're using to create the star shape.

Listing 9-9 .The User Interface for Our Motion Class Application

```
<phone:PhoneApplicationPage
    xmlns="http://schemas.microsoft.com/winfx/2006/xaml/presentation"
    xmlns:x="http://schemas.microsoft.com/winfx/2006/xaml"
    xmlns:phone="clr-namespace:Microsoft.Phone.Controls;assembly=Microsoft.Phone"
    xmlns:shell="clr-namespace:Microsoft.Phone.Shell;assembly=Microsoft.Phone"
    xmlns:d="http://schemas.microsoft.com/expression/blend/2008"
    xmlns:mc="http://schemas.openxmlformats.org/markup-compatibility/2006"
    xmlns:es="clr-namespace:Microsoft.Expression.Shapes;assembly=Microsoft.Expression.Drawing"
    x:Class="MotionSample.MainPage"
    FontFamily="{StaticResource PhoneFontFamilyNormal}"
    FontSize="{StaticResource PhoneFontSizeNormal}"
    Foreground="{StaticResource PhoneForegroundBrush}"
    SupportedOrientations="Portrait" Orientation="Portrait"
    mc:Ignorable="d" d:DesignHeight="768" d:DesignWidth="480"
    shell:SystemTray.IsVisible="True">
```

```
<Grid x:Name="LayoutRoot" Background="Transparent">
    <Grid.RowDefinitions>
        <RowDefinition Height="Auto"/>
        <RowDefinition Height="*"/>
    </Grid.RowDefinitions>

    <StackPanel x:Name="TitlePanel" Grid.Row="0" Margin="12,17,0,28">
        <TextBlock x:Name="ApplicationTitle" Text="MOTION SAMPLE" Style="{StaticResource
PhoneTextNormalStyle}"/>
        <TextBlock x:Name="PageTitle" Text="motion" Margin="9,-7,0,0"
Style="{StaticResource PhoneTextTitle1Style}"/>
    </StackPanel>

    <Grid x:Name="ContentPanel" Grid.Row="1" Margin="12,0,12,0">
            <es:RegularPolygon x:Name="Star" InnerRadius="0.47211"
Margin="100,175,100,175" PointCount="5" Stretch="Fill" Stroke="White"
UseLayoutRounding="False" StrokeThickness="6">
                    <es:RegularPolygon.Fill>
                            <SolidColorBrush Color="{StaticResource PhoneAccentColor}"/>
                    </es:RegularPolygon.Fill>
                <es:RegularPolygon.RenderTransform>
                    <RotateTransform CenterX="100" CenterY="128"></RotateTransform>
                </es:RegularPolygon.RenderTransform>
            </es:RegularPolygon>

        <TextBlock x:Name="yawValue" Text="YAW = 34.567" FontSize="40" Width="400"
Height="100" TextAlignment="Center" Margin="28,503,28,4" />
    </Grid>
</Grid>
</phone:PhoneApplicationPage>
```

Take the following steps to start building a sample application that uses the Motion class:

20. Create a new Windows Phone Application project named "MotionSample."

21. Replace the code in `MainPage.xaml` with the code in Listing 9-9.

You may notice that to render our Star polygon shape, we utilized a namespace specific to Expression Blend: `Microsoft.Expression.Shapes`. By using this namespace, you can create polygons with many different shapes without having to do the complicated math that is generally required to create something like a star (shown in Figure 9-9).

Figure 9-9. Our user interface for the Motion class applicationstar

The `es:RegularPolygon` element allows you to specify a `PointCount` for our shape. In the case of five points, it looks like a traditional solid pentagram. Adding or removing points will result in a star shape with any number of points from three to eighty. Anything more than about eighty continues to look the same, while anything with three or fewer points looks like the center of the Mercedes-Benz logo. For you *Star Wars* fans, it resembles the Empire's Imperial Shuttle as well (shown in Figure 9-10.)

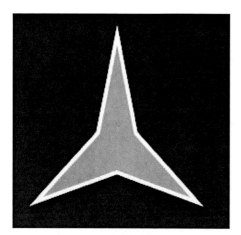

Figure 9-10 . A polygon shape with three or fewer points specified.

To make this Motion app work, we need to access the Motion class in our code-behind file. Listing 9-10 shows this code.

Listing 9-10. Using C# to Access the Motion Class

```
using System;
using System.Windows.Media;
using Microsoft.Phone.Controls;
using Microsoft.Devices.Sensors;
using Microsoft.Xna.Framework;

namespace MotionSample
{
    public partial class MainPage : PhoneApplicationPage
    {
        Motion motion;

        public MainPage()
        {
            InitializeComponent();

            if (Motion.IsSupported)
            {
                motion = new Motion();
                motion.TimeBetweenUpdates = TimeSpan.FromMilliseconds(20);
                motion.CurrentValueChanged += new
EventHandler<SensorReadingEventArgs<MotionReading>>(motion_CurrentValueChanged);
                motion.Start();
            }
        }
```

```
        void motion_CurrentValueChanged(object sender, SensorReadingEventArgs<MotionReading>
e)
        {
            Dispatcher.BeginInvoke(() => UpdateUI(e.SensorReading));
        }

        private void UpdateUI(MotionReading e)
        {
            ((RotateTransform)Star.RenderTransform).Angle =
MathHelper.ToDegrees(e.Attitude.Yaw);
            yawValue.Text = e.Attitude.Yaw.ToString();
        }
    }
}
```

To use this code in your application, you need to do the following:

22. Replace the code in your `MainPage.xaml.cs` file with the code in Listing 9-10.

23. Run your application (F5).

24. Discover, for the third time in this chapter, that the emulator does not currently support this sensor.

The Motion API works very similarly to the Accelerometer, Compass and Gyroscope objects. We need to create a new instance of a Motion object, and then create a new `CurrentValueChanged` event handler for it. Each time new data is received, this event receives a great deal of rich data. If you're investing in understanding the math that the Motion class is producing, you should further explore what the `MotionReading` class has to offer. The following is a short list:

- `Attitude`: Pitch, roll, and yaw; measured in radians.

- `DeviceAcceleration`: Measures the device's acceleration on the X, Y, and Z axes.

- `DeviceRotation`: Measures the device's rotation on the X, Y, and Z axes.

- `Gravity`: Measures the gravity vector of the device.

In our example, we are changing the angle of rotation of our star, basing it on the yaw value of the phone. Depending on the orientation of the phone, however, that value can vary significantly. For example, when the phone is faceup, the star moves at a reasonable speed when you tilt the device. However, if you hold the phone facedown and try similar movements, the star will appear to move twice as fast. This is because the calculation for yaw now includes a positive number instead of a negative one. Reference our discussion of the Accelerometer values for more information about how these positive and negative values come to be.

In this section, we've covered several powerful sensors available in Windows Phone devices. Table 9-3 reviews each of the sensors, their outputs, and what you will generally use each of them for in your applications.

Table 9-3. Comparing Windows Phone Location, Position, and Motion APIs

Class	Output	Best Use
Location	Longitude and latitude	For determining where the device is
Compass	TrueNorth Heading, MagneticNorth Heading, magnetic forces on X, Y, and Z axes	For compass and direction specific tasks
Accelerometer	Gravitational force on X, Y, and Z axes	For determining the orientation of the device
Gyroscope	Rotational velocity on X, Y, and Z axes	For determining the rotation of the device
Motion	Pitch, yaw, roll	For determining complete orientation of the device (combines Accelerometer, Compass, and Gyroscope)

Accessing Raw Camera Data

Above and beyond the camera tasks (see Chapter 7), we have the ability to tap into the raw camera feed from the device. This is handy for several reasons: we can grab both still images and video from this feed, as well as add our own data to the display for augmented reality-type applications. Combining the raw video feed with the Motion data we just learned to capture allows us to render objects, text, and other information into the real-time view of the user's camera. While a full Augmented Reality (AR) example is well beyond the scope of this book, Microsoft offers an excellent tutorial on the MSDN web site at http://msdn.microsoft.com/library/hh202984(v=VS.92).aspx.

In our example for this section, we will show you how to focus the camera and capture both photos and video from the raw camera feed. First, we need to display the camera's raw data on the screen of the device, as shown in Figure 9-11. We can do this by setting a VideoBrush as the Fill property of a rectangle, as shown in Listing 9-11.

Listing 9-11. Building the User Interface for a Camera Application

```
<Rectangle x:Name="ViewBox" Height="460" Margin="-22,-1,-131,148">
        <Rectangle.Fill>
                <VideoBrush x:Name="CameraSource" />
        </Rectangle.Fill>
        <Rectangle.RenderTransform>
                <RotateTransform Angle="90" CenterX="240" CenterY="240" />
        </Rectangle.RenderTransform>
</Rectangle>
<Button Foreground="Green" BorderBrush="Green" Content="Capture" Height="72"
HorizontalAlignment="Left" Margin="6,535,0,0" Name="CaptureButton" VerticalAlignment="Top"
Width="160" Click="CaptureButton_Click" />
```

To use the code in Listing 9-11, follow the next set of steps.

25. Create a new Windows Phone Application project named "CameraSample."

26. Add the Xaml in Listing 9-11 to the `ContentPanel` `Grid` in your `MainPage.xaml` file.

Figure 9-11. Our camera interface in the Windows Phone emulator

As you can see in the Xaml in Listing 9-11, we've added a `Rectangle` to the default page template, and defined its Fill property to be a `VideoBrush` named "CameraSource." You should also notice the `RenderTransform` we applied to the `Rectangle`. By rotating it 90 degrees, we are actually accommodating the fact that the cameras are mounted in the phone with a Landscape orientation. In our C# code-behind, we need to assign our camera data to that `VideoBrush`. We do this by creating a `PhotoCamera` object named "camera" and setting the source of our `VideoBrush` to be that `PhotoCamera` object (shown in Listing 9-12).

Listing 9-12. Accessing the Raw Camera Feed in Our Code-Behind File

```
using System;
using System.Windows;
using Microsoft.Phone.Controls;
```

```
using Microsoft.Devices;
using Microsoft.Xna.Framework.Media;

namespace Day7_RawCamera
{
        public partial class MainPage : PhoneApplicationPage
        {
                PhotoCamera camera;
                MediaLibrary library = new MediaLibrary();

                // Constructor
                public MainPage()
                {
                        InitializeComponent();
                        if (PhotoCamera.IsCameraTypeSupported(CameraType.FrontFacing))
                                camera = new PhotoCamera(CameraType.FrontFacing);
                        else
                                camera = new PhotoCamera(CameraType.Primary);
                        camera.CaptureImageAvailable += new
System.EventHandler<ContentReadyEventArgs>(camera_CaptureImageAvailable);
                        CameraSource.SetSource(camera);
                }

                private void CaptureButton_Click(object sender, System.Windows.RoutedEventArgs
e)
                {
                        try { camera.CaptureImage(); }
                        catch (Exception ex) { Dispatcher.BeginInvoke(() =>
MessageBox.Show(ex.Message)); }
                }

                void camera_CaptureImageAvailable(object sender, ContentReadyEventArgs e)
                {
                        Dispatcher.BeginInvoke(() => ThreadSafeImageCapture(e));
                }

                void ThreadSafeImageCapture(ContentReadyEventArgs e)
                {
                        library.SavePictureToCameraRoll(DateTime.Now.ToString() + ".jpg",
e.ImageStream);
                }
        }
}
```
To finish this sample camera application, follow the remaining steps.

27. Replace the contents of your `MainPage.xaml.cs` file with the code in Listing 9-11.

28. Run your application (F5).

29. On the emulator, you'll see the familiar white box with the small black square. On a real device, you'll see whatever the camera sensor sees.

Looking at Listing 9-12, we feed the raw data from the camera directly into the Rectangle without any complicated code maneuvers. In the code-behind, we create a new PhotoCamera object, and set the source (SetSource) of the VideoBrush equal to the new PhotoCamera object we created.

If you run our example code in the emulator, you're going to find the same type of output that you saw when you used the camera-related Launchers and Choosers (see Chapter 7). It will appear to be a white box with a black box traveling clockwise around the outside (shown in Figure 9-11). On an actual device, however, you will see the raw camera feed.

To grab a still image, we used the CaptureImage() method of the PhotoCamera class. For the simple purposes of our application, we're using the ApplicationBar to provide our buttons.

You will see that we are using the CaptureImageAvailable event handler on our PhotoCamera object. There is also a CaptureThumbnailAvailable event that you can use to grab a thumbnail of the image for gallery purposes. This is a nice additional feature, because it means you don't have to load each potentially giant image at a smaller size.

You should also notice that you *must* move the image capture to a separate thread. Leaving both the raw feed and the CaptureImage() method on the same thread will always result in an UnauthorizedAccessException, which means that you're trying to access data across different threads.

As you can see, we can call the CaptureImage() method, which, when completed, will fire the CaptureImageAvailable event handler. We pass the result of the event handlers to a separate thread, and gather the photo results. It's a very straightforward process that makes it easy to capture data from the raw video feed. This becomes especially handy when you want more than one image to be taken. For example, calling the CaptureImage() method once every second would provide an excellent way to capture a child running across your backyard. Or perhaps that amazing touchdown. There are tons of possibilities; it's up to you to be creative with these tools and come up with that next amazing app.

Summary

After reading this chapter, your mind should have been flooded with dozens of ideas for how you can improve your application idea. **One recommendation we can offer you is that making an application location-aware makes it better.** No matter your app, adding location data can make it better. Making a game? Play with other people that are nearby. Building a home-inventory app? Recommend nearby homeowner's insurance agents when they upload valuable property. Take the time as you're building your application to think about how you can incorporate a user's location into making your application richer.

As for the other sensors, if they don't have a direct purpose in your app, use that information for creating "Easter eggs" instead. The user turns the phone upside down? Give them a funny response that lets them know you noticed.

By using the orientation sensors with the camera, we end up with the opportunity to build augmented reality applications. Imagine holding your phone up in a crowded holiday parking lot, and using it like a viewfinder. When you point your phone in the direction of your car, there's a giant blue arrow pointing down from the sky to the top of your car. All you would need to do at this point is walk towards the arrow to find your vehicle. *This* is an example of augmented reality. There are an infinite number of ways we could enhance a user's view on the world around them by combining these technologies.

One great use of the accelerometer that we've seen was in a cycling application. The primary focus of the application was to track where a user was riding his bicycle. As a safety feature, you could enter an emergency phone number. If the application recognized an uncomfortably fast stop, followed by very little movement, it would automatically text the emergency phone number with the GPS coordinates of the device. Following that, it would prompt the phone to dial 911. This is an amazing use of both location and accelerometer data that will ultimately help to keep cyclists safer. Your app can use it too.

■   ■   ■

CHAPTER 10

Get Money: Profiting from Your Applications

Our hope is that as you've read this book, you've had a flurry of ideas for great applications that will make your users more productive, keep them more entertained, or perhaps just add to their knowledge of a subject. Now it's time to get it in front of millions of potential customers.

This chapter will focus on submitting your application to the Windows Phone Marketplace, as well as strategies for monetizing your applications. We'll show you how to advertise your app and release it to a select audience. We'll also introduce you to a new feature to Windows Phone, search extensibility; this addition to your app allows you to show up in your user's relevant search results, making your application both more visible and more useful to your users.

Submitting Your App to the Windows Phone Marketplace

Creating a great application is really only step number one in getting your software into the Windows Phone Marketplace. You still need to invest some time in your icons, descriptions, screenshots, keywords, and pricing. Microsoft has provided an amazing, step-by-step walk-through of the Marketplace submission process (http://create.msdn.com/home/about/app_submission_walkthrough), so this section will be dedicated to helping you navigate the pitfalls and curiosities you'll encounter along the way. We highly recommend that you read through the Microsoft walk-through before diving into this chapter.

As Microsoft describes the process, there are five steps you must to complete to submit an app to Microsoft Marketplace and gain approval, which are summarized by Figure 10-1.

Figure 10-1. Five steps to the Microsoft Marketplace

Before you upload your application, however, it's important to be aware of the Marketplace Test Kit. Using it will help you avoid many of the simple mistakes that get apps denied from the Marketplace.

Using the Marketplace Test Kit (Recommended)

Another new tool available to us is the Marketplace Test Kit. Integrated right into Visual Studio 2010 when you installed the Windows Phone 7.1 SDK, it provides a set of tests that we can run against our application to be certain that it will pass the Marketplace submission process on the first try. This tool is very similar to the one used by the Marketplace validation team. It checks your application for everything from its icons to its performance. To access this tool, click on your project in the Solution Explorer window, and open the Project menu from the Visual Studio toolbar, as shown in Figure 10-2.

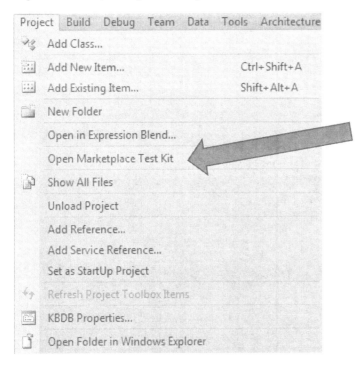

Figure 10-2. Opening the Marketplace Test Kit in Visual Studio 2010

Microsoft has provided an excellent walk-through of each of the individual tests in the Test Kit (http://msdn.microsoft.com/library/hh394032.aspx). We recommend using this tool before you ever start to submit your application to the Marketplace. It will help you avoid the common mistakes that many developers make. Once you've successfully uploaded your application, the next step will be to describe your application.

Now that you're familiar with the Microsoft Test Kit, you're ready to upload your app, the first step for any submission to the Marketplace.

Uploading Your App

The first step is always the toughest, and this is no exception. If this is your first time uploading an app, you're likely to struggle here. Figure 10-3 shows the first screen you will encounter in the application submission process. We will discuss each of the fields in Figure 10-3 in this section (an asterisk indicates that a field is required).

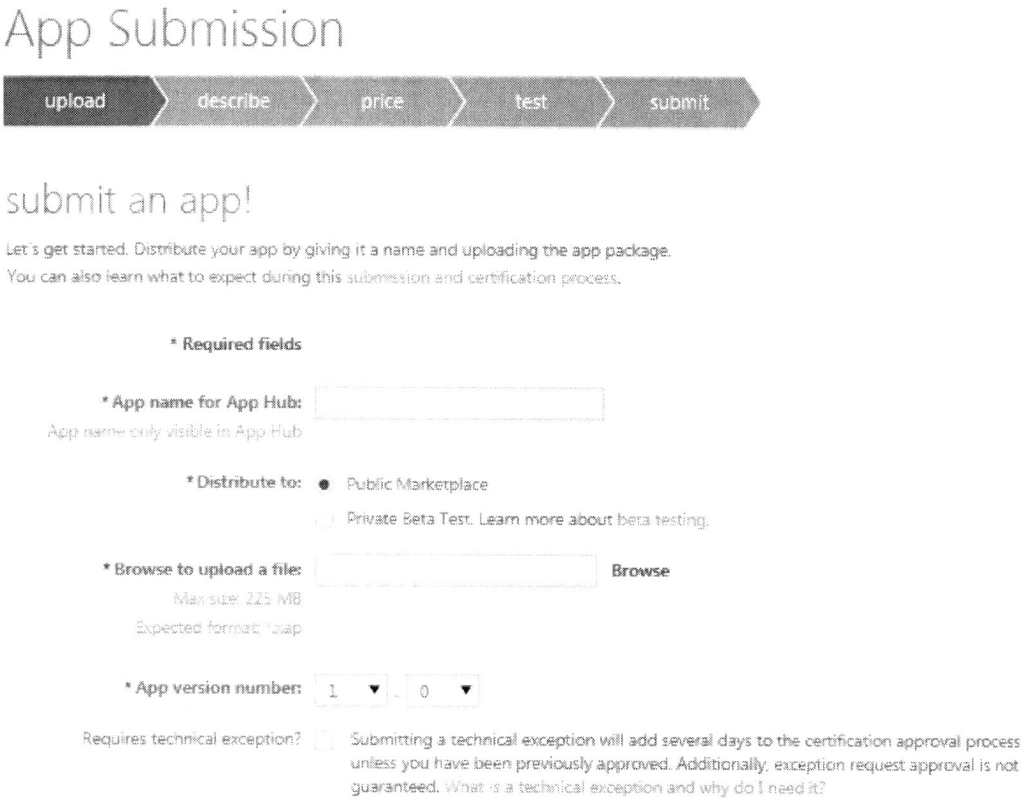

App Submission

| upload | describe | price | test | submit |

submit an app!

Let's get started. Distribute your app by giving it a name and uploading the app package.
You can also learn what to expect during this submission and certification process.

* Required fields

* App name for App Hub: [   ]
App name only visible in App Hub

* Distribute to: ● Public Marketplace
⦾ Private Beta Test. Learn more about beta testing.

* Browse to upload a file: [   ] Browse
Max size: 225 MB
Expected format: .xap

* App version number: 1 ▼ . 0 ▼

Requires technical exception? ☐ Submitting a technical exception will add several days to the certification approval process unless you have been previously approved. Additionally, exception request approval is not guaranteed. What is a technical exception and why do I need it?

Figure 10-3. The "upload" step of the Windows Phone App Submission process

*App name for App Hub

As you can see in Figure 10-3, we start by naming our application. This name is only seen by you in the App Hub, but there is one thing you'll want to remember when naming your application here: this is the name that will be displayed in all of your reports for this application, forever. Make sure it is meaningful enough to identify later because you won't be able to change it without deleting your application and starting over.

*Distribute to

This field allows you to decide how you want to distribute the application you're uploading. Choosing Public Marketplace will follow all of the expected rules: your app will be tested and certified, and upon approval, will be available in the public marketplace.

Private beta testing is a new feature to the Windows Phone Marketplace and we consider it to be a highly valuable *free* feature that you should use every time you create an application. It allows you to make your application available to up to 100 users that you choose. They don't need to be developers or have any special status whatsoever. All your beta testers need is a Windows Phone with an associated Windows Live ID. Your beta program runs for 90 days, at which point the beta version of your application will stop working on your user's phones.

The reason we find this process to be necessary to the development process is because you, as the developer, aren't always able to see past things like usability issues. As the person that created the interface for the app, it probably makes perfect sense to you. Putting this interface in front of a bunch of users that have never seen your application before, however, will be eye-opening. They will encounter issues and confusion that you never anticipated.

By correcting the issues that your beta testers encounter, you'll be able to prevent some of the negative feedback that users would have otherwise left on your application's review page. Better reviews result in better sales, so beta testing is always recommended.

When choosing the Public Beta Test option, it is important to remember that you will want to avoid using the App Hub name that you will use for your final, public application. All App Hub names have to be unique within your account, so we recommend appending the word "BETA" to your App Hub name when submitting a beta application. Also, a beta application does not go through the same rigorous certification and validation that your final application will.

*Browse to upload a file

This is the step that requires you to upload your application. If you haven't already noticed it, open up your project folder on your PC, and look inside the Bin   Release folder. You should find a XAP file there; this is the file you want to upload. If there is not a file in this folder, you've likely not performed a Release build of your application. To do this, change the dropdown in Visual Studio 2010 from Debug to release, as shown in Figure 10-4. The reason to choose the Release build is for the optimizations (and removal of debugging code) that it provides. A Debug build will work perfectly fine, and in most cases will be unnoticeable, but using Release is still the best practice for releasing your software.

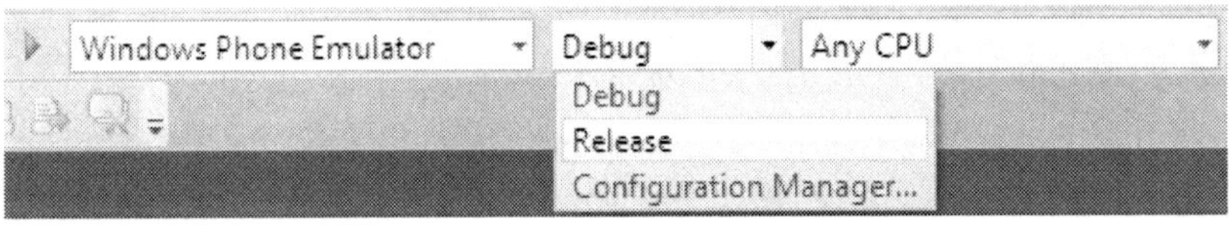

Figure 10-4. Changing Visual Studio from Debug to Release build

When you finish this first screen of the app submission process, there is an automated validator that will run on your XAP file. The validator checks to make sure that you're not forgetting some of the simpler requirements for an application, like using the default icons for your app, or setting your NeutralResourceLanguage. The tests performed here are the same ones that you checked your app with using the Marketplace Test Kit at the beginning of this chapter. For example, you need to use custom icons for your app every time, and those small star icons cannot be used (we'll cover this in the Describing Your Application section of this chapter.)

Another common omission, and probably the one most likely to catch you, is a value called the NeutralResourceLanguage. This defines the default language that your application uses. To change this, you need to open the properties page of your application. You can do this by right-clicking on your project's name in the Solution Explorer. You should see a dialog that looks like the one in Figure 10-5.

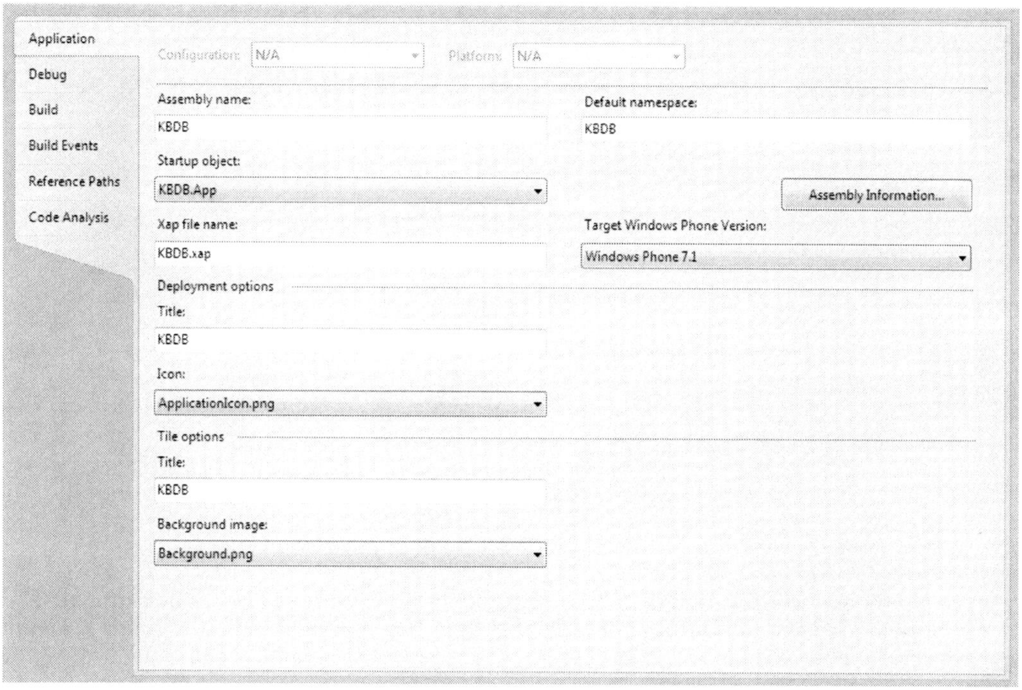

Figure 10-5. The Windows Phone properties page

Clicking on the Assembly Information… button will bring up a dialog box that allows you to visually set all of the values that are stored in your project's `Properties/AssemblyInfo.cs` file. You can select your default language from the dialog, as shown in Figure 10-6.

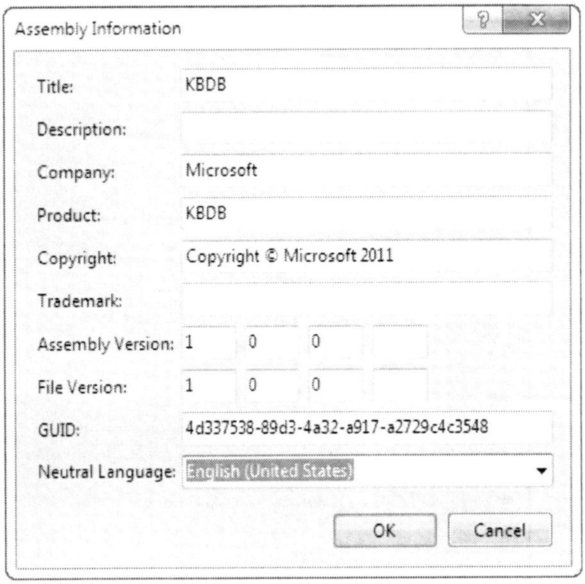

Figure 10-6. Selecting your default language in the Assembly Information dialog

Or you can simply add one line of code to the end of your `AssemblyInfo.cs` file, like in Listing 10-1, using the appropriate language code for your default language. This is what changing the value in Figure 10-6 does for you behind the scenes.

Listing 10-1. Adding NeutralResourceLanguage to AssemblyInfo.cs

```
[assembly: NeutralResourcesLanguageAttribute("en-US")]
```

*Version Number

We don't have much specific guidance about version number, but a beta application should be less than 1.0. Many times, you will find beta applications will use 0.9 or 0.8 (anticipating a second beta release at 0.9), and when the final application is ready for a public submission, the 1.0 version number should be used.

Minor future edits generally receive a bump of .1 in the version number, so fixing some small bugs and typos in your application should change the version number of a new application to 1.1. Major releases move up to the next largest integer, so when you have the next major release of your app, it should be 2.0.

Having said all of that, it is entirely up to you what version number you give your application. There are not any specific rules about version numbers, other than that future releases must have a higher version number than the previous release.

Requires Technical Exception

Sometimes, we run into a situation where we need to break the rules. If you're not familiar with the rules for Windows Phone applications, make sure you check out the Application Certification Requirements for Windows Phone (`http://msdn.microsoft.com/library/hh184843.aspx`). Maybe you've got a specific reason that black text should be displayed on a black background. (This is generally not allowed for readability purposes.)

We've also seen examples where the application needs an Exit button for a specific reason, and the only way to accomplish that is to crash your application. You can apply for an exception to the Application Requirements by filling out the Technical Exception Request form found on the App Hub site, and uploading it with your application. You can find the Technical Exception Request form at `http://go.microsoft.com/fwlink/?LinkID=201159`.

Describing Your Application

Your first inclination is going to be to hurry through this section. It asks for simple information like a short and detailed description of your application, as well as all of the artwork that your application will require in the Marketplace. Don't hurry. In fact, spend a great deal of time on this. The descriptions that you write for your application might be the only thing that potential users will see before deciding whether or not to buy your application. You want the description and artwork to entice, excite, and encourage your Marketplace visitors to download it. Figure 10-7 shows the top half of the form you will be filling out.

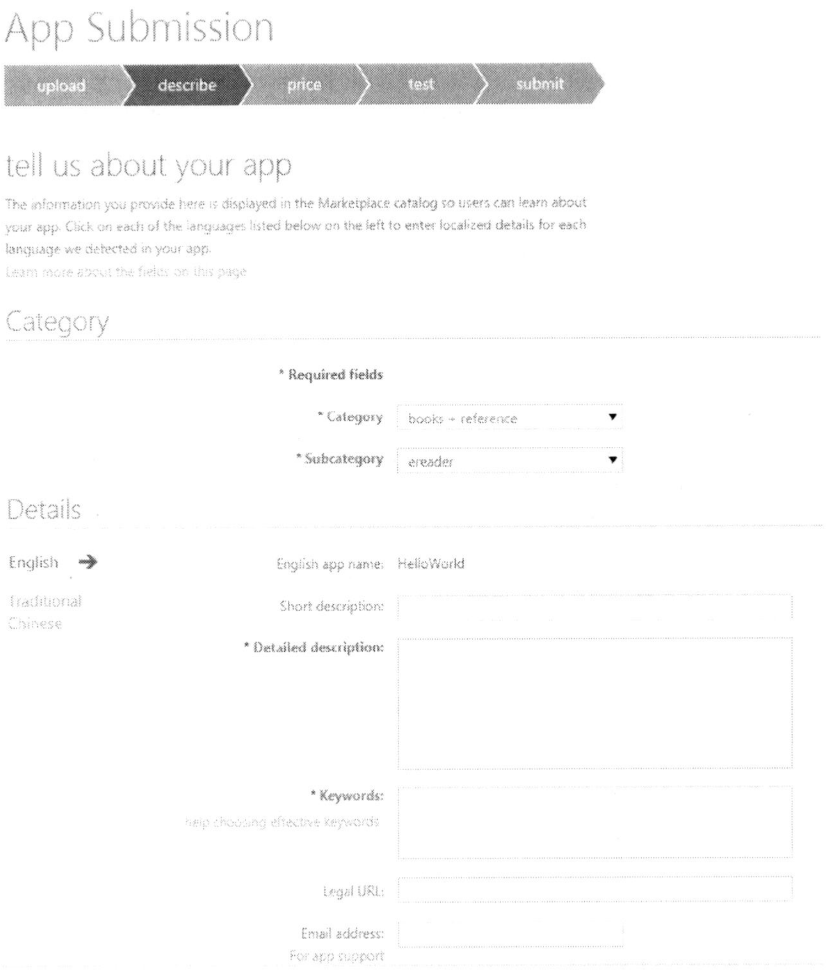

App Submission

upload   >   describe   >   price   >   test   >   submit

tell us about your app

The information you provide here is displayed in the Marketplace catalog so users can learn about
your app. Click on each of the languages listed below on the left to enter localized details for each
language we detected in your app.

Learn more about the fields on this page

Category

* Required fields	
* Category	books + reference ▼
* Subcategory	ereader ▼

Details

English →   English app name: HelloWorld

Traditional   Short description: [   ]
Chinese

* Detailed description: [   ]

* Keywords: [   ]
help choosing effective keywords

Legal URL: [   ]

Email address: [   ]
For app support

Figure 10-7. The first half of the form you will use to describe your app

*Category

Aside from being a required field, the category determines where in the Marketplace your application
will be listed. This could be a difficult choice, but you can only have your application listed in one
category. Some categories have subcategories, in which case you will get to select one of those as well.
You can choose any category you want, but our recommendation is to choose the category that your
users would be most likely to be looking for your app.

*Details

Your short description should be very concise, but very descriptive. Think of this as an elevator speech. You have 25 characters to describe the functionality of your application. What is the most important thing about your application that your potential user needs to know?

The long description should be everything. You get 2,000 characters, so use them. It should start very specific (much like your short description), and as you progress, it should expand on the points you made in the beginning. Avoid generic filler terms and phrases like "this app," or "when you download." Save your words for what your app does. We also recommend keeping an update history in your long description as well. It not only demonstrates all of the additional features that have been added to the application, but it also shows that this application is being supported going forward.

The following are examples of a short and a long description for the Home Inventory app we built in Chapter 2:

Short Description

> Save your stuff.

Long Description

> Do you know the model number of your television? What about the appraised value of your great-grandmother's ring? Your insurance company certainly will want that information. Store your info with My Stuff, and you won't have to worry if something terrible happens.
>
> My Stuff allows you to quickly take pictures of all of your valuable possessions. Tag them by room and category. Add descriptions, serial, and model numbers. When you need it, e-mail the entire list, with photos, to yourself or your insurance agent. Your data is encrypted on your phone, and is never shared with anyone. You do have the option to store all of your data in the cloud, but this is not required.
>
> My Stuff is your final line of defense against disaster. Protect yourself and your stuff. You won't regret it.
>
> To see My Stuff (and our other applications) in action, check out our YouTube channel at http://youtube.com/jeffblankenburg.
>
>
> Update Notes: December 12, 2010
>
> Version 1.1
>
> - Added the ability to take more than one photo of each item.
>
> - Improved performance of scrolling in the items list.
>
> - Added the ability to categorize an item in multiple categories.
>
>
> Update Notes: January 17, 2011
>
> Version 1.2

> - Added email export functionality. You can now email one or all categories to multiple email addresses.
>
> - Added secure cloud storage for offsite backup of your data.
>
>
> Update Notes: March 31, 2011
>
> Version 1.3
>
> - Added the ability to extract tears from unicorns.- Fixed a bug that prevented users from lying about the size of their televisions.

The keywords field of this form is to help your search results. If there is a search term that should lead a user to your app, you'll want to include it here. As an example, the following is a list of keywords we used for the home inventory application: home, stuff, insurance, fire, inventory, tornado, flood, gear, serial number, model number, library, home inventory.

Finally, you have the option to provide a legal URL and an e-mail address for your users in case they need that information. A legal URL is entirely up to you, but if you think that there could be legal implications to someone using your app, that information should be made available to them. As for the e-mail address, although it is not required, you should always provide one, even if you create a new inbox just for this purpose. You want to give your users a way to reach you if they are having issues, and an e-mail address is the perfect way to do this. Don't miss out on making your customers happy.

Now we get to move on the images and icons for your application in the Marketplace. Figure 10-8 shows the second half of the form we are currently working on. To upload the images in this section, click on the gray, plus sign (+) icon next to each heading.

Figure 10-8. The artwork portion of our "describe your app" form

Add Artwork

As developers, very few of us have any idea where to start regarding artwork for our application. If you're lucky, you're working with a designer on your app, and they've been able to help you make your app look significantly better than the mess of buttons and textboxes that it may have been before. There are three pieces of artwork that are required by the Marketplace, but you can also add up to seven more app screenshots. We recommend always providing as many screenshots as you can. The better the picture you can draw for your potential user about what their experience will be with your application, the more likely they are to give it a try.

The first three images—Large Mobile App Tile, Small Mobile App Tile, and Large PC App Tile—could very easily be the same image in different sizes. Many developers will create one image, resize it to the three appropriate sizes, and consider the task done. For you, however, it's important to evaluate each of these icon "opportunities" and leverage each for its appropriate use. For example, the Small

Mobile App Tile will only be used in the Marketplace's app list. In that case, your icon should be perfectly centered in the 99 × 99 pixels square. Figure 10-9 is an example of where it would be used.

Figure 10-9. The usage of the Small Mobile App Tile

For the Large Mobile App Tile, the story is a little different. This 173 × 173 pixels image will be used when a user selects your application in the Marketplace. This image is much larger and can convey much more information. For example, if you offer a trial mode, this might be the place to highlight that. Figure 10-10 shows what the Marketplace looks like when your user dives in to look at your app in more detail.

Figure 10-10. Using the Large Mobile App Tile

For the Large PC App Tile, this is only going to be displayed in the Zune software on a user's machine. It is shown when they see your application in the Zune Marketplace. This icon is huge at 200 × 200 pixels, which means you can leverage text even more than you did on the other two icons. Make sure that each of these images conveys the important information that you want the user to know, as shown in Figure 10-11.

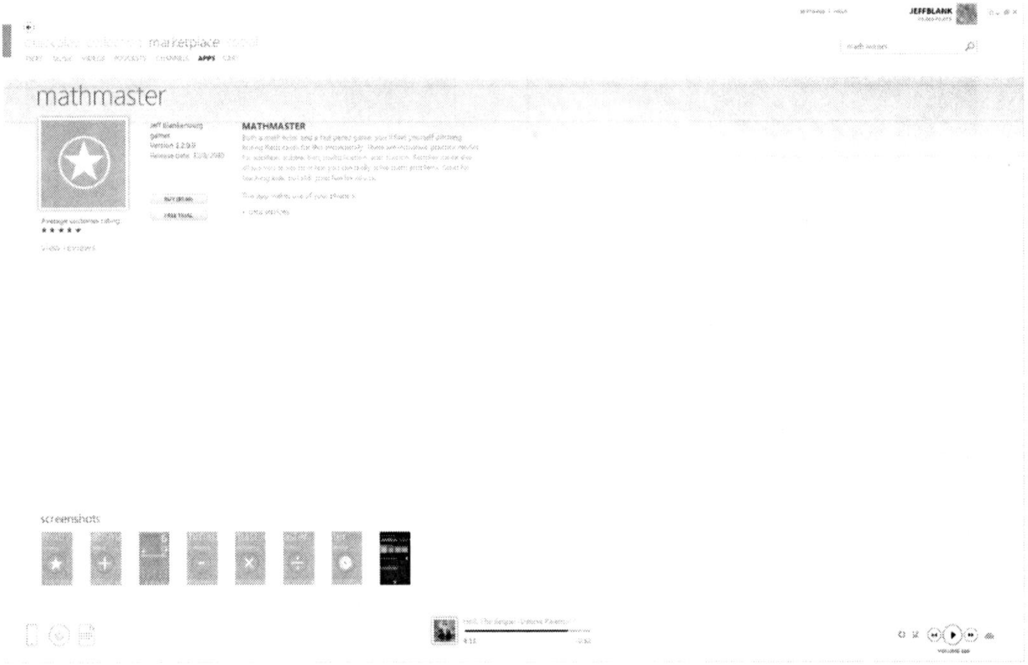

Figure 10-11. Using the Large PC App Tile

Notice in Figure 10-11 that in the background of the Marketplace, there's a large background image (it looks like lined paper), as well as eight screenshots listed at the bottom. You can add all of these to your application, but only one of the screenshots is required. Again, in our opinion, if they give you an opportunity to show off your application, you absolutely should. Next, let's look at how we price our application in the Marketplace.

Pricing Your Application

Pricing is a very tricky part of making an application successful. Price it too high and you're unlikely to sell many; price it too low, and you're leaving money on the table. Prices can range from $0 all the way up to $499 USD. Most applications in the Marketplace range from $0.99 to $2.99, depending on the functionality, brand, and popularity of the application. The form you will see is shown in Figure 10-12.

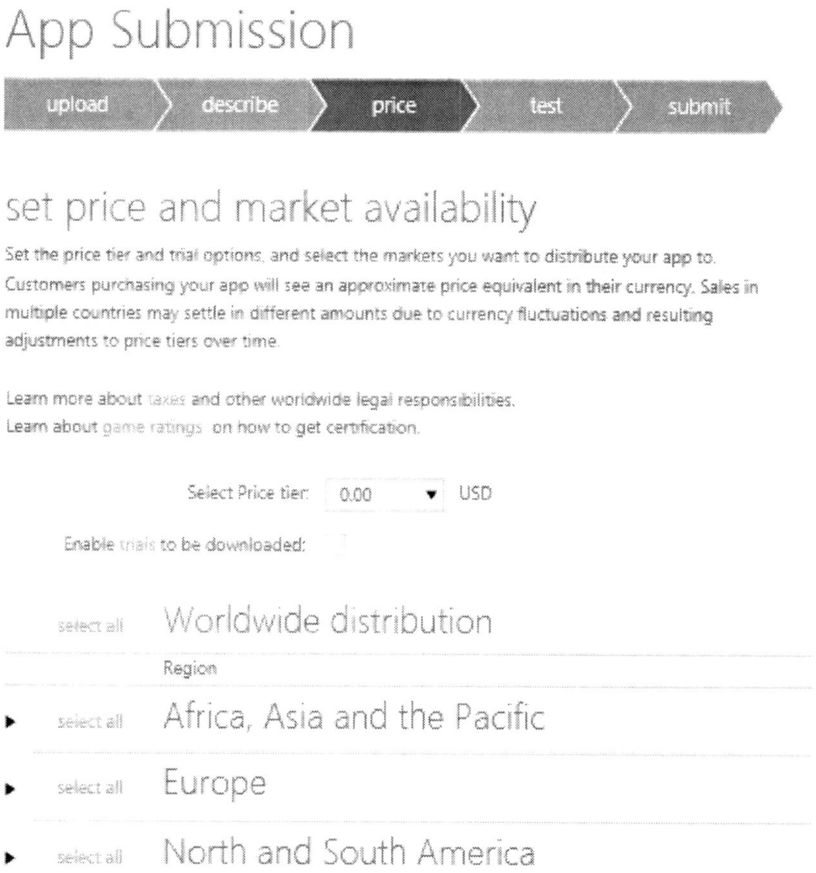

App Submission

| upload | describe | price | test | submit |

set price and market availability

Set the price tier and trial options, and select the markets you want to distribute your app to.
Customers purchasing your app will see an approximate price equivalent in their currency. Sales in
multiple countries may settle in different amounts due to currency fluctuations and resulting
adjustments to price tiers over time.

Learn more about taxes and other worldwide legal responsibilities.
Learn about game ratings on how to get certification.

Select Price tier: 0.00 ▼ USD

Enable trials to be downloaded:

select all   Worldwide distribution

Region

▶   select all   Africa, Asia and the Pacific

▶   select all   Europe

▶   select all   North and South America

Figure 10-12. Pricing your application and choosing distribution

It's our opinion that you're always better off starting a little higher with your price at $1.29 or $1.99 because it leaves you room to lower your price if you don't feel you're getting the traction that you were hoping for. If you start out at $0.99, raising your price will be received negatively from those that saw it at the lower price, which generally manifests itself as negative comments, the death knell of an application in the marketplace.

Once you've decided on a price, the form shown in Figure 10-12 will allow you to choose where you want your application to be distributed. Unless you have a very specific reason for excluding a country or region of the world, we recommend selecting *all* of the available countries, which is currently at 35, and will probably have grown since you purchased this book. The tool will automatically translate your USD price to all of the other currencies. This means you won't be able to charge higher prices in one region and lower prices in another. You have to have a consistent global price for your application.

We will cover trial mode and free applications in "Monetizing Your Application" later in this chapter, so let's continue through to the next step of the submission process: testing.

Testing Your Application

Depending on the choice you made in the Uploading Your App step, this step will take one of two forms: beta testing or certification.

Beta Testing

If you chose to upload your application for beta testing in the first step of the submission process, this step will ask you to provide up to 100 e-mail addresses for distribution of your application. These e-mail addresses must be the Live ID that is associated with a beta tester's Windows Phone. It is highly recommended that you only provide the addresses of friends and acquaintances that would be expecting this type of message from you. The system will send an e-mail to your list of beta testers, inviting them to download the application. Sending unsolicited beta invitations to complete strangers will be received poorly, and will be unlikely to get you the feedback you're looking for.

Certification

If you are uploading your application to be available in the public Windows Phone Marketplace, this step is merely a form field for you to leave notes or instructions for the testers. This is very important if there are passwords, tricks, or secrets in your application that would be time-consuming or impossible to determine otherwise. You want to make it very easy for the testers to be able to navigate your application, and verify that everything is working. A screenshot of this screen is shown in Figure 10-13.

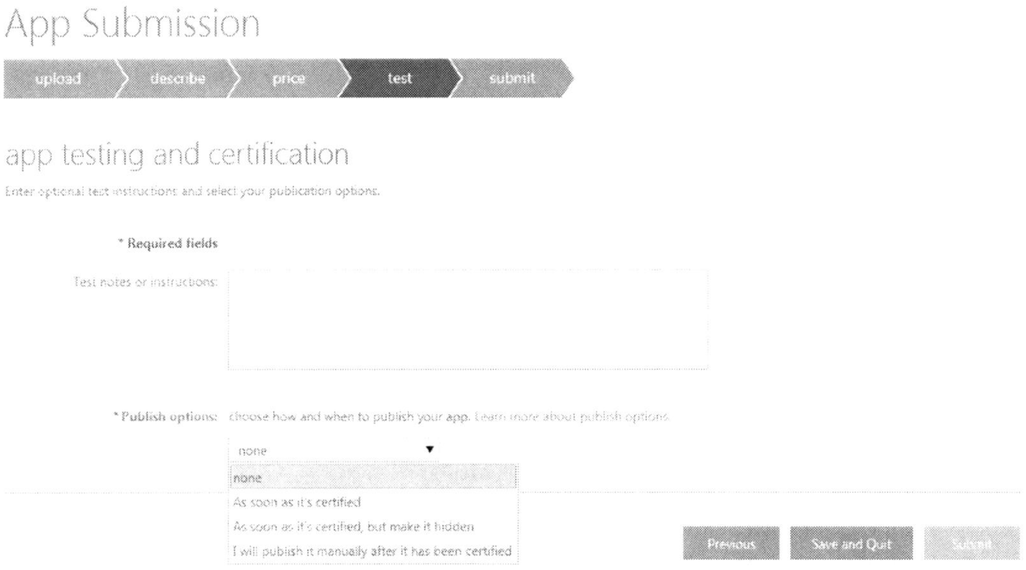

Figure 10-13. The app testing and certification form

You are also presented with choices on your publication options. We recommend that you allow your application to be published as soon as it is certified. This is because otherwise you'll have to wait for the certification e-mail and return to the App Submission portal to publish your application to the Marketplace. Unless you have a very specific reason for waiting, there's really no reason to wait. You're submitting this application to get it in the marketplace, so you may as well make it as easy as possible to make that happen.

At the bottom of the Testing and Certification section, you're presented with a Submit button instead of the standard Next button you've seen thus far. Pressing this button will submit your application for evaluation, so make sure you're ready and that you've gotten everything uploaded, written, and included before you press the button. Once you do, you'll see a screen like the one shown in Figure 10-14..

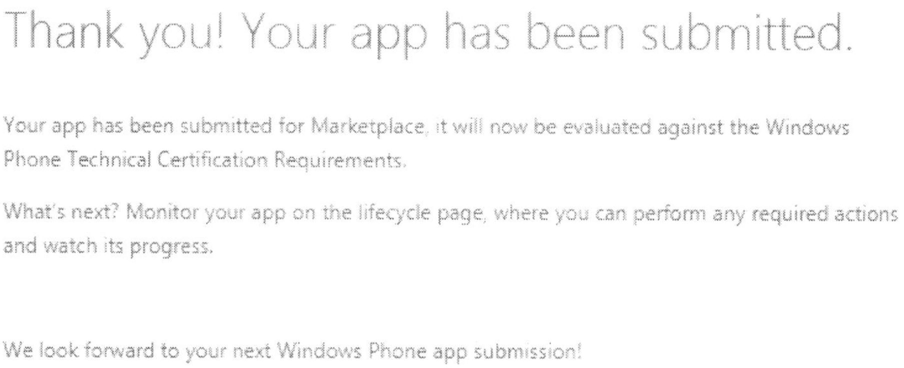

Thank you! Your app has been submitted.

Your app has been submitted for Marketplace, it will now be evaluated against the Windows Phone Technical Certification Requirements.

What's next? Monitor your app on the lifecycle page, where you can perform any required actions and watch its progress.

We look forward to your next Windows Phone app submission!

Figure 10-14. App submission congratulations screen

That's it! Your app will go through the certification and evaluation process (the lifecycle of your app is shown in Figure 10-15),. and if you were thorough in following the rules in the Windows Phone Application Certification Requirements, and made a point of running the Marketplace Test Kit, you can be confident that your application will make it into the Marketplace on your first try.

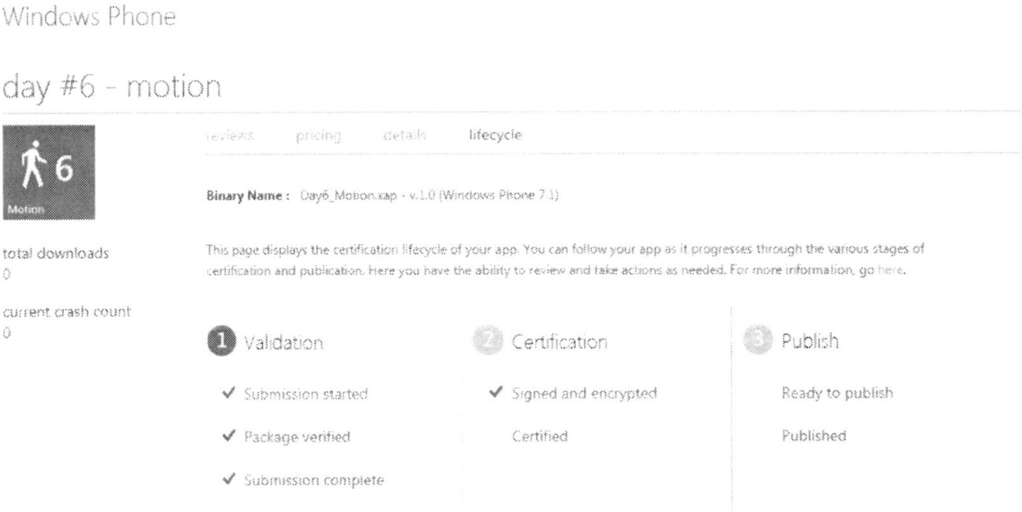

Windows Phone

day #6 - motion

reviews   pricing   details   lifecycle

Binary Name : Day6_Motion.xap - v.1.0 (Windows Phone 7.1)

total downloads
0

current crash count
0

This page displays the certification lifecycle of your app. You can follow your app as it progresses through the various stages of certification and publication. Here you have the ability to review and take actions as needed. For more information, go here.

1 Validation

✔ Submission started

✔ Package verified

✔ Submission complete

2 Certification

✔ Signed and encrypted

Certified

3 Publish

Ready to publish

Published

Figure 10-15. The application lifecycle page

Dealing with Rejection.

Sometimes an application gets denied from the Marketplace. There are thousands of reasons why this might happen, but the good news is that they're all based on objective criteria. When your application fails certification, you will get an incredibly detailed report e-mailed to you by the tester.

The report will include the specific portion of the Application Certification Requirements that you failed, and will also include a specific, repeatable set of instructions on how to re-create the issue. It will be absolutely clear as to why your application failed, and it also describes what you need to do in order to pass certification. There's no guessing required whatsoever, and that makes it easier for you to fix the issue and resubmit your application quickly. Don't be discouraged. It's much better for your application to fail certification than it is to have users get frustrated with an issue in your application. This is a very positive, rewarding learning experience.

The other reward of going through this entire submission process is the obvious one: monetary gain. The next section of this chapter focuses on Trial Mode, free apps, and using the Advertising SDK to make money from advertising in your applications.

Monetizing Your Application

In the first part of this chapter, we focused on how you get your application into the Windows Phone Marketplace and how you can price your apps to make money. This is only one option when it comes to making money selling Windows Phone apps. In this section, we'll explore three others: Trial Mode, Paid Trial, and Ad-Supported.

Trial Mode

Windows Phone also offers another unique feature called Trial Mode. This is a feature that you can enable in your application to create one codebase that can function as both a limited trial, as well as the full version of the app. On other platforms, you will often see a "Lite" or "Free" version of an app, alongside the "Full" version, which costs money. In some cases, you may find this same experience in the Windows Phone Marketplace.

The Windows Phone Trial Mode allows you to have one project, one codebase, and two versions of your application. By implementing this feature, you can show ads when the user doesn't pay for your app, and remove them when they finally pay for it. You can also remove some of the core functionality so that your user can try your app, but in order to get the full experience, they need to purchase the full version. Listing 10-2 shows how you implement Trial Mode in your applications.

Listing 10-2. Implementing Trial Mode in Your Code-Behind File

```
using System;
using System.Windows;
using Microsoft.Phone.Controls;
using Microsoft.Phone.Marketplace;

namespace KBDB
{
    public partial class MainPage : PhoneApplicationPage
    {
                LicenseInformation li = new LicenseInformation();

                // Constructor
        public MainPage()
        {
            InitializeComponent();

                        if (li.IsTrial())
                        {
                                //DO SOMETHING SPECIFIC TO TRIAL MODE, LIKE SHOWING
ADVERTISEMENTS
                        }
                        else
                        {
                                //DO SOMETHING THAT ONLY PAID USERS CAN DO.
                        }
        }
    }
}
```

As you can see, Trial Mode was made to be easy to implement. We need a reference to Microsoft.Phone.Marketplace, as well as a new LicenseInformation object. LicenseInformation exposes an IsTrial method that checks to see if the user has paid for your application. This is a great opportunity to show ads or display a Buy the Full Version button. (You can use the MarketplaceDetailTask to accomplish this. We covered that in Chapter 6.)

Paid Trial

It's important to remember that although you *can* offer a Trial version of your app, it might not always be in your best interest. We think this is especially true for low-priced utility applications and games. If you are intending to sell your app for 99 cents, you might want to reconsider utilizing Trial Mode.

Many users are very willing to participate in what we refer to as a "paid trial," or an impulse buy. Let's look at the potential math problem this creates.

If 1,000 people are willing to try your application by paying the 99 cents, do you expect that more or fewer people will pay 99 cents once they've tried the trial version of the app?

The answer, in almost all cases, is fewer. Twenty-five percent of all applications that a user installs on their phones are used less than once. Think about your own mobile device right now. How many of the applications you've installed actually get used on a regular basis? Our bet is less than ten. Is your application good enough to make it into someone's top ten? Even if you offer a trial version of your application with advertising, if it only gets used once, you're unlikely to see any real revenue from the user. Instead, we suggest *not* offering a trial for low-priced, minimally-featured applications. Sell it for 99 cents instead. You're bound to make more money that way.

The primary reason for this thinking is because Trial apps don't get exposed in the Marketplace the way that free applications do. A user that is looking for some new, free applications will be looking in the Free category of the Marketplace. Trial mode applications are not listed there. Therefore, this means that the users that *will* discover your application were already prepared to spend some money. Offering one version for a small price is probably your best bet to make money with your app.

For those applications that you think will get a ton of your user's screen time, we highly recommend advertising.

Advertising Supported

The place you're going to want to get started is the Microsoft Advertising pubCenter (`http://advertising.microsoft.com/mobile-apps`). They will walk you through getting the SDK, registering your application, and implementing the ads in your application. But, because this is a book on development, we're going to show you the implementation here as well. If you've downloaded the latest version of the Windows Phone tools, you've already got the Advertising SDK installed.

Once you have added `Microsoft.Advertising.Mobile.UI` as a reference to your project, you can start adding `AdControls` to your pages. Listing 10-3 shows the Xaml you need to put an ad in your app.

Listing 10-3. Adding an AdControl to Your Xaml Page

```
<phone:PhoneApplicationPage
    x:Class="KBDB.MainPage"
    xmlns="http://schemas.microsoft.com/winfx/2006/xaml/presentation"
    xmlns:x="http://schemas.microsoft.com/winfx/2006/xaml"
    xmlns:phone="clr-namespace:Microsoft.Phone.Controls;assembly=Microsoft.Phone"
    xmlns:shell="clr-namespace:Microsoft.Phone.Shell;assembly=Microsoft.Phone"
    xmlns:d="http://schemas.microsoft.com/expression/blend/2008"
    xmlns:mc="http://schemas.openxmlformats.org/markup-compatibility/2006"
    mc:Ignorable="d" d:DesignWidth="480" d:DesignHeight="768"
    FontFamily="{StaticResource PhoneFontFamilyNormal}"
    FontSize="{StaticResource PhoneFontSizeNormal}"
    Foreground="{StaticResource PhoneForegroundBrush}"
    SupportedOrientations="Portrait" Orientation="Portrait"
```

```
    shell:SystemTray.IsVisible="True"
    xmlns:ad="clr-
namespace:Microsoft.Advertising.Mobile.UI;assembly=Microsoft.Advertising.Mobile.UI">

    <Grid x:Name="LayoutRoot" Background="Transparent">
            <ad:AdControl AdUnitId="Image480_80" ApplicationId="test_client" Height="80"
HorizontalAlignment="Left" Margin="-12,527,0,0" Name="adControl1" VerticalAlignment="Top"
Width="480" />
        </Grid>
</phone:PhoneApplicationPage>
```

It's important to note that you need to include the XML namespace for the
`Microsoft.Advertising.Mobile.UI` in order to use the `AdControl` control. There are some important
things to know about the values in the `AdControl`, so let's look at that next.

Using Test Values in Your AdControl

While we're testing, we shouldn't use our *actual* `AdUnitId` values, because that would be like illegally
clicking on our banner ads on a web page. The `AdControl` is smart enough to recognize when it's running
in the emulator, and won't show ads in that case. Instead, you should use the values in Table 10-1. There
are actually three different types of test values, depending on what size/shape of ads you want to show.
Table 10-1 summarizes the entire list.

Table 10-1 .The test values you should use when building and testing your app.

Ad Type	Ad Model	Size (W × H)	Test ApplicationId	Test AdUnitId
Text Ad	Contextual	480 × 80	test_client	TextAd
XXL Image Banner	Contextual	480 × 80	test_client	Image480_80
XL Image Banner	Contextual	300 × 50	test_client	Image300_50

For our purposes, as you see in Table 10-1, we are using the 480 × 80 XXL Image Banner. We have
positioned it to take up the bottom 80 pixels of our application's screen, showing ads from the specific
ad unit.

What Is an Ad Unit?

Ad Units are specific "campaigns" that you might want to run. For example, Jeff has an application
called *Toothbrush Timer*. It's meant to show kids how long to brush each region of their mouths.
Because he is expecting parents to put it on the counter, and watch it with their kids as they brush,
advertising seems like a perfect way to catch their eye.

The best part about the Ad Units is the ability to define categories of advertisements to be shown. In
the toothbrush example, Jeff wants to show ads that are relevant to parents and their children.

Thankfully, there are tons of different ad categories to choose from (there are 385, ranging from politics to health and fitness), and you can even have multiple categories (up to three) in one Ad Unit.

So, once you've created some Ad Units in the pubCenter, grab those `AdUnitId` and `ApplicationId` values, and plug them into your `AdControl`. Then your code, fully formatted, should look more like Listing 10-4.

Listing 10-4. AdControl with Real AdUnit Values

```
<ad:AdControl x:Name="AdBox" AdUnitId="10018171" ApplicationId="350b8257-d92a-4978-a218-
f3650bd485df" Margin="-12,528,-12,0" Width="480" Height="80" />
```

And Figure 10-16 shows what the ad looks like in a sample application (note the sample ad used inside the emulator).

Figure 10-16. A sample ad using the Advertising SDK

Finally, Profit.

Just by adding the `AdControl` to your application (assuming your application is actually downloaded by users), you should start seeing activity in the pubCenter. It will show impressions, click-throughs, and other reporting metrics. The most important number, revenue, shows as you enter the site. Now, let's look at the toughest of questions: How do we attract users?

Promoting Your Application

Getting users to find your application might seem like something that's out of your hands, but you're wrong. There are plenty of things you can do to drive awareness of your application. This section focuses on a few best practices that you should utilize for every application that you create.

Make the Most of Week One

Unless your app becomes a runaway sensation, it's highly likely that your app's first week in the Marketplace will also see your highest number of daily downloads. Getting exposure in the *New* category is a one-time opportunity, and you need to make sure that you leverage this in a way that will make your app shine for much longer than a few days. Ultimately, your goal is to catapult from the New category to the Top Apps category. The four to five days that you will wait for your application to be approved should be spent executing a specific strategy for making the public aware of your application.

Use a Marketplace Link in Your Communications

When you first submit your application to the Marketplace, even before the app is approved, you are assigned a *deep link* that you can use to direct people to your app using a standard web URL. An example of the deep link to *MathMaster*, one of Jeff's applications, can be found at

```
http://windowsphone.com/s?appid=f08521cd-1cff-df11-9264-00237de2db9e
```

This link takes you to a page for your app in the Marketplace. This link will *not* work until your application is approved. We recommend using this link everywhere you can, especially on the custom web site you created for your apps. You were planning on doing that, right? To find your deep link, look on the Details tab of your application's submission page in the App Hub, as shown in Figure 10-17.

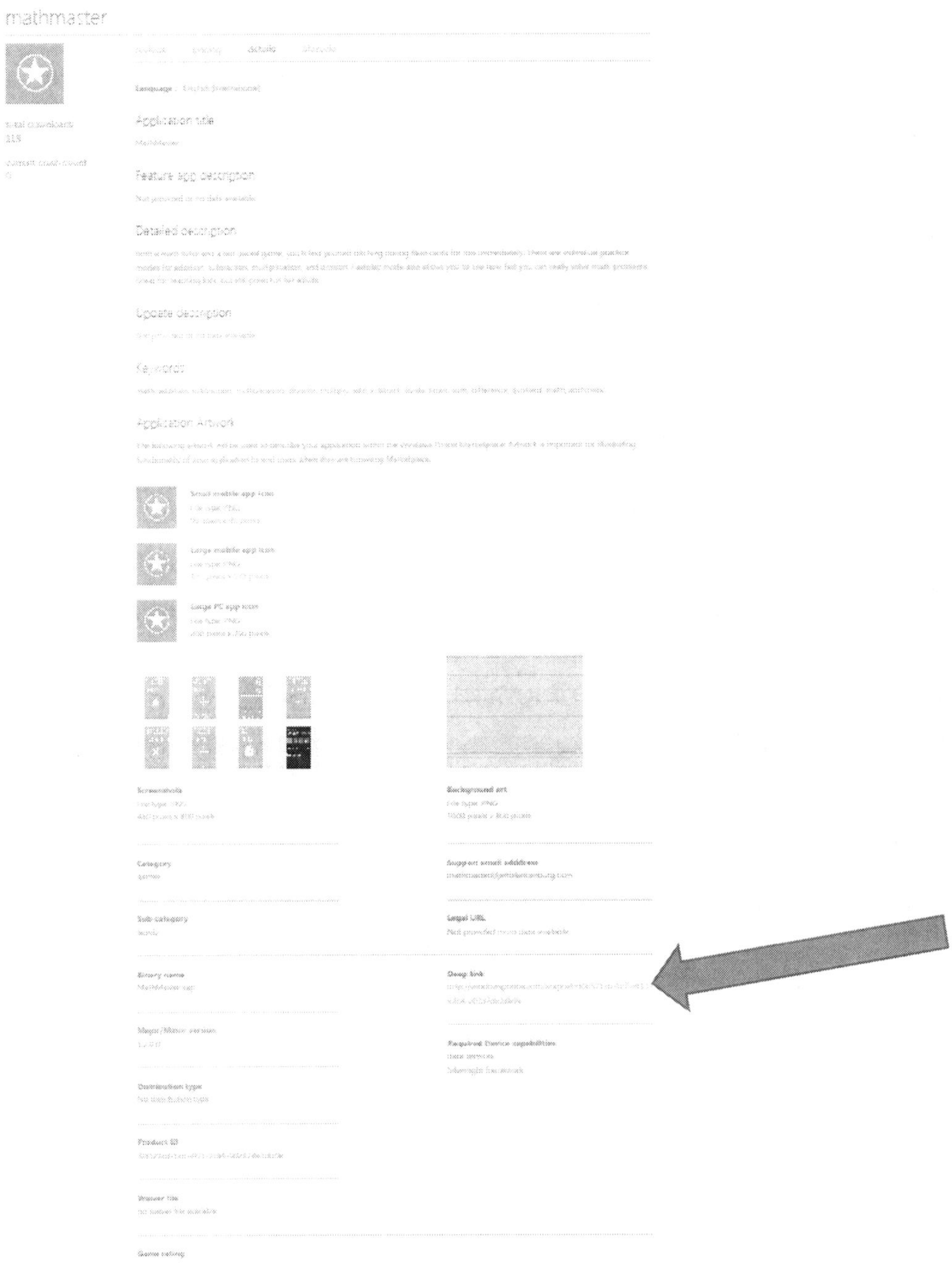

Figure 10-17. The details page of your application in App Hub

Create a Web Portal for Your Apps

An important thing that you should have learned from the Marketplace walk-through earlier in this chapter was that your ability to discuss your apps is pretty limited. A few screenshots, and approximately 2,000 characters is all you have. By creating a web site for your applications, you create several new opportunities for yourself.

1. You can create real connections with your users. The Windows Phone Marketplace doesn't give you any indication who your users are, only a total number of app sales. A web site allows you to interact with your fans.

2. You can provide a rich amount of information about your app, including videos and other promotional content that might make your app more appealing.

3. You can cross-sell your applications. The Marketplace doesn't always do a great job at promoting your other applications to potential customers, so leverage your web site to make that happen.

4. Your app is now discoverable by people that aren't actively looking for it in the Marketplace.

5. This web site doesn't have to be a web site at all. There's nothing wrong with creating a page on Facebook or another social network that you can customize. The ultimate goal of this process is to provide a destination for your fans, so that they can spread the word about your awesome app.

Create a Walk-through Video for Your App

One of the important features your web site should include is a video walk-through of your app. Screenshots in the Marketplace are good, but allowing a user to see the actual experience in a controlled way will always provide them with more information. Our recommendation is to use a video-screen capture tool like TechSmith's Camtasia, which makes it easy to not only capture the video feed from the emulator, but to edit the results, add background music, and introduce information before and after the video. There are probably plenty of tools that will do this for you, but in our experience, Camtasia is the perfect tool for the job. You can see an example of Jeff's *MathMaster* video on YouTube at `http://youtu.be/uMlyUn3sgJU`.

Have fun with it. Your video can add a level of excitement to your app that screenshots can never provide. Now that we've focused on web sites and videos, let's discuss the things you can do inside your application to help promote it.

Encourage Reviews of Your Applications

We discussed reviews earlier in this chapter; they can be the deciding factor as to whether or not your application gets the downloads that you're looking for. Unfortunately, there's not a built-in mechanism for reminding users to review your app. You need to do this yourself. We recommend making it a fun addition to your application rather than an annoyance to your user.

One idea we recommend is to make it an achievement within your app. Litter fun little surprises throughout your application, and you'll hook an otherwise passive user. Give points for reading the credits of the app. Give more for using the app ten times. By adding achievements to *any* application, you'll find that your users will find themselves coming back again and again. You might also unlock a specific piece of functionality that would otherwise be unavailable when they review your app.

A second idea is to count the number of times your user has launched your application, and prompt them at the second, fifth, and tenth times to review your application. Ask gently. You don't want to annoy the user, but you do want their review. You can even use the `MarketplaceReviewTask` to take them directly to the review page for your application.

Great reviews generate more traffic. Oftentimes, a star review can be just as valuable as a written one. The average star rating (1–5) is displayed everywhere your application is, so a high rating often generates more traffic. Encouraging your users to leave a review will have a positive effect on your application's download rates.

Cross-Sell Your Applications

Within your app, you should provide a place where the user can find information about your company, support contacts, and other data, like version number. In this place, or certainly in a more prominent location, you have an opportunity to promote the other applications you've created. Use your icons. Use the deep links or the `MarketplaceDetailTask` launcher. Provide a simple way for your user to find and download your other application offerings.

If you really want to get fancy, create an XML file on your web server that contains all of the information about your apps, and consume this in your apps to create the list of your applications. This way, when you add a new app to your catalog, you won't have to update all of your apps just to do this cross-promotion.

Summary

After you've finished your application, there are plenty of things you need to do in order to get your application ready. Make sure that you've considered your promotion strategy before you push the final Submit button on your app. Building a community around your application will only help to make your audience grow, because enthusiastic users are also powerful evangelists of your efforts.

If you've taken the time to create an amazing new application for Windows Phone, you need to be certain that it's going to have the potential impact you're hoping for. If you've built your big idea, followed our carefully-crafted advice throughout this book, and successfully passed Marketplace certification, you're ready to start raking in the cash.

It was our distinct honor to share our knowledge about Windows Phone development with you in this book, and we hope that as the money starts to pile up, you'll remember your trusted guides in this process, Jesse Liberty and Jeff Blankenburg. As it turns out, apps make far more money than writing about them does.

A sincere thank you for buying and reading our book. We hope it was as enjoyable for you to use as it was for us to write.

Index

■ ■ ■

CPSIA information can be obtained at www.ICGtesting.com
Printed in the USA
LVOW050316020112

261965LV00001B/1/P